# CHRÉTIEN STUDIES

Problems of form and meaning

in

*Erec, Yvain, Cligés* and the *Charrete*

*by*

Z. P. Zaddy

UNIVERSITY OF GLASGOW
PRESS
1973

Published with the recommendation of the
Monograph Committee of the Modern
Humanities Research Association

Printed by Robert MacLehose and Co. Ltd., Anniesland, Glasgow
for
University of Glasgow Press

# Contents

# Illustrations

# Foreword

CHRÉTIEN DE TROYES, the twelfth-century poet who is the subject of these studies, has long been regarded as a major French author. Though practically nothing is known about him, it is clear that in his own day and well beyond it, Chrétien ranked as one of the foremost writers of courtly romance. At least two princely patrons – Marie de Champagne and Philippe d'Alsace, the count of Flanders, both with a taste for Arthurian tales and a desire to propagate a new ideal among the chivalric classes – commissioned works from him. The extent to which he was plagiarised, translated, 'continued' and adapted by contemporaries and successors alike testifies in itself to his standing and success. In their turn, the references that his fellow poets make to him – some acknowledging his mastery and claiming only to glean where he had reaped, others insisting on the superiority of their subject matter over his – show equally clearly that they saw him as the yardstick by which their own achievements would be measured.

In our own times, when various editions of his works have made them readily available, Chrétien's importance as a literary figure has become increasingly apparent. The general reader finds him agreeably accessible and unexpectedly akin to La Fontaine. He has the same quick eye for the absurdities of human pretensions, the same ready sympathy for sincerity and sheer goodness of heart, and, outside the rhetorical passages which so impressed his contemporaries, the same deftness in handling word and metre. Furthermore, for those who have lived through these last few decades when all values seem to have been called into question, the moral issues raised by Chrétien have acquired a relevance and an interest they could not have for older readers born into a more settled world. As for the scholars, they have found a particularly rich field of study in Chrétien. His works provide an excellent starting point for an exploration of the Middle Ages and have been the cause of endless discussion and debate. Indeed, after nearly a hundred years of scholarly investigation, opinions are still divided over such crucial questions as Chrétien's originality or the purpose behind his tales. The critics cannot even agree over the plots of the romances or the most elementary facts of their organisation. They remain undecided over their dating.

It is hoped that these studies will make sense to anyone who has access to Chrétien's works, although they are intended for the specialist rather than the general reader. As an introduction to Chrétien for the non-specialist Professor Frappier's book *Chrétien de Troyes* is admirable. My own purpose is more particularly to explore some of the problems concerning the form and content of the romances which have not been satisfactorily resolved so far. For having studied Chrétien's texts closely in an attempt to analyse his psychological vocabulary, I am convinced that a perfectly satisfactory solution can be found for most of the problems which bedevil Chrétien scholarship – provided one pays more regard to what his texts actually say than to what critics commonly feel should be said there.

The topics discussed here by no means exhaust the list of those that call for investigation. For the moment, I only propose to look at certain basic points which have to be elucidated before the wider and more interesting issues can be considered. But I hope eventually to deal with these remaining problems in a further series of studies that will complement the present one.

## Acknowledgements

MY THANKS are due to:

The Modern Humanities Research Association and the editors of the *Modern Language Review*, for permission to reprint 'The Structure of Chrétien's *Erec*', and 'The Structure of Chrétien's *Yvain*'.

The Society for the Study of Mediæval Languages and Literature and the editor of *Medium Aevum*, for permission to reprint 'Chrétien de Troyes and the verb *Esprover*'.

Mouton & Co., Publishers, The Hague, for permission to quote from F. D. Kelly, '*Sens*' and '*Conjointure*' in the '*Chevalier de la Charrette*'.

Mrs Dorothy B. Loomis, for permission to use illustrations from *Arthurian Legends in Medieval Art* by Roger Sherman Loomis.

I also wish to acknowledge the help given by the Modern Humanities Research Association who first gave these studies its *imprimatur* and that of the Publications Committee of Glasgow University which has made it possible for them to appear now under the imprint of the University.

Finally, I must thank Mr Jack Baldwin of Glasgow University Library who so willingly put himself and the resources of his Special Collections at my disposal, Mr J. A. MacFarlane who made the prints reproduced here – and, last but not least, the various long-suffering friends who have assisted at the protracted birth of this book.

Z. P. Z.
*University of Glasgow* 1971

# Editions of Texts Used

Except where otherwise stated, the editions of the texts used in these studies are as follows:

Beroul. THE ROMANCE OF TRISTRAN. A POEM OF THE TWELFTH CENTURY. Edited by A. Ewert. Vol. I. 4th ed. Oxford: Blackwell, 1958.

Chrétien de Troyes. LE CHEVALIER DE LA CHARRETE. Edited by Mario Roques. Vol. III of *Les romans de Chrétien de Troyes édités d'après la copie de Guiot* (Bibl. nat. fr. 794). Classiques Français du Moyen Age 86. Paris: Champion, 1958.

    CLIGÉS. Edited by Alexandre Micha. Vol. II of *Les romans de Chrétien de Troyes édités d'après la copie de Guiot* (Bibl. nat. fr. 794). Classiques Français du Moyen Age 84. Paris: Champion, 1957.

    EREC ET ENIDE. Edited by Mario Roques. Vol. I of *Les romans de Chrétien de Troyes édités d'après la copie de Guiot* (Bibl. nat. fr. 794). Classiques Français du Moyen Age. 80. Paris: Champion, 1952.

    YVAIN (LE CHEVALIER AU LION). Edited by T. B. W. Reid. French Classics. 2nd ed. Manchester University Press, 1948.

——GEREINT SON OF ERBIN in THE MABINOGION. Translated by Gwyn Jones and Thomas Jones. Everyman's Library No. 97. 3rd ed. London: Dent, 1966.

*Note*
    Since different editions use different spellings of proper names, these will appear in quotations from other critics in the forms used by those critics.

# The Romance of Erec and Enide: An Essay in Interpretation

*Erec* has long been the subject of much controversy among the critics. There have been many attempts to discover a connecting theme behind the adventures and festivities which follow one another in breathless succession; but so far no one interpretation has been able to command general acceptance. Indeed, Chrétien's last editor carefully refrains from committing himself on this issue and suggests that the various views which have been advanced may perhaps be less irreconcilable than they seem:

> ...c'est bien à Chrétien qu'appartiendrait la signification, le "sens" du roman, malheureusement difficile à dégager avec certitude et sur lequel il ne fournit aucune claire indication. Les commentateurs n'en ont eu que plus de liberté pour imaginer et construire les thèses et les symboles qu'ils se sont plu à attribuer à l'auteur d'*Erec*. . . . Ces opinions ne sont pas absolument inconciliables.[1]

A close study of the text has persuaded me, however, that the romance has a very definite theme and that the key to it is provided by an understanding of four points:

(1) The motivation of Erec's second quest (namely, the expedition he undertakes with Enide when she accuses him of *recreantise*).

(2) Erec's role in the romance.

(3) Enide's role in the romance.

(4) The significance of the ending Chrétien gives to Erec's quest for the 'Joie de la Cort'.

The purpose of this present study is to make a detailed examination of these four points. By this means I hope to show that part of Chrétien's meaning in claiming in the preface to *Erec* that he had turned a mere adventure story into a 'molt bele conjointure' (vs 13–4) was that he had provided it with a theme to hold the interest of men right down the ages.

## I  THE MOTIVATION OF EREC'S SECOND QUEST[2]

The key to any understanding of the romance of Erec and Enide is the motive behind Erec's second quest. For until we realise why Erec decides to set off into the unknown with Enide, it is impossible to make any sense of the story. Yet this crucial question is one that Chrétien leaves his readers to answer for themselves. There is no explanatory comment at the time that Erec's decision is taken, and no explanation is provided when the main events of the expedition are recapitulated on Erec's return to court (vs 6416–38). Indeed, Chrétien flatly refuses to give one on the grounds that his story makes everything perfectly clear:

> Erec ancomance son conte:
> ses avantures li reconte,
> que nule n'en i antroblie.
> Mes cuidiez vos que je vos die
> quex acoisons le fist movoir?
> Naié; que bien savez le voir
> et de ice, et d'autre chose,
> si con ge la vos ai esclose.                    (vs 6417–24)

One feels, in fact, that he is providing his patrons with a talking point, much as Thomas does in *Tristan* when he invites his public to decide which of the four unhappy lovers is the most to be pitied: Mark, the queen, Tristan or Tristan's wife.[3]

In the absence of any definite ruling from the author, the critics have felt themselves at liberty to read what motive they will into his story. Ferdinand Lot, for example, states that 'la conduite d'Erec est difficilement compréhensible' and then observes in a footnote that 'Chrétien de Troyes ne daigne même pas l'expliquer et laisse au lecteur le soin d'interpréter sa conduite';[4] whilst E. S. Sheldon maintains even more forcibly that:

> Since Chrétien does not plainly tell us why he makes Erec act as he does after Enide has told him what people are saying of him, any attempt to find out what was in the poet's mind must be more or less conjectural, and only a certain degree of probability can be attained.[5]

Accordingly, a number of theories have been put forward to account for Erec's departure. For some his aim is to test Enide's love and put an end to the torturing doubts aroused by her criticisms of him;[6] for others it is to assert his authority as a husband which he feels has been challenged by her.[7] Some critics see him as a man wounded in his self-esteem and determined to vindicate himself;[8] others maintain that his concern is to resume his duties as a knight and re-instate Enide in her rightful role as his lady.[9] Finally it has even been claimed that Erec's aim is to test Enide's veracity.[10] But of all the various explanations advanced so far, not one has proved entirely satisfactory, not one has been found conclusive enough to command general support. The result has been that Chrétien's more recent commentators have either turned to compromise for a solution, ascribing Erec's departure to a combination of motives (as in passage (a) below); or have been driven to despair of ever finding one at the plot-level (as can be seen from passage (b)).

(a) Les raisons qui déterminent la prompte décision d'Erec sont moins simples: elles se conjuguent, mais elles sont diverses. Le héros a été profondément blessé dans sa fierté, son honneur de chevalier. La revanche de son amour-propre se manifeste par sa froideur, son laconisme impérieux, sa dureté. Il est d'autant plus irrité qu'il reconnaît la justesse des reproches qui lui sont faits. ... Il arrive que rien n'exaspère au même point le mécontentement de soi et le désir d'une réhabilitation, fût-ce aux dépens d'autrui, qu'une critique légitime entendue à contretemps. Erec a douté aussi de l'amour d'Enide ... il a conclu de la "parole" perçue dans son demi-sommeil, de cet inquiétant "con mar fus", du trouble et de la réticence d'Enide, ..., qu'elle s'est laissé aller à subir l'influence des autres, qu'elle lui échappe peut-être et ne l'aime pas assez. Le sentiment d'une faille possible dans la perfection de leur amour lui est insupportable. Pour détruire ce tourment raffiné, pour savoir s'il est fondé ou vain, il se résout sur-le-champ, selon l'exigence de son coeur et de son esprit, à "essayer" Enide, à l'éprouver. A ces mobiles très clairs, s'ajoute une nuance qui était plus immédiatement intelligible au Moyen Age que de nos jours: l'idée que dans le mariage c'est l'homme qui doit commander. En se faisant l'écho du reproche de *recreantise*, en se plaignant du dommage qui l'atteint elle aussi, en se présentant quelque peu comme une victime, en réclamant, au lieu de la suggérer, le réhabilitation qui lui paraît être désormais le devoir impérieux de son mari, Enide a commis non seulement une maladresse qu'elle aurait pu réparer par des explications plus habiles, mais aussi une faute: acte d'orgueil, de "sorcuidance". A un point de vue qui n'est plus nécessairement le nôtre, Erec a le droit d'estimer qu'il se trouve atteint dans sa "souveraineté" d'époux: il ne lui paraît pas injuste qu'Enide subisse un purgatoire d'obéissance.[11]

(b) It is difficult to believe that Chrestien is incapable of writing clearly, for nothing is more lucid than his expositions. Nothing could be arranged with more care and order than this romance of Erec and Enide. Yet there remains this obscure motivation for the episodes and hence there persists a vague uneasiness about the meaning of the poem. Apparently the answer does not lie within the plot elements, and one should look to the *sans* [i.e. the symbolic meaning] for a solution – or concede that the romances are just a series of loosely connected adventures with no overall meaning or thesis.[12]

For my part, however, I would suggest that a more positive stand than either compromise or despair should be taken over the question of the motivation of Erec's second quest. A careful reading of the text shows that there is in fact no justification for claiming that Chrétien 'a laissé les sentiments d'Erec dans une ombre mystérieuse'.[13] On the contrary, one finds that his story provides all the clues needed to build up a very clear picture of what was in Erec's mind as he set off into the blue with his wife – provided, and this is all important, that the passages are read in context and are approached without any pre-conceived ideas as to how a twelfth-century hero should act, or a twelfth-century poet write or think.

The passages which enable us to determine why Erec undertakes his expedition with Enide occur between vs 2762 (when he leaves his father's court) and vs 5212 (when he decides to return to Arthur). They include Erec's remarks to Enide; Enide's impressions of Erec; and the comments Chrétien makes from time to time about Erec's reactions. Their value as evidence differs considerably. Some passages provide mere straws-in-the-wind which indicate but give no definite proof of Erec's mood and intentions. Others are of capital importance and make it possible to establish once and for all why Erec treats his wife as harshly as he does.

The first clue to Erec's behaviour comes at the outset of his journey. It is Enide's conviction that he is furious with her since he refuses to speak to her:

> "Mes de ce sui morte et traïe,
> que mes sires m'a anhaïe.
> Anhaïe m'a, bien le voi,
> quant il ne vialt parler a moi."          (vs 2785–8)

Enide's conclusion here is natural enough. It cannot, however, be taken as definite proof of Erec's displeasure, since she could conceivably be mistaken in her interpretation of his instructions to ride ahead and not to speak unless spoken to:

> Erec s'an va, sa fame an moinne,
> ne set ou, mes en avanture.
> "Alez, fet il, grant aleüre,
> et gardez ne soiez tant ose
> que, se vos veez nule chose,
> ne me dites ne ce ne quoi;
> tenez vos de parler a moi,
> se ge ne vos aresne avant.
> Alez grant aleüre avant
> et chevauchiez tot a seür."          (vs 2762–71)

The description of Erec's encounter with the first robber-band provides three pointers to his mood and intentions:

(1) There is an indication that at the start of the quest Erec's attention is turned in upon himself and is not directed towards Enide, as one might expect it to be if his main concern were to test her love. When the robbers approach, Enide is convinced that Erec is too preoccupied to have noticed them and attempts to call him back to an awareness of outer realities:

> "Cil le ferra ja demenois,
> que mes sires ne s'an prant garde.
>       .     .     .     .     .
> Vers lui se torne en es le pas
> et dist: "Biau sire, ou pansez vos?
> Ci vienent poignant aprés vos
> troi chevalier qui molt vos chacent;
> peor ai que mal ne vos facent."          (vs 2834–44)

Here again, however, we are dealing with a mere straw-in-the-wind. There is nothing at present to show whether Enide is correct in her surmise.

(2) Erec's reply to Enide's warning is a clear statement of his exasperation at her disobedience. He tells her he sees it as an act of sheer insubordination, as a flouting of his authority, and warns her not to repeat the offence, although he is prepared to overlook it this time:

> "Cui? fet Erec, qu'avez vos dit?
> Or me prisiez vos trop petit.
> Trop avez fet grant hardemant,
> qui avez mon comandemant
> et ma desfanse trespassee.
> Ceste foiz vos iert pardonee,
> mes, s'autre foiz vos avenoit,
> ja pardoné ne vos seroit."          (vs 2845–52)

But however explicit Erec's displeasure may seem here, there has, as yet, been nothing to show if his words are to be taken at their face value. They may possibly belie his true feelings, as those who maintain that he is testing Enide claim they do:

> ... cette dureté n'est qu'une attitude que prend Erec, afin de rendre l'épreuve plus efficace; c'est un jeu cruel, mais nécessaire, pour éprouver la force de cet amour.[14]

(3) Erec's treatment of Enide after the fight shows that his victory has done nothing to alter his tone or manner. He orders her to ride ahead with the captured horses, and cautions her to keep silent unless she is told she may speak:

> A son chemin est repeiriez,
> la ou Enyde l'atandoit.
> Les trois chevax li comandoit
> devant li mener et chacier,
> et molt la prist a menacier
> qu'ele ne soit plus si hardie
> c'un seul mot de la boche die,
> se il ne l'an done congié.          (vs 2910–7)

The description of Erec's encounter with the second robber-band provides three further pointers to Erec's state of mind:
(1) A comment from Chrétien shows that Erec is on his guard and is watching Enide when the attack comes. We are told that Erec sees the first of his assailants bearing down on him but conceals the fact:

> Erec le vit et sanblant fist
> qu'ancor garde ne s'an preïst.          (vs 2957–8)

From this we can infer that on the previous occasion Erec had indeed been caught unawares, and that it took the first encounter to put him on his guard and also to direct his attention to Enide.

(2) Erec's reply to Enide's second warning is an even plainer statement of his exasperation at her disobedience. He complains bitterly of her lack of respect for himself and his wishes, and tells her bluntly that he thoroughly resents her officiousness. The tirade ends with an injunction to keep quiet in future, since he has no wish to hear anything from her:

> Erec respont: "Mar le pansastes,
> que ma parole trespassastes
> ce que desfandu vos avoie;
> et ne por quant tres bien savoie
> que gueres ne me priseiez.
> Cest servise mal anpleiez,
> que ge ne vos an sai nul gré;
> bien sachiez que ge vos an hé;
> dit le vos ai et di ancore.
> Ancor le vos pardonrai ore;
> mes autre foiz vos an gardez,
> ne ja vers moi ne regardez,
> que vos feriez molt que fole,
> car je n'aim pas vostre parole."     (vs 2993–3006)

Yet however obvious Erec's resentment may seem here, we are still in no position to tell whether it is genuine or not.

(3) For Enide, however, there are no doubts about the reality of Erec's displeasure. She obeys without a word when he orders her, once again, to ride ahead with the captured horses and to beware of speaking to him (vs 3070–8). Later, we find she has no doubts either about the cause of Erec's anger. Her reflections as she keeps watch over him that night indicate that she is convinced that he has been offended by her criticism of his *recreantise*. She bitterly regrets taking him to task for his sloth, and feels that she is being justly punished for her presumption:

> Et molt s'est blasmee et maudite
> de la parole qu'ele ot dite:
> molt a, ce dit, mal esploitié,
> "que n'ai mie de la mité
> le mal que je ai desservi.
> Lasse, fet ele, si mar vi
> mon orguel et ma sorcuidance!
> Savoir pooie sanz dotance
> que tel chevalier ne meillor
> ne savoit l'an de mon seignor.
> Bien le savoie. Or le sai mialz;
> car ge l'ai veü a mes ialz,
> car trois ne cinc armez ne dote.
> Honie soit ma leingue tote,
> qui l'orguel et la honte dist
> dont mes cors a tel honte gist."     (vs 3097–3112)

Although it is impossible to subscribe to Enide's view of herself as presumptuous and overweening, she could very well be right in thinking that Erec had taken exception to her reproaches.

If the clues which have been considered so far have proved mere straws-in-the-wind, the evidence provided by the next episode, the encounter with the amorous count, is conclusive and enables us to establish three points:

(1) There is proof that Erec is not jealous of his wife. When the count asks to be allowed to pay his respects to Enide, Chrétien states that Erec saw no cause for jealousy in the request:

> Erec ne fu mie jalous,
> que il n'i pansa nule boise. (vs 3296–7)

This disposes of the claim that Erec's expedition was motivated by jealousy:

> Et Erec? Derrière le silence du poète, qui ne nous montre que ses actions, pouvons-nous en pénétrer les motifs? Le conte gallois dit expressément qu'il soupçonne sa femme ... ce motif paraît bien être celui que Chrétien a eu aussi dans l'esprit: Erec doute de l'amour d'Enide, et n'est rassuré que quand il l'a mis à une longue et multiple épreuve: voyez le passage ... où il lui déclare qu'après l'avoir *essaiee* il ne doute plus qu'elle ne l'aime *parfitement*. ... C'est donc ce doute sur l'amour d'Enide qui tourmente l'Erec français comme le Gereint gallois; seulement Chrétien, employant un procédé qu'il a toujours affectionné, nous le laisse deviner, au lieu que le conteur gallois le dit expressément.[15]

In accusing Erec of jealousy, Gaston Paris allowed himself to be over-influenced by the example of Gereint – unless he was just following the Gallic tendency to *chercher l'homme* when difficulties arise between man and wife.

(2) There is a clear indication that Erec's resentment at Enide's disobedience in the previous episodes was genuine enough. When Enide warns him of the count's intentions, Chrétien states that Erec suddenly realises that she is devoted to him:

> Or ot Erec que bien se prueve
> vers lui sa fame lëaumant. (vs 3480–1)

This shows that hitherto he had been quite sincere in accusing her of flouting his authority. It thereby invalidates the claim that Erec has merely been testing Enide, and is secretly gratified by her successive acts of disobedience.

> ... chaque fois que, chevauchant en tête à vive allure, elle sera la première à voir un danger, ... , chaque fois elle rompra le silence imposé. Si Erec n'est pas mécontent qu'elle obéisse, il est plus heureux encore qu'elle désobéisse: c'est sa désobéissance qui prouve son amour.[16]

(3) There is also a clear indication that the recognition of Enide's devotion is gradually disarming Erec and causing his anger to evaporate.

When he turns on her for telling him that the count and his men are on their heels, he qualifies his usual threats by admitting to the possibility of a change of heart in himself:

> Erec respont: "Po me prisiez,
> quant ma parole despisiez;
> je ne vos sai si bel prïer
> que je vos puisse chastïer.
> Mes, se Dex ait de moi merci
> et eschaper puisse de ci,
> ceste vos iert molt chier vandue,
> *se corages ne me remue.*"                    (vs 3553–60)

The description of the encounter with Guivret contains a passage of vital importance for the understanding of Erec's behaviour in both the earlier and the later stages of his quest. It is Chrétien's statement that, when Erec turns on Enide for warning him of Guivret's arrival, his threats are meaningless since he knows that she loves him more than anything else in the world and that he loves her with all his might:

> Ele li dit; il la menace;
> mes n'a talant que mal li face,
> qu'il aparçoit et conuist bien
> qu'ele l'ainme sor tote rien,
> et il li tant que plus ne puet.              (vs 3751–5)

This passage has a threefold significance:

(1) It proves once again, and this time beyond all dispute, that Erec's threats were uttered in anger on the earlier occasions and that his harshness was genuine enough and not assumed as has been claimed.

(2) It proves that it is the recognition of Enide's devotion to himself that has mollified Erec and brought back all his old tenderness for her. This is a point of some importance. It shows that those who see Erec as a husband who feels he must assert his authority over his wife have no grounds for claiming that it is the recognition of her submissiveness, the discovery that she does accept his authority, which appeases his anger:

> . . . Erec is hurt, hurt at Enide's siding with his detractors; his pride or his sense of *soveraynétee* is aroused; he asserts it in both directions: (1) as to Enide by humbling her, (2) as to himself, by proving his valor, which I see no reason to think he has seriously doubted; *and learning in the course of the ride that Enide can submit, he forgives and reinstates her in her former position.* . . .[17]

(3) Finally, vs 3751–5 make it clear that from now on only the shame and embarrassment of admitting himself to have been in the wrong are holding Erec back from making his peace with his wife. The fact that he maintains an outward show of anger when his resentment is dead within him; the fact that he continues to expose Enide to further hardship and danger when his heart is full of tenderness towards her, can only mean

that Erec is casting round for some occasion which will allow him to put an end to their estrangement with the minimum loss of dignity and face. Such a reaction is human enough. It is never easy to acknowledge that one has been in the wrong, particularly for so proud a man as Erec. It is equally understandable that the urgency of finding an opportunity for a reconciliation should make Erec refuse Guivret's offers of hospitality after their fight (vs 3878–90); insist on spending only one night in Arthur's camp, when he needs a full fortnight to recover from his wounds (vs 4209–20); and risk exposing Enide to death and worse when he is in no fit state to protect her.

Some critics, it is true, have seen Erec's final adventures as a quest for some supreme proof of Enide's devotion, which he eventually obtains at Limors:

> A Limors, Erec passant pour mort, Enide n'a plus rien à redouter de lui. Rien ne l'empêche donc de montrer ses véritables sentiments. ... C'est l'épreuve finale, le triomphe de l'amour conjugal, plus fort que la mort. *Aussi Erec ne peut-il plus douter à présent.* L'aventure s'achève donc ici dans le pardon et dans l'amour.[18]

But such critics either disregard vs 3753–5 which show that Erec is already convinced of Enide's absolute devotion before he meets Guivret, or they overlook the fact that in making him demand still further proof, as is done in the following commentary, they turn him into a monster of suspicion, a pathological case:

> Erec, ému et attendri, sans oser le montrer encore, touche déjà au seuil du pardon. Le poète nous dit de lui:
>
> > ... Cil la menace
> > mes n'a talant que mal li face;
> > qu'il aparçoit et conoist bien
> > qu'ele l'aimme sor tote rien,
> > et il li tant que plus ne puet.          (vs 3765–9)
>
> Et c'est là comme un éclair qui jaillit du fond de son âme où la flamme de l'amour, voilée par la douleur, obscurcie par la méfiance, ne s'est jamais éteinte. Mais pour que cette flamme déchire enfin les ténèbres qui l'enveloppent, il faut une révélation éblouissante de la part de la femme, un acte d'héroïsme qui couronnera toute son oeuvre de tendresse et fera tomber à jamais la barrière qui sépare deux coeurs aimants.[19]

The final clue to Erec's motives in setting out on his expedition with Enide is found in the description of their encounter with Oringles. It is provided by Erec himself as he rides off from Limors, with Enide in his arms, and at last finds himself able to make his peace with her now that he has saved her from the clutches of the count. First he assures her that her term of trial is over and that now she need fear no more, for he loves her more dearly than ever before and is certain of her absolute devotion to himself (vs 4882–7). Then, having reassured her that she is completely

reinstated in his affections and favour (vs 4888–90), he adds that he freely
and fully forgives the offence caused by any untimely remark she may have
made about his conduct (vs 4891–3):

4879   Et Erec, qui sa fame an porte,
l'acole et beise et reconforte;
antre ses braz contre son cuer
4882   l'estraint, et dit: "Ma dolce suer,
bien vos ai de tot essaiee.
Or ne soiez plus esmaiee,
c'or vos aim plus qu'ainz mes ne fis,
et je resui certains et fis
que vos m'amez parfitemant.
4888   Or voel estre d'or en avant,
ausi con j'estoie devant,
tot a vostre comandemant;
4891   et se vos rien m'avez mesdit,
je le vos pardoing tot et quit
del forfet et de la parole."
4894   Adons la rebeise et acole.
Or n'est pas Enyde a maleise,
quant ses sires l'acole et beise,
et de s'amor la raseüre.

The all-important lines in this passage are 4891–3 with their reference to
the offence given by Enide's criticisms and the all-revealing attempt to
pass them off as calumnies – in spite of the fact that they were justified
and that Erec himself had admitted as much at the time (vs 2572–3).
They make it perfectly clear that Enide was right to think that Erec's
anger had been caused by her comments on his *recreantise*. And this,
surely, should come as no surprise. Nothing is more difficult to brook
than criticism. It is hard enough to accept it with a good grace even from
an acknowledged superior; it is harder still for most men to take it from a
woman. Moreover, in Erec's case, the inevitable resentment of wounded
pride is exacerbated by the fear that he has forfeited Enide's esteem and
thereby her love; for in twelfth-century eyes 'seignor ne crient qui ne le
prise, / et qui nel prise ne l'a chier'.[20] Nor again should we be surprised to
find that Erec makes no apology for his harshness, for his callous disregard
of Enide; but talks instead of calumnies to be pardoned and a test that
has been passed. It is, after all, natural enough to try to save appearances
with a discreet lie, to keep face in one's own eyes and in those of the
world. The twelfth century, at all events, was fully aware of the human
tendency to rationalise misconduct. There is the case of the Duke of
Saxony in *Cligés*, whose one thought is to save his skin, but whose talk is
all of sparing his young adversary; there is the description Marie de
France gives of Equitan casting round for an excuse to seduce his seneschal's wife; and above all, there is Thomas' masterly study of Tristan's
attempt to justify himself in breaking his oath to the Queen and seeking
oblivion in the arms of the second Ysolt.[21]

And now that it has been established that Erec's anger was indeed the resentment of wounded self-esteem (the self-esteem of a proud man caught in the wrong, the self-esteem of a husband who finds he may have lost his wife's respect), it is easy enough to arrive at the motive behind his second quest. The inevitable reaction of anyone who has been criticised, particularly when the charges are justified, is to strive to vindicate himself and give his critics the lie. As La Bruyère reminds us:

> Il est pénible à un homme fier de pardonner à celui qui le surprend en faute et qui se plaint de lui avec raison. Sa fierté ne s'adoucit que lorsqu'il reprend ses avantages et qu'il met l'autre dans son tort.[22]

So if Erec forces Enide to set out with him in search of adventure when he learns from her that he is accused of *recreantise*, the reason must surely be that he is determined to give her proof of his hardihood and so win the satisfaction of hearing her say that her charges were ill-founded (just as he claims they were at the moment of reconciliation), and at the same time reconquer her esteem. It is this need to vindicate himself that makes Erec resent Enide's interventions so fiercely; for he sees them as further and flagrant proof that he has lost her confidence and respect. And it is because he must prove himself in Enide's eyes that Erec can only make his peace with her when he has put her in his debt. Once that has been done and his pride has been finally assuaged, he will be prepared to be her debtor, even to the extent of owing his life to her (vs 4983–5024), but not before.

Although vs 4879–97 provide the final clue to Erec's intentions in undertaking the expedition with Enide, they have all too often proved a trap for the unwary. As often as not, the critics have taken vs 4882–3 as proof positive that Erec has been testing Enide in order to put an end to the torturing doubts aroused by her criticisms of him.

> G. Paris a indiqué depuis longtemps le principe de la seule explication possible: il faut qu'Erec ait douté de l'amour d'Enide puisqu'il déclarera lui-même avoir voulu l'"essayer".[23]

> Il y a, en effet, un passage, où Chrétien d'un seul mot explique l'attitude énigmatique d'Erec et le sens qu'il entendait donner à toute la tournée d'aventures. Il a placé l'explication, comme cela se convient, dans la bouche d'Erec, mais elle rend évidemment la propre pensée de l'auteur, et il l'a mise au seul endroit où elle était possible, c'est-à-dire au moment de la réconciliation des deux époux. Car c'est alors seulement qu'Erec peut avouer à Enide le fond de sa pensée et lui faire comprendre l'attitude déconcertante qu'il avait prise à son égard. C'est donc à la fin de l'épisode de Limors, quand Erec, revenu à la vie, serre Enide sur son coeur, qu'il lui déclare: "Bien vos ai del tot essaiee" (v. 4921). Essaiee! Donc il ne s'agit pas d'un châtiment, mais d'une épreuve à laquelle il a soumis sa femme. Épreuve de quoi? Les vers suivants le disent avec la même précision:

> Ne soiez de rien esmaiee
> Qu'or vos aim plus qu'ains mes ne fis,
> Et je resui certains et fis
> Que vos m'amez parfitement.                    (vs 4922–5)

L'accent porte sur *or*: "car maintenant je vous aime plus que jamais, et de mon côté je suis sûr et certain que vois m'amez parfaitement". C'est l'amour même de sa femme qu'il a voulu éprouver.[24]

But to take Erec at his word here when he speaks of testing Enide is to read the whole passage out of context. The theory that he forces Enide to undergo the rigours of a quest more in sorrow than in anger just will not square with the facts of Chrétien's story. The evidence of the text has shown that up to the encounter with Guivret Erec acts in anger. Moreover, if proof of Enide's love were all that he required such proof has been his since the encounter with Guivret and even before it. That Erec should go on after this to search for some irresistible, some ultimate demonstration of Enide's devotion is monstrous and utterly incredible. Indeed, the prolongation of Enide's ordeal beyond the point where Erec is fully convinced of her love for him and of his love for her, is one of the reasons why W. S. Woods abandoned all hope of making sense of *Erec*.[25]

No doubt the objection will be raised here that Chrétien himself describes Erec as having made trial of his wife in vs 5096–8:

> Or ne li set que reprochier
> Erec, qui bien l'a esprovee:
> vers li a grant amor trovee.

For these lines are generally thought to mean: 'Now Erec knows no further reason to reproach her, for he has tried her well and found that she bears great love to him' (with 'esprover' taken in the sense of 'testing' and the 'li' of vs 5098 seen as a mistake for the masculine form 'lui' – a confusion which actually does occur in vs 1120 of *Erec*).[26] This objection, however, will not hold. It overlooks the fact that in Old French the verb 'esprover' has a variety of meanings besides that of deliberately testing something. In particular, it overlooks the fact that with a personal object 'esprover' can be used in the sense of assessing (or of knowing) someone's character or worth.[27] This, for instance, is the way the word is employed by the heroine of *Cligés* when she explains why she has full confidence in the discretion of her nurse:

> "Mestre, fet ele, je sai bien
> que chose que je ci vos die
> n'iert ja par vos avant oïe,
> car molt vos ai bien esprovee
> et molt vos ai sage trovee:
> tant m'avez fet que molt vos aim."    (*Cligés* vs 5350–5)

In this particular case, it is highly unlikely that the girl has been subjecting her nurse to a series of searching tests. It is far more likely that her claim: 'molt vos ai bien esprovee' merely means that her everyday dealings with her nurse have given her an insight into the woman's character and enabled her to form a clear idea of her worth. A still clearer case of 'esprover' being used in the sense of assessing, or knowing, someone's character and worth is found in the proverb quoted by the heroine of *Yvain* when she turns to her companion for help:

> ". . . se De plest, ore i verrons
> vostre consoil et vostre san;
> *qu'au besoing, toz jorz le dit an,*
> *doit an son ami esprover.*"          (*Yvain* vs 6598–601)

Here there can be no question of 'esprover' meaning 'to test'. It would be ludicrous to take the adage to mean that misfortune should be used as an occasion for deliberately testing the sincerity of one's friends. It can only mean: 'the time to assess (or to recognise) the true worth of a friend is when things are going badly'. At all events, this interpretation is borne out by the following passages where the proverb appears in variant forms and which make it very clear that a man can only hope to recognise his friends for what they are really worth from the way they behave in his hour of need:

> Ainc nel sot, mais or le sara,
> se il nul verai ami a;
> *car nus ne set s'il aime seus*
> *si bien com fait li besoigneus,*
> qu'ami ne se püent celer
> quant l'uns voit l'autre mesmener.
> *Ne puet savoir cui riens ne faut*
> *s'en l'aime ou het,* se Diex me salt.
> (*First Continuation of the Perceval*, edited by
> W. Roach, vs 151–8)

> "Si vos prie et mande sanz faille
> que la le veigniez garantir.
> Guiromelant velt desmentir
> qui s'est de lui honir vantez.
> Bien le vos dit, si est vertez,
> vos ne Gavains ne vostre ami
> n'avez plus mortel anemi.
> *Au besoing pert qui est amis.*
> Mesire Gavains m'a tramis
> a celui qui les besoigneus
> maintient contre les orgueilleus."
> (*First Continuation of the Perceval* vs 58–68)

Since 'esprover' can be used both in the sense of testing someone and in the sense of assessing or recognising someone's character or worth, it follows that the statement 'or ne li set que reprochier / Erec, qui bien l'a esprovee' is open to two interpretations if it is considered out of context.

(a) It can mean: 'Erec, who has tested her thoroughly, has nothing to criticise in her now'.

(b) It can also mean: 'Erec, who has formed a true estimate of her worth (or, has come to know her thoroughly), has nothing to criticise in her now'. In this case, the connection with Chrétien's next remark: 'he has come to feel a very great love for her' ('vers li a grant amor trovee') is both apparent and logical.

Once the words 'or ne li set que reprochier / Erec, qui bien l'a esprovee' are considered in their context, it is immediately clear that only the second of these two interpretations holds. Whilst it is true that Enide has been put to the proof in the course of the quest and has given abundant proof of her love, her courage and good sense, this proving of Enide has been the unexpected result of the expedition rather than its primary objective.[28] As we have seen, Erec's attention at the outset of the journey was fixed upon himself rather than his wife, so that it took the shock of his first encounter with a robber-band to direct it towards her. And, as we have seen, the discovery of Enide's true feelings towards him came as an unexpected revelation to Erec, which disarmed him in spite of himself. To argue, therefore, from line 5097 that Erec set out to test his wife is to mistake result for cause.

The review of the evidence contained in Chrétien's account of Erec's second quest is now complete. It has shown that wounded pride and not a torturing doubt drove Erec to go off into the unknown with Enide. It has also shown that the story Chrétien has to tell is a perfectly coherent and human one. It is the story of a man taken to task by his wife, who sets out resentfully to vindicate himself in her eyes; but who comes in the process to recognise her love and worth, and is so disarmed by his discovery that he is left, with the semblance of a quarrel on his hands, to look around for an occasion for reconciliation.

## 2    EREC'S ROLE IN THE ROMANCE

Though one might expect resentment to be the inevitable reaction of a man who finds himself taken to task as baldly and as tactlessly as Erec is, there has been much opposition to the idea that his harsh treatment of Enide reflects the bitterness of his wounded self-esteem. This opposition stems in the first place from two widely held assumptions that are closely allied to one another:

(i) It is taken for granted that the hero of a medieval romance must act at all times from the worthiest of all possible motives, and is necessarily exempt from all human foibles and weaknesses.

(ii) It is assumed that, whereas it is fitting enough for a man to treat his wife harshly in order to allay his doubts about her love, it is not becoming for him to do so in a resentful attempt to counter her criticisms of himself.

The first of these assumptions expresses itself very clearly in the following passage. Here Nitze's view that Erec is trying to reassert his authority as a husband is rejected out of hand by E. S. Sheldon on the score that however natural it might be, such conduct would be below a courtly hero:

> The psychological correctness of Erec's behaviour urged in the same paper (p. 448) needs some comment. I am quite willing to grant that the conduct of Erec is psychologically explicable, that such a man might be unjust as he is (according to the sovereignty theory), though he has no plausible excuse. But this does not meet the real difficulty for me in the poem, which stands in the way of this theory. *We are concerned in the present discussion not so much with the question whether Erec's conduct is psychologically natural or explicable as with the question whether the poet Chrétien made him act as he does with that reason (i.e. that it is so explicable though it is unjust) in his (Chrétien's) mind.* Nitze grants that Enide does not deserve (according to his and Foerster's theory) the very unjust treatment she gets, but he urges, in palliation of Erec's injustice, that it is not unnatural under the circumstances. *But could the poet represent his hero as falling so far short of the ideal conduct of a good knight?* We can see that a good man under tension may fall short of ideal conduct, but any intelligent outsider looking at the situation here presented must see that, in spite of the extenuating circumstances, Erec's conduct is distinctly discreditable, being flagrantly unjust. And Chrétien was such an intelligent outsider, and his readers were and are outsiders, and some of them in his own time must have been intelligent enough to see the unpardonable injustice Erec is, on this theory, guilty of toward Enide.[29]

As for the assumption that harshness is acceptable in the treatment of a wife if it is to test her love, but unbecoming if it is to assuage wounded pride, this expresses itself equally clearly in the next two passages. In the first of these, the view that Erec acts out of pique and bitterness is rejected out of hand on the score that such a reaction would be absurd; and in the second, on the ground that it would be unfair:

> Sans ce doute d'Erec, sa conduite est impossible à comprendre: il ne peut, *sous peine d'être absurde*, en vouloir à sa femme, s'il ne doute pas de son amour, d'avoir eu le courage de lui conseiller de vivre moins pour elle et plus pour sa gloire; il peut être quelque peu froissé de ce qu'elle le lui ait dit aussi nettement, mais cela ne saurait suffire à expliquer son étrange voyage.[30]

> ... l'on explique la colère d'Erec par une blessure d'amour-propre, qui ne saurait *justifier* les dangereuses épreuves auxquelles il soumet sa femme. G. Paris a indiqué depuis longtemps le principe de la seule explication possible: il faut qu'Erec ait douté de l'amour d'Enide puisqu'il déclarera lui-même avoir voulu l'"essayer".[31]

But for all that these two assumptions have been generally subscribed to – and so far only Nitze seems to have contested the view that a hero of romance must at all times be a dignified figure[32] – the fact remains that Chrétien's story plainly shows Erec behaving as absurdly and as unfairly as human beings all too often do. In the circumstances it would surely seem more logical to question the validity of the assumptions than deny the evidence of the text. And it is all the more necessary to do this when the attempts to provide more flattering interpretations of Erec's conduct fail to square with the facts of the story, or do so only at the cost of turning him into a monster of suspicion.

A second cause for the opposition to the idea that Erec acts out of resentment in making Enide share the rigours of a quest is the failure of the critics to consider the estrangement of the lovers in the context of the romance as a whole. When it is seen in context, Erec no longer appears as a husband who cuts a rather sorry figure in a tiff with his wife, but as a young man who passes before our eyes from youth to maturity. In the course of Chrétien's story we watch Erec learn two lessons: first, that he has obligations beyond his private pleasures and inclinations;[33] and second, that his wife is someone to be treated with consideration and respect.

That Erec has to learn the need for self-discipline is obvious from the way he gives himself up entirely to the pleasures of honeymooning with Enide when he withdraws from Arthur's court to his father's domains. In the preface to his account of the estrangement, Chrétien stresses that Erec is so completely absorbed in the delights of bed that it is often well past midday before he and Enide get up, and that though he continues to supply his men with the horses and arms they need for tourneying, he himself is no longer interested in such activities. Clearly there has been a sad falling off in the man Arthur had esteemed as the foremost knight of his court after Gauvain (vs 2230–6), and not surprisingly his men complain bitterly of his *recreantise*:

> . . . tant l'ama Erec d'amors,
> que d'armes mes ne li chaloit,
> ne a tornoiemant n'aloit.
> N'avoit mes soing de tornoier:
> a sa fame volt dosnoier,
> si an fist s'amie et sa drue;
> en li a mise s'antendue,
> en acoler et an beisier;
> ne se quierent d'el aeisier.
> Si conpaignon duel en avoient;
> sovant entr'ax se demantoient
> de ce que trop l'amoit assez.
> Sovant estoit midis passez,
> einz que de lez lui se levast;
> lui estoit bel, cui qu'il pesast.
> Molt petit de li s'esloignoit;
> mes ainz por ce moins ne donoit
> de rien nule a ses chevaliers
> armes ne robes ne deniers.
> Nul leu n'avoit tornoiemant
> nes anveast, molt richemant
> aparelliez et atornez.
> Destriers lor donoit sejornez
> por tornoier et por joster,
> que qu'il li deüssent coster.

> Ce disoit trestoz li barnages
> que granz diax ert et granz domages,
> quant armes porter ne voloit
> tex ber com il estre soloit.                    (vs 2430–58)

In the circumstances, Enide's strictures are well-founded, tactless though
they may be. There is, as she claims, an obvious need for reform, a need
for Erec to curb his self-indulgence, to put an end to his *recreantise*,
i.e. his sloth, and regain his former standing in the world:

> "Par ceste terre dïent tuit,
> li blonc et li mor et li ros,
> que granz domages est de vos
> que voz armes antrelessiez.
> Vostre pris est molt abessiez:
> tuit soloient dire l'autre an
> qu'an tot le mont ne savoit l'an
> meillor chevalier ne plus preu;
> vostres parauz n'estoit nul leu;
> or se vont tuit de vos gabant,
> juesne et chenu, petit et grant;
> recreant vos apelent tuit.
> Cuidiez vos qu'il ne m'an enuit,
> quant j'oi dire de vos despit?
> Molt me poise, quant an l'an dit,
> et por ce m'an poise ancor plus
> qu'il m'an metent le blasme sus;
> blasmee an sui, ce poise moi,
> et dïent tuit reison por coi,
> car si vos ai lacié et pris
> que vos an perdez vostre priz,
> ne ne querrez a el antandre.
> Or vos an estuet consoil prandre,
> que vos puissiez ce blasme estaindre
> et vostre premier los ataindre,
> car trop vos ai oï blasmer."       (vs 2540–65)

Erec's behaviour after his convalescence at Guivret's shows that he has
taken Enide's criticisms to heart – for all he affects to pass them off as
slanders at the time of their reconciliation (vs 4891–3). His first thought on
recovering his strength is to resume the active life he abandoned to give
himself up to amorous dalliance. A determination to make amends for
his past lapse shows itself in the urgency of his decision to return to Arthur.
This is clearly as pressing a matter for him now as the need to set out on
his quest with Enide had been before:

> "Sire, je ne puis plus atandre
> que je ne m'an aille an ma terre;
> feites apareillier et querre
> que j'aie tot mon estovoir:
> je voldrai par matin movoir,
> tantost com il iert ajorné.

> Tant ai antor vos sejorné
> que je me sant fort et delivre.
>
> .    .    .    .    .
>
> Je ne cuit nul leu demorer,
> se ne sui pris ou retenuz,
> tant qu'a la cort soie venuz
> le roi Artus, que veoir vuel
> a Quarrois ou a Quaraduel."          (vs 5218–34)

The same determination is also betrayed by the eagerness with which Erec accepts the challenge of the *Joie de la Cort* when he learns of that adventure from Guivret:

> Or ot Erec ce qui li siet.          (vs 5399)
>
> "Dex! an joie n'a se bien non,
> fet Erec; ce vois je querant.
> Ne m'alez ci desesperant,
> biax amis, ne de ce ne d'el,
> mes feisons prandre nostre ostel,
> que granz biens an puet avenir.
> Rien ne me porroit retenir
> que je n'aille querre la Joie."          (vs 5418–25)

And it is later still further emphasised by Erec's steadfast refusal to be influenced by the forebodings of the crowds who watch him riding through Brandigan (vs 5469–81; 5652–79), or to be deterred from his purpose by King Evrain:

> Erec l'antant et bien l'otroie
> que li rois a droit le consoille;
> mes con plus granz est la mervoille
> et l'avanture plus grevainne,
> plus la covoite et plus s'an painne.          (vs 5594–8)

In coming to see that knighthood cannot be set aside for the pleasures of love, Erec has learnt rather more than the fact that his prestige and his vocation must be paramount for a knight. The lesson he has been taught by Enide's criticisms is the more general one that duty must take precedence over private inclination. This can be seen from his behaviour at his father's funeral where he restrains his grief, as a king must, to carry out his public obligations:

> Erec an pesa plus asez
> qu'il ne mostra sanblant as genz,
> *mes diaus de roi n'est mie genz,*
> *n'a roi n'avient qu'il face duel.*
> La ou il ert, a Tintajuel,
> fist chanter vigiles et messes,
> promist et randi les promesses,
> si com il les avoit promises,
> as meisons Deu et as eglises.
> Molt fist bien ce que fere dut:          (vs 6466–75)

In other words, the coronation at Nantes marks the end of an apprentice-ship which has fitted Erec for the responsibilities he must assume with the crown.

As for the second lesson that Erec learns in the course of the romance, the progress he makes as a lover can be gauged by comparing his attitude to Enide before and after their estrangement. In the early days of their relationship Erec's behaviour left something to be desired. Though he shows a lively appreciation of the physical pleasure she can offer him, he seems to have small regard for her as a person and shows little consideration for her feelings.

Where Alexander is fearful of forcing himself on Soredamors and hesi-tates to ask for her hand in marriage, although he knows his request would be granted (*Cligés* vs 2187–97), Erec asks Enide's father for her hand – much as he asked for the loan of his armour – without once con-sulting her wishes:

> "Mes ancor vos voel querre un don,
> don ge randrai le guerredon,
> se Dex done que je m'an aille
> a tot l'enor de la bataille."
> Et cil li respont franchemant:
> "Demandez tot seüremant
> vostre pleisir, comant qu'il aut:
> riens que je aie ne vos faut."
> Lors dist Erec, que l'esprevier
> vialt par sa fille desresnier,
>
> .    .    .    .    .
>
> Puis dist: "Sire, vos ne savez
> quel oste herbergié avez,
> de quel afeire et de quel gent.
> Filz sui d'un riche roi puissant:
> mes peres li rois Lac a non,
> Erec m'apelent li Breton;
>
> .    .    .    .    .
>
> ... je vos promet et otroi,
> se vos armes m'aparelliez
> et vostre fille me bailliez
> demain a l'esprevier conquerre,
> que je l'an manrai an ma terre,
> se Dex la victoire m'an done;
> la li ferai porter corone,
> s'iert reïne de dis citez.
> – Ha! biax sire, est ce veritez?
> Erec, li filz Lac, estes vos?
> – Ce sui mon, fet il, a estros."
> Li ostes molt s'an esjoï
> et dist: "Bien avomes oï
> de vos parler an cest païs.
>
> .    .    .    .    .
>
> ja de moi n'iroiz escondiz:
> tot a vostre comandemant

> ma bele fille vos comant."
> Lors l'a prise par mi le poing:
> "Tenez, fet il, je la vos doing."
> Erec lieemant la reçut,
> or a quanque il li estut.          (vs 631–80)

Again, in insisting that she appear at court in her ragged gown, Erec gives no thought to the embarrassment this will cause Enide, even though he has heard her cousin call attention to the indignity of it:

> "Demain droit a l'aube del jor,
> an tel robe et an tel ator,
> an manrai vostre fille a cort:
> je voel que ma dame l'atort
> de la soe robe demainne,
> qui est de soie tainte an grainne."
> Une pucele estoit leanz,
> molt preuz, molt saige, molt vaillanz,
>
>         .       .       .       .
>
> A parole en a mis le conte:
> "Sire, fet ele, molt grant honte
> sera a vos, plus qu'a autrui,
> se cist sires an mainne o lui
> vostre niece, si povrement
> atornee de vestemant."
> Et li cuens respont: "Je vos pri,
> ma dolce niece, donez li,
> de voz robes que vos avez
> la mellor que vos i savez."
> Erec a la parole oïe
> et dist: "Sire, n'an parlez mie.
> Une chose sachiez vos bien:
> ne voldroie por nule rien
> qu'ele eüst d'autre robe point
> tant que la reïne li doint."          (vs 1331–58)

Finally, when the crisis comes, Erec is remarkably insensitive in his handling of Enide. Her attempt to evade the issue makes him resort to angry threats to wring the truth from her:

> "Dites moi, dolce amie chiere,
> por coi plorez an tel meniere?
> De coi avez ire ne duel?
> Certes, je le savrai, mon vuel.
> Dites le moi, ma dolce amie,
> gardez nel me celez vos mie,
> por qu'avez dit que mar i fui?
> Por moi fu dit, non por autrui;
> bien ai la parole antandue."
> Lors fu molt Enyde esperdue,
> grant peor ot et grant esmai:
> "Sire, fet ele, je ne sai
> neant de quanque vos me dites.

> – Dame, por coi vos escondites?
> Li celers ne vos i valt rien:
> ploré avez, ce voi ge bien;
> por neant ne plorez vos mie;
> et an plorant ai ge oïe
> la parole que vos deïstes.
> – Ha! biax sire, onques ne l'oïstes,
> mes je cuit bien que ce fu songes.
> – Or me servez vos de mançonges:
> apertemant vos oi mantir;
> mes tart vandroiz au repantir,
> se voir ne me reconuissiez."            (vs 2511–35)

After the reconciliation, one is aware of a marked change in Erec's attitude to his wife. The physical attraction is there as strong as ever and Erec's recovery is marked by a second honeymoon (vs 5196–208), but his love has grown and deepened with the knowledge of her that the quest has brought him. Erec, in fact, says as much at the time of their reconciliation:

> "Or ne soiez plus esmaiee,
> c'or vos aim plus qu'ainz mes ne fis."    (vs 4884–5)

and as much is said by Chrétien in his comment on Erec's feelings towards his wife as she tends him in the safety of Guivret's camp:

> Son seignor desarme et desvest;
> si li a ses plaies lavees
> ressuiees et rebandees,
> car n'i leissa autrui tochier.
> Or ne li set que reprochier
> Erec, qui bien l'a esprovee:
> vers li a grant amor trovee.            (vs 5092–8)

We see more plainly what they both have in mind when Erec stops to speak to Enide before riding off alone into the enchanted orchard:

> A tant li rois Evrains le leisse;
> 5778 et cil vers Enyde se beisse,
> qui delez lui grant duel feisoit,
> ne por quant s'ele se teisoit;
> .  .  .  .  .  .
> Et cil, *qui bien conuist son cuer,*
> 5784 li a dit: "*Bele douce suer*
> *gentix dame lëax et sage,*
> bien conuis tot vostre corage:
> 5787 peor avez grant, bien le voi,
> si ne savez ancor por coi.
> Mes por neant vos esmaiez
> jusqu'a itant que vos voiez
> que mes escuz iert depeciez

et ge dedanz le cors bleciez,
. . . .
que plus ne me porrai desfandre,
ainz m'estovra merci atandre
et deprier outre mon vuel.
Lors porroiz fere vostre duel,
que trop tost comancié l'avez.
Douce dame, ancor ne savez
que ce sera, ne ge nel sai :
5804    de neant estes an esmai,
car bien sachiez seüremant,
s'an moi n'avoit de hardemant
fors tant con vostre amors m'an baille,
ne crienbroie je an bataille,
cors a cors, nul home vivant.
5810    Si fais folie, qui m'an vant,
mes je nel di por nul orguel,
fors tant que conforter vos vuel :
confortez vos, lessiez ester.
Je ne puis plus ci arester,
ne vos n'iroiz plus avoec moi,
car avant mener ne vos doi,
si con li rois l'a comandé."
Lors la beise et comande a Dé,
et ele i recomande lui.                    (vs 5777–819)

The very fact that Erec stops to comfort his wife although she has said nothing of her distress (vs 5778–83), reveals in him a new awareness of her that contrasts sharply with his insensitivity at the time of their quarrel. The very words Erec uses to address Enide: 'Bele, douce suer, / gentix dame, lëax et sage', betoken the respect that has grown in him with the discovery in her of these self-same qualities of loyalty, resourcefulness, courage and tender affection (which he now knows to be the mainspring of all her actions). Then, after the gentle reminder that her grief is a little premature (vs 5787–803), there comes the acknowledgement that she is a source of strength to him and a constant inspiration in battle (vs 5804–9), and with it the assurance that, in saying this, his desire is to comfort her, not to boast of his prowess (vs 5810–12). In short, there is evidence here of a new tenderness, a new esteem. It is obvious that Enide is no longer a mere bed-fellow for Erec, but a consort whose worth he has come to recognise and whose counsels he will henceforth be prepared to listen to and accept.

As the somewhat self-centred youth who comes to see that he has obligations beyond his immediate pleasures and inclinations; as the selfish lover who comes to recognise his wife as a person in her own right and not just as a source of pleasure, Erec is surely worthy to appear as the central figure in a courtly romance. The fact that he is not perfect from the start and appears only at the end of the story as a man fit for kingship and as a truly courteous lover means that Chrétien has offered us a much more interesting hero than the paragon of unvarying perfection his critics have expected him to provide. This surely should be an occasion for discarding unwarrantable preconceptions and for accepting the agreeable reality that in Erec Chrétien created a character to hold the interest and wry sympathy of men down the ages – or as he puts it himself: "tant con durra chrestientez".

## 3    ENIDE'S ROLE IN THE ROMANCE

In vs 19 of *Erec*, Chrétien announces that the story he is about to relate is that of Erec, the son of Lac:

> D'Erec, le fil Lac, est li contes.

But when he comes to refer to his first romance in *Cligés*, he describes it as the story of Erec and Enide:

> Cil qui fist d'Erec et d'Enide
> et les comandemanz d'Ovide
> .    .    .    .    .
> un novel conte rancomance.                    (*Cligés* vs 1–8)

This association of Enide's name with her husband's in the opening line of *Cligés* may, of course, signify nothing more than a need to provide a rhyme for the 'Ovide' which comes at the end of vs 2. On the other hand, it could well be an acknowledgement of the fact that, in the longest and most important section of *Erec*, Enide's role is as important as her husband's. The truth is that, in the account of his second quest, attention is equally divided between the hero and his wife. Enide's feelings and activities are described there in as much detail and with as much interest as Erec's battles, and her part in averting disaster is equal to his. Indeed, as one reads *Erec*, one realises that it is the story of a joint venture, a joint apprentice-ship where Enide, no less than Erec, has a lesson to learn and a fault to expiate.[34]

It has been suggested that the fault Enide has to expiate is that she allows herself to doubt Erec's valour and to under-estimate his love:

Un fait y apparaît comme certain: la culpabilité d'Enide. Ni Erec ni Enide, *ni par conséquent Chrétien lui-même*, n'ont le moindre doute à cet égard. . . .
   Troublée par les paroles qu'elle a entendu dire autour d'elle et qui lui sont d'autant plus pénibles que les reproches retombent en partie sur elle-même, Enide a accueilli sans hésiter le blâme qu'on a infligé à son mari; elle se l'est approprié en quelque sorte et elle le lui a répété. Or, ses paroles renferment, sans qu'elle s'en fût rendu compte, un doute blessant pour la vaillance d'Erec, que cependant elle devait connaître mieux que tout autre. Mais il y a plus: en même temps elle méconnaissait aussi le profond amour que lui portait Erec. S'il a

renoncé à la gloire des armes, c'était bien pour l'amour d'elle. Elle s'en rend compte presque aussitôt. . . . Mais le mal est fait et il ne lui reste plus qu'à en porter les conséquences. Aussi le traitement qu'Erec lui impose est-il aux yeux d'Enide elle-même la juste conséquence de son action. Ce n'est pas chez elle la résignation passive d'une Griseldis, à laquelle on la compare souvent; non, c'est l'humble soumission d'une femme qui se sait coupable et qui pense ainsi expier sa faute.[35]

But this and similar claims that Enide is guilty of under-valuing Erec overlook two points: first, that Erec was as guilty as Shakespeare's Mark Antony of neglecting his calling to give himself up to the delights of love; and second, that sloth was considered as reprehensible as cowardice in a warrior in the twelfth century. The evidence for the first point is provided in vs 2439–58 (the preface to the lovers' estrangement). The evidence for the second can be found in *Cligés* and *Yvain*. In the one romance we have Alexander urging his father to let him go and prove himself at Arthur's court on the grounds that inactivity and honour are incompatible:

> "Maint haut home par lor peresce
> perdent grant los qu'avoir porroient
> se par la terre cheminoient.
> Ne s'acordent pas bien ansanble
> repos et los, si com moi sanble,
> car de nule rien ne s'alose
> riches hom qui toz jorz repose,
> ensi sont contraire et divers."          (*Cligés* vs 152–9)

In the other, Gauvain succeeds in seducing Yvain away from his bride by an argument which could be taken for a comment on Erec's case. It is, he maintains, a disgrace for a knight to let his reputation be ruined through marriage or a love-affair. A woman, be she mistress or wife, has every right to withdraw her esteem and affection from a man who allows this to happen. Love should act as a spur, not as a curb, to a knight.

> "Comant? Seroiz vos or de çaus,"
> ce disoit mes sire Gauvains,
> "qui por lor fames valent mains?
> Honiz soit de sainte Marie,
> qui por anpirier se marie!
> Amander doit de bele dame,
> qui l'a a amie ou a fame,
> ne n'est puis droiz, que ele l'aint,
> que ses pris et ses los remaint.
> Certes, ancor seroiz iriez
> de s'amor, se vos anpiriez;
> que fame a tost s'amor reprise,
> ne n'a pas tort, s'ele desprise
> celui, qui de neant anpire,
> quant il est del reaume sire.
> Or primes doit vostre pris croistre!

Ronpez le frain et le chevoistre,
s'irons tornoiier moi et vos,
que l'an ne vos apiaut jalos.
Or ne devez vos pas songier,
mes les tornoiemanz ongier,
anprandre estorz et fort joster,
que que il vos doie coster!
Assez songe, qui ne se muet.
Certes venir vos an estuet;
que je serai an vostre ansaingne.
Gardez, que an vos ne remaingne
biaus conpainz! nostre conpaignie." (*Yvain* vs 2484–511)

By now it ought to be obvious that no blame should be attached to Enide for taxing Erec with his *recreantise*. Her criticisms were both justified and necessary. Where she was at fault was, in fact, in failing to raise the matter with Erec when the murmurings of his men first reached her ears. For this meant that he was left to continue in his sloth until he discovered, by sheer chance, that something was amiss, and then had to drag the truth out of her. The whole position is, indeed, made perfectly clear in vs 2459–519 – provided one is prepared to accept the fact that the hero of a courtly romance can be guilty at times of self indulgence and worse. First we learn of Enide's distress when the complaints about Erec came to her notice, and then of her fear of angering him which kept her from telling him anything about them:

Tant fu blasmez de totes genz,
de chevaliers et de sergenz,
qu'Enyde l'oï antre dire
que recreant aloit ses sire
d'armes et de chevalerie:
molt avoit changiee sa vie.
*De ceste chose li pesa;*
*mes sanblant fere n'an osa,*
*que ses sire an mal nel preïst*
*asez tost, s'ele le deïst.*                    (vs 2459–68)

So we find that the whole matter was kept from him until one day Enide was reminded of Erec's disgrace as she lay by his side. The thought of it filled her with distress – and here the text makes it perfectly plain that her concern was solely for Erec, her wretchedness solely at finding herself to be the cause of his downfall:

Tant li fu la chose celee
qu'il avint une matinee,
la ou il jurent an un lit,
qu'il orent eü maint delit;
boche a boche antre braz gisoient,
come cil qui molt s'antre amoient.
Cil dormi et cele veilla;
de la parole li manbra

> que disoient de son seignor
> par la contree li plusor.
> Quant il l'an prist a sovenir,
> de plorer ne se pot tenir;
> tel duel en ot et tel pesance
> qu'il li avint par mescheance
> qu'ele dist lors une parole
> dom ele se tint puis por fole;
> mes ele n'i pansoit nul mal.
>
>   •    •    •    •    •
>
> "Lasse, fet ele, con mar fui!
> de mon païs que ving ça querre?
> Bien me doit essorbir la terre,
> quant toz li miaudres chevaliers,
>
>   •    •    •    •    •
>
> li plus lëax, li plus cortois,
> a del tot an tot relanquie
> por moi tote chevalerie.
> *Dons l'ai ge honi tot por voir;*
> *nel volsisse por nul avoir."*
> Lors li dist: "Amis, con mar fus!"
> A tant se tot, si ne dist plus.     (vs 2469–504)

Roused by Enide's last words, 'Amis, con mar fus!", Erec naturally enough demanded to know what she meant by them and what cause she had to weep:

> Et cil ne dormi pas formant,
> la voiz oï tot an dormant;
> de la parole s'esveilla
> et de ce molt se merveilla
> que si formant plorer la vit.
> Puis li a demandé et dit:
> "Dites moi, dolce amie chiere,
> por coi plorez an tel meniere?
> De coi avez ire ne duel?
> Certes, je le savrai, mon vuel.
> Dites le moi, ma dolce amie,
> gardez nel me celez vos mie,
> por qu'avez dit que mar i fui?
> Por moi fu dit, non por autrui;
> bien ai la parole antandue."     (vs 2505–19)

It was Enide's panic-stricken attempt to evade this question which then provoked Erec into wringing the truth from her (vs 2520–71).

The reason for Enide's reluctance to speak to Erec about his *recreantise* is not hard to discover. It obviously stems from a deep-seated conviction that it is not her place to criticise her husband.[36] For on three different occasions we find her accusing herself of presumption in daring to reproach Erec – in spite of the fact that her criticisms were as necessary as they were justified.

The first occasion is when Erec orders her to prepare for a journey after hearing the charges against him. Enide is convinced that he intends to send her away and bitterly regrets the ill-timed remarks which have put an end to her happiness. At the same time, we find that she accepts this fate as the inevitable and justifiable answer to her presumption in daring to tax Erec with his sloth:

> "Ha! fet ele, fole malveise,
> or estoie je trop a eise,
> qu'il ne me failloit nule chose.
> Ha! lasse, por coi fui tant ose,
> qui tel forssenaige osai dire?
> Dex! don ne m'amoit trop mes sire?
> Par foi, lasse, trop m'amoit il.
> Or m'estuet aler an essil;
> mes de ce ai ge duel greignor
> que ge ne verrai mon seignor,
> qui tant m'amoit de grant meniere
> que nule rien n'avoit tant chiere.
> Li miaudres qui onques fust nez
> s'estoit si a moi atornez
> que d'autre rien ne li chaloit.
> Nule chose ne me failloit;
> molt estoie boene eüree,
> *mes trop m'a orguialz alevee,*
> *quant ge ai dit si grant oltraige;*
> *an mon orguel avrai domaige*
> *et molt est bien droiz que je l'aie:*
> ne set qu'est biens qui mal n'essaie."         (vs 2585–606)

The next occasion occurs when Enide is watching over Erec and their ten chargers in the forest. This time we find her accepting the hardships which have been forced upon her as a fitting punishment for her presumptuous allegations, which she now feels were entirely unwarranted – just as Erec had intended she should:

> Cil dormi, et cele veilla,
> onques la nuit ne someilla;
> chascun cheval tint an sa main
> tote nuit jusqu'a l'andemain;
> et molt s'est blasmee et maudite
> de la parole qu'ele ot dite:
> molt a, ce dit, mal esploitié,
> "que n'ai mie de la mité
> le mal que je ai desservi.
> *Lasse, fet ele, si mar vi*
> *mon orguel et ma sorcuidance!*
> Savoir pooie sanz dotance
> que tel chevalier ne meillor
> ne savoit l'an de mon seignor.
> Bien le savoie. Or le sai mialz;
> car ge l'ai veü a mes ialz,
> car trois ne cinc armez ne dote.

> *Honie soit ma leingue tote,*
> *qui l'orguel et la honte dist*
> dont mes cors a tel honte gist."        (vs 3093–112)

The third occasion on which we find Enide accusing herself of presumption in criticising Erec comes when he rejoins her after rescuing Cadoc from the giants and falls apparently lifeless at her feet. Her immediate reaction is to see herself and her untimely remarks as the cause of his death:

> "Ha! fet ele, dolante Enyde,
> de mon seignor sui omecide;
> par ma folie l'ai ocis:
> *ancor fust or mes sires vis,*
> *se ge, come outrageuse et fole,*
> *n'eüsse dite la parole*
> *por coi mes sires ça s'esmut;*
> ainz boens teisirs home ne nut,
> mes parlers nuist mainte foiee:
> ceste chose ai bien essaiee
> et esprovee an mainte guise."        (vs 4585–95)

If one now asks why Enide should stand in such awe of her husband for it to seem an unpardonable liberty to criticise him, the answer is, once again, easy enough to find.

In the first place, she is by nature the most modest and unassuming of women. This can be seen from her confusion on first meeting Erec (vs 443–7), or on being presented to Arthur's assembled knights:

> Quant la bele pucele estrange
> vit toz les chevaliers au range
> qui l'esgardoient a estal,
> son chief ancline contre val;
> vergoigne an ot, ne fu mervoille,
> la face l'an devint vermoille.        (vs 1707–12)

Added to this, she has been well-schooled in obedience and self-effacement at her father's house. This much is clear from the fact that her wishes are not consulted in the matter of her marriage. She is handed over to Erec without further ado when her father learns who has asked for her in marriage:

> ... "Bien avomes oï
> de vos parler an cest païs.
> Or vos aim assez plus et pris,
> car molt estes preuz et hardiz;
> ja de moi n'iroiz escondiz:
> tot a vostre comandemant
> ma bele fille vos comant."
> Lors l'a prise par mi le poing:
> "Tenez, fet il, je la vos doing."
> Erec lieemant la reçut.        (vs 670–9)

And it is typical that in the general rejoicing that follows, Enide's satisfaction and contentment are kept to herself:

> Grant joie font tuit par leanz:
> li peres an ert molt joianz,
> et la mere plore de joie,
> *et la pucele ert tote coie,*
> *mes molt estoit joianz et liee*
> *qu'ele li estoit otroiee,*
> por ce que preuz ert et cortois,
> et bien savoit qu'il seroit rois
> et ele meïsme enoree,
> riche reïne coronee.                    (vs 681–90)

Once Enide has been entrusted to the care of Erec, she submits to his authority as completely as she did to her father's. And typically, it is left to her cousin to protest at the indignity of her appearing at court in her rags; she herself says nothing (vs 1331–86).

The deference Enide is prepared by inclination and training to pay her husband is further increased by the sense of obligation she feels towards Erec. How acutely she is aware of the honour he has conferred upon her in raising her from poverty to high estate can be gauged from what she has to say of him to her cousin when they meet after the battle for the *Joie de la Cort*:

> "Onques ancor ne me soi faindre
> de lui amer, ne je ne doi:
> voir, mes sires est filz de roi,
> et si me prist et povre et nue;
> par lui m'est tex enors creüe
> qu'ainz a nule desconseilliee
> ne fu si granz apareilliee."              (vs 6256–62)

Indeed, on comparing Chrétien's story with the Welsh version of the tale, it is found that he has been at particular pains to emphasise the disparity in rank and fortune between his hero and heroine – albeit he is equally careful to stress that they are evenly matched in all other respects (vs 1484–96). Where Gereint merely sees that his father-in-law's earldom and possessions are restored to him by the nephew he had tried to dispossess (*Gereint* pp. 240–1), Erec's father-in-law, as an honourable, if impoverished, vavasour, is entirely beholden to Erec's liberality for the change in his fortunes:

> Erec le vavasor apele,
> parole li dist boene et bele,
> et si li comança a dire:
> "Biax amis, biax ostes, biax sire,
> vos m'avez grant enor portee,
> mes bien vos iert guerredonee:
>
> .    .    .    .    .

Mener vos ferai an ma terre,
qui mon pere est et moie aprés;
loing de ci est, non mie pres.
Illuec vos donrai deus chastiax,
molt boens, molt riches, et molt biax;
sires seroiz de Roadan,
qui fu fez des le tans Adan,
et d'un autre chastel selonc
qui ne valt mie moins un jonc;
la gent l'apelent Montrevel,
mes peres n'a meillor chastel.
Einz que troi jor soient passez
vos avrai anvoié assez
or et argent et veir et gris
et dras de soie et de chier pris
por vos vestir et vostre fame,
qui est ma chiere dolce dame."                    (vs 1303–30)

Finally, Erec is a formidable person for a shy and diffident girl to have to take to task.[37] Throughout the romance he is presented as a singularly intractable young man, more disposed to impose his will on others – equals and superiors alike – than to accept guidance from anyone, least of all from a wife he seems to look upon as a mere bedfellow.[38] Erec's intractability is best seen when Enide and himself are tricked by Gauvain into spending the night at Arthur's forest camp. For here a comparison with the Welsh tale shows how much Erec's intransigence is stressed in Chrétien. Where Gereint is constrained by Arthur to spend a month at the camp for his wounds to be healed, and is only permitted to go when the physicians pronounce him fit, Erec cannot be prevailed upon to spend more than one night there. When Arthur presses him to stay, he puts an end to the discussion with a finality that seems unparalleled in its rudeness: even when one realises how urgent a matter it is for him to find an occasion for making his peace with Enide, and can see that, meanwhile, the company of others would be intolerably irksome:

'This is Gereint', said Gwalchmei, 'and of his own free will he would not have come to see thee to-day.' 'Aye,' said Arthur, 'he lacks counsel.' ... 'Lord,' said Gereint, 'with thy leave, we will be on our way.' 'Whither will that be?' asked Arthur, 'Thou canst not go at present unless thou go to complete thy death.' 'He would not suffer me to bid him stay,' said Gwalchmei. 'He will suffer me,' said Arthur, 'and further, he shall not go hence till he is whole.' 'It would please me best, lord,' said Gereint, 'if thou gave me leave to depart.' 'I will not, between me and God,' he replied. ... And he called on Cadyrieith and bade him pitch a tent for Gereint and his physicians, and charged him to have ready plenty of everything, as it might be requested of him. And Cadyrieith did so, even as he was bidden in all. And he brought Morgan Tud and his disciples to Gereint.
    And then Arthur and his company spent close on a month healing Gereint. And when Gereint's flesh was strong, he came to Arthur and asked leave to go his way. 'I know not whether thou art yet quite well.' 'In faith I am, lord,' said Gereint. 'It is not thou that I will believe in that matter, but the physicians

who have tended thee.' And he summoned the physicians to him and asked them whether that was true. 'True enough,' said Morgan Tud.

On the morrow Arthur gave him leave to depart, and he went to finish his journey.

(*Gereint* pp. 265–6)

> Li rois lui et Enyde an mainne
> en la soe chanbre demainne,
> et dist que por la soe amor
> vialt an la forest a sejor
> sejorner .xv. jorz toz plains,
> tant que toz soit gariz et sains.
> Erec de ce le roi mercie,
> et li dist: "Sire, je n'ai mie
> plaie de coi je tant me duelle
> que ma voie lessier an vuelle.
> Retenir ne me porroit nus;
> demain, ja ne tardera plus,
> m'an voldrai par matin aler,
> lors que le jor verrai lever."
> Li rois en a levé le chief,
> et dist: "Ci a molt grant meschief,
> quant vos remenoir ne volez;
> je sai bien que molt vos dolez;
> remenez, si feroiz que sages,
> car il sera trop granz domages,
> se vos an ces forez morez.
> Biax dolz amis, car remenez
> tant que vos soiez respassez."
> Erec respont: "*Or est assez.*
> *Je ai si ceste chose anprise*
> *ne remanroie en nule guise.*
> *Or lessiez la parole ester,*
> et si comandez aprester
> le souper et les tables metre;
> li vaslet s'an vont antremetre."

(vs 4207–36)

Since Arthur himself meets with such a rebuff from Erec when he tries to counsel him for his own good, there is little wonder that Enide quailed at the thought of broaching the subject of his *recreantise* ('mes sanblant fere n'an osa / que ses sire an mal nel preïst / asez tost, s'ele le deïst'); or that it provoked so violent a reaction in him when she eventually did so.

Once we realise that it is the excessive deference she feels for Erec that keeps Enide from speaking to him of his sloth, and then makes her handle the matter so badly when she is forced into discussing it, it is plain enough what lesson it is that she has to learn. Clearly her task is to overcome her diffidence in her dealings with her husband and to acquire the confidence to act as she sees best when his own interests demand it. And this is precisely what she is forced to do throughout the quest that Erec makes her share with him. The various encounters which call upon him to display his physical prowess, oblige Enide to prove her mettle in the

moral sphere. She is driven, successively, to brave Erec's wrath by disobeying his orders in the interests of his own safety; to act on her own
initiative without his knowledge or consent; and finally, to assert herself
and her rights when an attempt is made to dispose of her against her wishes.

On the arrival of the first robber-band, Enide is torn between her fear
of Erec and her fears for him. On the one hand, she has received strict
instructions not to speak until she is spoken to (vs 2764–9). On the other
hand, she cannot allow him to be taken unawares. Inevitably, concern for
Erec triumphs over concern for herself, and she turns to call his attention
to the danger that threatens:

> Enyde vit les robeors:
> molt l'an est prise granz peors.
> "Dex, fet ele, que porrai dire?
> Or iert ja morz ou pris mes sire,
> car cil sont troi et il est seus;
> n'est pas a droit partiz li jeus
> d'un chevalier ancontre trois;
> cil le ferra ja demenois,
> que mes sires ne s'an prant garde.
> Dex! serai je donc si coarde
> que dire ne li oserai?
> Ja si coarde ne serai;
> jel li dirai, nel leirai pas."
> Vers lui se torne en es le pas
> et dist: "Biau sire, ou pansez vos?
> Ci vienent poignant aprés vos
> troi chevalier qui molt vos chacent;
> peor ai que mal ne vos facent."                (vs 2827–44)

The arrival of the second robber-band again proves an occasion for
love to overcome self-interest. This time the conflict between Enide's
fears for herself and her anxiety for Erec's welfare is sharper, for her
first intervention received but small thanks from him: only an angry
complaint that she shows no respect for his wishes (vs 2845–9) and equally
angry threats, repeated after his victory, that she had better obey him in
future (vs 2850–2, 2914–7):

> Quant Enyde les ot veüz,
> tot li sans li est esmeüz;
> grant peor ot et grant esmai:
> "Lasse, fet ele, que ferai?
> Ne sai que die ne que face,
> que mes sires molt me menace
> et dit qu'il me fera enui,
> se je de rien paroil a lui.
> Mes se mes sires ert ci morz,
> de moi ne seroit nus conforz:
> morte seroie et mal baillie.
> Dex! mes sire ne le voit mie;
> qu'atant je dons, malveise fole?

> Trop ai or chiere ma parole,
> quant je ne li ai dit pieç'a.
> Bien sai que cil qui vienent ça
> sont de mal faire ancoragié.
> Ha! Dex, comant li dirai gié?
> Il m'ocirra. Asez m'ocie!
> ne leirai que je ne li die."
> Lors l'apele dolcemant: "Sire.
> – Cui? fet il, que volez vos dire?
> – Sire, merci! dire vos vuel
> que desbunchié sont de ce bruel
> cinc chevalier, don je m'esmai;
> bien pans et aparceü ai
> qu'il se voelent a vos conbatre;
> arrieres sont remés li quatre,
> et li cinquiesmes a vos muet
> tant con chevax porter le puet;
> ne gart l'ore que il vos fiere;
> li catre sont remés arriere,
> mes ne sont gaires de ci loing:
> tuit le secorront au besoing."          (vs 2959–92)

The end of the first day of the quest brings an occasion for Enide to counter an order of Erec's. When he instructs her to sleep whilst he keeps watch, she insists that it would be better for him to rest since his need is greater than hers; a counter-proposal he is pleased to accept:

> Chevauchié ont jusqu'a la nuit
> ne vile ne recet ne virent;
> A l'anuitier lor ostel prirent
> desoz un arbre an une lande.
> Erec a la dame comande
> qu'ele dorme, et il veillera;
> ele respont que nel fera,
> car n'est droiz, ne feire nel viaut:
> il dormira, qui plus se diaut.
> Erec l'otroie, et bel li fu.          (vs 3080–9)

In the encounter with the amorous count (vs 3276–652), Enide finds herself forced into acting entirely on her own initiative. When her rejection of the count's proposal that she should become his mistress makes him resort to ugly threats of murdering Erec before her eyes (vs 3308–51), Enide quickly adapts her tone and tactics to meet the situation. With remarkable resourcefulness ('bien sot par parole enivrer / bricon, des qu'ele i met l'antante'), she convinces the man that she is ready enough to fall in with his proposition, but was merely testing his intentions (vs 3352–63). She then persuades him that it would look better for both of them if he arranged to have Erec ambushed the next day, rather than murder him there and then (vs 3364–406). In point of fact, of course, she is playing for time; time for Erec to get a night's rest, and time for them both to make good their escape before the arrival of the count and his men. For the rest of

the night Erec sleeps whilst Enide stays waiting for the dawn and the
moment to rouse him and warn him of their danger:

> Erec dormi molt longuemant,
> tote la nuit, seüremant,
> tant que li jorz molt aprocha.
> Lors vit bien Enyde et soucha
> que ele pooit trop atandre;
>
> . . . .
>
> ele se vest et aparoille,
> a son seignor vient, si l'esvoille:
> "Ha! sire, fet ele, merci!
> Levez isnelemant de ci,
> que traïz estes antreset
> sanz acoison et sanz forfet.
> Li cuens est traïtres provez;
> se ci poez estre trovez,
> ja n'eschaperoiz de la place
> que tot desmanbrer ne vos face:
> avoir me vialt, por ce vos het;
> mes se Deu plest, qui toz biens set,
> vos n'i seroiz ne morz ne pris.
> Des her soir vos eüst ocis,
> se creanté ne li eüsse
> que s'amie et sa fame fusse.
> Ja le verroiz ceanz venir:
> prandre me vialt et retenir,
> et vos ocire, s'il vos trueve."          (vs 3453–79)

Enide's warning shows Erec that she is completely loyal to him (vs 3480–1),
and he acts on it immediately. This does not, however, stop him from
cautioning her again to hold her peace as soon as they are fairly on their
way (vs 3509–13). The arrival of the count and his men drives Enide nonetheless into disobeying her husband's orders once more:

> Erec chevalche; cil le virent,
> einz qu'il se fust anforestez;
> lors s'an est li uns dessevrez,
> par contançon le leissent tuit.
> Enyde ot la noise et le bruit
> de lor armes, de lor chevax,
> et vit que plains estoit li vax.
> Des que cele les vit venir,
> de parler ne se pot tenir:
> "Haï! sire, fet ele, haï!
> Con vos a cist cuens anvaï,
> qui por vos amainne tel ost!
> Sire, car chevalchiez plus tost
> tant qu'an cele forest fussiens;
> espoir tost eschaperïens:
> cil sont ancore molt arriere.
> Se nos alons an tel meniere
> ne poez de ci eschaper,
> car n'iestes mie per a per."          (vs 3534–52)

Enide's final act of disobedience is committed on the arrival of Guivret. It comes after the sharpest and most difficult struggle of all, for Enide is convinced that Erec is capable of abandoning her in the forest if she defies him again. Ironically enough, however, his anger has completely evaporated by now, as Chrétien reveals in his comment on Erec's reaction to her warning:

> Enyde ot la noise et l'esfroi;
> a po que de son palefroi
> ne cheï jus pasmee et vainne;
> an tot le cors de li n'ot vainne
> don ne li remuast li sans,
> si li devint pales et blans
> li vis con se ele fust morte.
> Molt se despoire et desconforte,
> car son seignor dire ne l'ose,
> qu'il la menace molt et chose
> et comande qu'ele se teise.
> De deus parz est molt a male eise,
> qu'ele ne set lequel seisir
> ou le parler ou le teisir.
> A li meïsmes s'an consoille;
> sovant del dire s'aparoille
> si que la leingue se remuet,
> mes la voiz pas issir n'an puet,
> car de peor estraint les danz,
> s'anclost la parole dedanz,
> et si se justise et destraint:
> la boche clot, les danz estraint
> que la parole hors n'an aille;
> a li a prise grant bataille
> et dit: "Seüre sui et certe
> que trop recevrai leide perte,
> se je ici mon seignor pert.
> Dirai li donc tot en apert?
> Nenil. Por quoi? Je n'oseroie,
> que mon seignor correceroie;
> et se mes sires se corroce,
> il me leira an ceste broce
> seule et cheitive et esgaree:
> lors serai plus mal eüree.
> Mal eüree? Moi que chaut?
> Diax ne pesance ne me faut
> ja mes, tant con je aie a vivre,
> se mes sires tot a delivre
> an tel guise de ci n'estort
> qu'il ne soit mahaigniez a mort.
> Mes se je tost ne li acoint,
> cist chevaliers qui ci apoint
> l'avra einz mort que il se gart,
> que molt sanble de male part.
> Lasse, trop ai or atandu.

Si le m'a il molt desfandu,
mes ja nel leirai por desfansse:
je voi bien que mes sires pansse
tant que lui meïsmes oblie;
donc est bien droiz que je li die."
Ele li dit; il la menace;
mes n'a talant que mal li face,
qu'il aparçoit et conuist bien
qu'ele l'ainme sor tote rien,
et il li tant que plus ne puet.                  (vs 3701–54)

In the next two adventures Enide has no active part to play. In the
encounter with Arthur and the court, it is left to the King to try to persuade Erec to stay long enough with them for his wounds to heal (and he
meets, as we know, with as little success as Enide herself would have done).
In the encounter with the giants, Enide is left to wait for Erec, fearful
lest she should find herself abandoned to her fate (vs 4545–7). In the
encounter with Oringles, however, Enide becomes the centre of attention:
first with her grief and lamentations (vs 4559–635) which attract the
attention of the count, who arrives in time to prevent her from committing
suicide (vs 4636–703); and then by the stand she puts up at Limors where
she is finally driven into asserting her right to dispose of herself and her
feelings as she sees fit. When Oringles tries to bully her into acquiescing
gracefully in the marriage he has forced upon her, she refuses to be
browbeaten, and meets his blows with spirited defiance:

Aprés vespres, un jor de mai,
estoit Enyde an grant esmai.
Onques ses diax ne recessoit,
et li cuens auques l'angressoit,
par proiere et par menacier,
de pes fere et d'esleescier;
            .     .     .
"Dame, fet il, il vos estuet
cest duel lessier et oblïer:
            .     .     .
Voirs est que morz est vostre sire;
se vos en avez duel et ire,
cuidiez vos que je m'an mervoil?
Nenil. Mes ge vos doing consoil
le meillor que doner vos sai:
quant je espousee vos ai,
molt vos devez esleescier;
gardez vos de moi correcier:
mangiez, quant je vos an semoing.
– Sire, fet ele, n'an ai soing.
Sire, ja tant con je vivrai,
ne mangerai ne ne bevrai,
se ge ne voi mangier einçois
mon seignor, qui gist sor ce dois.
– Dame, ce ne puet avenir.

Por fole vos fetes tenir,
quant vos si grant folie dites;
vos en avroiz males merites,
s'ui mes vos an fetes semondre."
Cele ne li vialt mot respondre,
car rien ne prisoit sa menace.
Et li cuens la fiert an la face;
ele s'escrie, et li baron
an blasment le conte an viron:

    .   .   .   .

"Teisiez vos an tuit! fet li cuens;
la dame est moie et je sui suens,
si ferai de li mon pleisir."
Lors ne se pot cele teisir,
einz jure que ja soe n'iert;
et li cuens hauce, si refiert;
et cele s'escria an haut:
"Ahi! fet ele, ne me chaut
que tu me dïes ne ne faces:
ne criem tes cos ne tes menaces.
Asez me bat, asez me fier:
ja tant ne te troverai fier:
que por toi face plus ne mains
se tu or androit a tes mains
me devoies les ialz sachier
ou tote vive detranchier."

                            (vs 4741–814)

Enide's stand at Limors, her foiling of the amorous count and her repeated acts of disobedience when Erec's safety is at stake, confirm that it was sheer diffidence that kept her from speaking to Erec of his *recreantise*, and not any lack of courage, loyalty or resourcefulness. By forcing her to exercise these very qualities, which she may well be unaware of in herself, the quest proves to be a training in self-assurance, a lesson in self-assertion, for Enide. By the end of it, she is prepared to intervene without a moment's hesitation in the fight between Erec and Guivret, showing a spirit that wins Guivret's admiration:

Enyde, qui a pié estoit,
quant son seignor a terre voit,
morte cuide estre et mal baillie:
hors de la haie estoit saillie,
et cort por aidier son seignor.
S'onques ot duel, lors l'ot graignor;
vers Guivret vient, si le seisist
par la resne, lors si li dist:
"Chevaliers, maudiz soies tu,
c'un home seul et sanz vertu,
dolant et pres navré a mort
as anvaï a si grant tort
que tu ne sez dire por coi.
Se ci n'eüst ore fors toi,
que seus fusses et sanz aïe,

car fust feite ceste anvaïe,
mes que mes sires fust heitiez!
Or soies frans et afeitiez,
si lesse ester par ta franchise
ceste bataille qu'as anprise;
que ja n'an valdroit mialz tes pris,
se tu avoies morz ou pris
un chevalier qui n'a pooir
de relever, ce puez veoir,
car d'armes a tant cos soferz
que toz est de plaies coverz."
Cil respont: "Dame, ne tamez.
Bien voi que lëaumant amez
vostre seignor, si vos an lo;
n'aiez garde, ne bien ne po,
de moi ne de ma conpaignie."          (vs 4983–5013)

Similarly, after the battle for the *Joie de la Cort*, it is Enide who takes the initiative in consoling Mabonagrain's disconsolate 'amie' (vs 6146–54), and her lead is soon followed by the other ladies of Evrain's court (vs 6155–66).

Enide's silence over Erec's decision to seek the *Joie de la Cort* (vs 5628–33; 5778–82) makes it quite clear that she will never try to influence him for purely selfish motives: in matters of duty he will be left to act as he knows he must. Indeed, Enide's conversation with her cousin after the battle in the enchanted orchard shows that she is content to take second place to Erec and to know that she loves him rather more than he loves her (vs 6254–62). But it seems safe to assume that when the occasion arises, she will, henceforth, put out a restraining hand – a hand which Erec is now prepared to heed.

In other words, the coronation at Nantes finds Enide ready to take her place by Erec's side and discharge her duties as his consort with the dignity and assurance that befit a queen.

Enide's lack of self-confidence is a problem all too commonly met with in everyday life. It is somewhat surprising, then, that, up to now, no one should have realised that the adventures she shares with Erec are a training in self-assurance for her, an exercise in self-assertion. But the point has been missed even by those who see Chrétien as preaching that 'a wife may be also the mistress of her husband and the inspirer of his valour'.[39] Hitherto, the critics have tended to see Enide merely as a wife who allays her husband's doubts about the love (or, alternatively, the respect) she bears him by her steadfast devotion in the face of the hardships she is compelled to endure:

> Les sept aventures ont d'ailleurs toutes pour but et pour effet de mettre en lumière la tendresse d'Enide pour son mari et de dissiper dans l'âme de celui-ci la méfiance qui s'y est introduite et qui est devenue la cause déterminante de son voyage aventureux.[40]

Some critics, indeed, have gone so far as to cast Enide explicitly in the role of a Griselda. One description of her reads:

> Enide est d'abord la jeune fille dont aucune imperfection n'entache la beauté physique et morale et qui, dans le mariage, sera le type, parfait aussi, de la fidelité et de la soumission. Toute épreuve que lui infligera son mari, pour une faute qui peut nous paraître vénielle, la trouvera respectueuse et inébranlable: aucune prouesse de séducteur, aucun appât de richesse et de pouvoir ne sauraient la détourner de son attachement à l'époux. *Elle est déjà une Grisélidis, sur qui ne plane même aucun soupçon.*[41]

A similar but rather more accurate picture of Enide is provided by the following passage and its accompanying footnote:

> Vierge, elle avait toutes les pudeurs de l'amour, épouse, elle en a tous les dévouements.[1] Peu à peu, son âme s'épanouit. Le calvaire, dont elle a franchi toutes les étapes, montant toujours plus haut, aboutit à une apothéose à l'apothéose de l'amour invincible.
>
> [1] Enide ici nous rappelle de près le type si profondément populaire de la femme injustement persécutée que l'on retrouve dans les chansons de geste (le thème de Berthe aux grands pieds) et que Boccace a immortalisé dans sa Griselidis. La transformation courtoise de ce type dans le roman de Chrétien ne change rien à son origine même.[42]

But as in the case of Erec, one finds, on re-examining Enide's role, that Chrétien has provided a far more subtle and interesting study than his critics have been prepared to expect from him. Once again, this should be an occasion for sacrificing preconceptions and for accepting the reality that the men and women of the twelfth century were not so very different from ourselves, and that the poets of the twelfth century were as able as their modern counterparts to recognise and describe the problems which beset them.

4    THE SIGNIFICANCE OF THE CONCLUSION
     TO THE *JOIE DE LA CORT* EPISODE

On comparing the accounts of the adventures in the enchanted orchard given in *Erec* and *Gereint*, one finds a considerable difference in their endings.

In *Gereint*, the hero spares his opponent's life when he begs for mercy on condition that there be an end to the enchantment and the 'game'. This he achieves by sounding the horn which hangs in the orchard; for the moment this is blown, the orchard and the mists surrounding it vanish into thin air:

> And swiftly he [Gereint] drew his sword, intending to cut off his head. 'Alas, lord', said he, 'thy mercy, and thou shalt have what thou wilt.' 'I wish for

nothing,' he replied, 'save that this game never be here, nor the hedge of mist, nor the charm nor the enchantment that has been.' 'That thou shalt have gladly, lord.' 'Then do thou see to it,' said he, 'that the mist disappear from the place.' 'Sound yonder horn,' said he, 'and the moment thou dost sound it, the mist will disappear. And until a knight who had overthrown me should sound it, the mist would never disappear from thence.'

And sad and anxious was Enid in the place where she was, with anxiety for Gereint. And then Gereint came and sounded the horn, and the moment he blew one blast thereon the mist disappeared. And the company came together, and peace was made between each one of them and his fellow. And that night the earl invited Gereint and the little King, and on the morrow they parted and Gereint went towards his own domain. (*Gereint* p. 273)

In Chrétien's story, Erec's victory is followed by a long conversation in the course of which he learns what his opponent was doing in the orchard and what he has achieved by his victory. The knight, who later proves to be King Evrain's nephew, Mabonagrain, explains that his presence in the orchard was the idea of his mistress, the girl on the silver couch. When they were both quite young, she had asked him to promise to grant her a boon, and this, as a true lover, he had willingly done:

> "Cele pucele, qui la siet,
> m'ama des enfance et je li.
>
> .  .  .  .  .
>
> . . . ele me demanda
> un don, mes el nel noma mie.
> Qui veheroit neant s'amie?
> N'est pas amis qui antresait
> tot le boen s'amie ne fait,
> sanz rien leissier et sanz faintise,
> s'il onques puet an nule guise.
> Creantai li sa volanté."       (vs 6002–13)

On the day he was knighted, he discovered that he had committed himself to staying with her in the orchard until such time as he should be defeated in battle (vs 6018–28). This he felt compelled to do, since it would have been dishonourable for him to break his word, and since he was unwilling to alienate his mistress's affections by any show of reluctance:

> "Reisons fu que je remainsisse,
> ainz que ma fïance mantisse,
> ja ne l'eüsse je plevi.
> Des que ge soi le boen et vi
> a la rien que ge oi plus chiere,
> n'an dui feire sanblant ne chiere
> que nule rien me despleüst;
> car, se ele l'aparceüst,
> el retraissist a li son cuer,
> et je nel volsisse a nul fuer
> por rien qui poïst avenir."       (vs 6029–39)

The girl had hoped thereby to keep him with her in the orchard for the rest of his days, since neither had expected that he would ever meet his match, and, for his part, he had scorned to seek release by deliberately courting defeat:

> "Ensi me cuida retenir
> ma dameisele a lonc sejor:
> ne cuidoit pas que a nul jor
> deüst an cest vergier antrer
> vasaus qui me deüst outrer;
> par ce me cuida a delivre,
> toz les jorz que j'eüsse a vivre,
> avoec li tenir an prison.
> Et ge feïsse mesprison,
> se de rien nule me fainsisse
> que trestoz ces ne conqueïsse
> vers cui ge eüsse puissance:
> vilainne fust tex delivrance."          (vs 6040–52)

As for the joy Erec has achieved by defeating Mabonagrain, this is nothing less than the satisfaction of his uncle's court at having him restored to liberty:

> ". . . sachiez bien, n'est pas petite
> l'enors que vos avez conquise.
> Molt avez an grant joie mise
> la cort mon oncle et mes amis,
> c'or serai hors de ceanz mis;
> et por ce que joie an feront
> tuit cil qui a la cort vanront,
> Joie de la Cort l'apeloient
> cil qui la joie an atandoient.
> Tant longuemant l'ont atandue
> que premiers lor sera randue
> par vos, qui l'avez desresniee."          (vs 6066–77)

This in fact proves to be the case when Erec sounds the horn that gives the signal for his victory: the jubilation is universal (vs 6109–39). The only person who does not share in it is the girl on the couch; she, Chrétien tells us, is grief stricken at the thought that her lover will no longer be able to devote his whole time and attention to herself:

> Mes celi mie n'atalante
> qui sor le lit d'argent seoit:
>
> .    .    .    .    .
>
> por ce qu'il li estoit a vis
> c'or ne seroit mes ses amis
> avoec li tant con il soloit,
> quant il del vergier issir doit.
> A cui qu'il onques abelisse
> ne puet müer qu'il ne s'an isse,

> que venue est l'ore et li termes:
> por ce li coroient les lermes
> des ialz tot contreval le vis.          (vs 6140–71)

Seeing her grief, Enide is moved to try and comfort her (vs 6146–54).
When the girl recovers her composure sufficiently to return Enide's greeting, a long conversation takes place between the two young women. In the
course of this, the girl discovers Enide is her cousin and then proceeds to
tell her story (vs 6183–213). She explains how she and Mabonagrain fell
in love when he went to Laluth to serve Enide's other uncle, the count;
and how they agreed that she should steal away with her lover when he returned to Brandigan, without saying anything to anybody:

> "Li cuens vostre oncles avoit guerre,
> si vindrent a lui an soldees
> chevalier de maintes contrees.
> Ensi, bele cosine, avint
> que avoec un soudoier vint
> li niés le roi de Brandigan;
> chiés mon pere fu pres d'un an,
> bien a, ce croi, douze ans passez.
> Ancor estoie anfes asez,
> et il ert biax et avenanz;
> la feïmes noz convenanz
> antre nos deus, tex con nos sist.
> Einz ne vos rien qu'il ne volsist,
> tant que amer me comança,
> si me plevi et finaça
> que toz jorz mes amis seroit
> et que il ça m'an amanroit;
> moi plot et a lui d'autre part.
> Lui demora et moi fu tart
> que ça m'an venisse avoec lui;
> si nos an venimes andui
> que nus ne le sot mes que nos."          (vs 6214–35)

Asked in her turn to explain her relationship with Erec, Enide replies that
they were married with the full consent and approval of her whole family,
since Erec is one of the most famous knights of the day; that he loves her
dearly and she loves him more dearly still – as is only right, since he raised
her from poverty to high estate:

> "Bele cosine, il m'espousa,
> si que mes peres bien le sot
> et ma mere qui joie an ot.
> Tuit le sorent et lié an furent
> nostre parant, si com il durent;
> liez an fu meïsmes li cuens,
> car il est chevaliers si buens
> qu'an ne porroit meillor trover;
> ne n'est or pas a esprover

de bonté ne de vaselage:
ne set l'an tel de son aage,
ne cuit que ses parauz soit nus.
Il m'ainme molt, et je lui plus,
tant qu'amors ne puet estre graindre.
Onques ancor ne me soi faindre
de lui amer, ne je ne doi:
voir, mes sires est filz de roi,
et si me prist et povre et nue;
par lui m'est tex enors creüe
qu'ainz a nule desconseilliee
ne fui si granz apareilliee."                (vs 6242–62)

By the time Enide has finished describing the circumstances of their meeting and marriage, her cousin is sufficiently reconciled to her lot for Enide
to lead her towards the rest of the company to join in the general celebrations (vs 6267–310).

Chrétien's purpose in making the *Joie de la Cort* adventure end as it
does is not explicitly stated by him. Accordingly, opinions have differed
as much over this point as they have over the motivation of Erec's second
quest.

For Gaston Paris, Chrétien was merely trying to rationalise a story he
had found in his sources and to explain it, though with remarkably little
success, in purely human terms. For him, 'l'histoire aussi déraisonnable
que peu claire de Mabonagrain et de son amie'[43] has no significance whatsoever except as an 'explication qui n'explique rien'.

Il est assurément impossible d'imaginer quelque chose de plus absurde, de
plus incohérent et en même temps de moins intéressant que ce récit, allongé
d'ailleurs par le poète à grand renfort de détails inutiles et raconté avec une
fatigante prolixité. *Il est clair qu'on se trouve en présence d'un vieux conte mal
transmis, que le poète français ne comprenait plus et qu'il a rendu encore plus
inintelligible en essayant de l'expliquer.* Qu'est-ce que ce mur d'air dans lequel
il y a une porte et qui n'empêche personne d'entrer? Pourquoi Mabonagrain
ne se contente-t-il pas, suivant son engagement, de vaincre ceux qui se présen-
tent, et leur coupe-t-il la tête? Comment s'est produit cet enchantement qui
fait surgir un nouveau pieu au fur et à mesure que le dernier reçoit son sinistre
trophée? A quoi sert ce cor que sonne Erec? Comment Evrain et les siens,
qui montrent une telle joie de la délivrance de Mabonagrain, n'ont-ils pas
averti Erec de ne pas le tuer s'il est vainqueur? Comment concilier la sympathie
que montre Enide à l'amie de Mabonagrain avec l'extravagante férocité que
révèle la conduite de celle-ci? Que désire au juste Mabonagrain: être vainqueur
ou être délivré? Tout cela n'a aucun sens. *Le poète, ici comme dans d'autres
épisodes de ses romans, en essayant d'atténuer le merveilleux des contes qu'il
recueillait et rimait, en rapprochant de l'humanité réelle les personnages fantastiques
de ses récits, n'a fait que rendre les contes et leurs héros à la fois plus invraisem-
blables et plus plats* (pp. 154–5, my italics).

A few critics have subscribed to the view that Chrétien is merely trying to
rationalise a folk-tale in this episode.[44] The majority, however, have felt
that its ending was devised to allow him to compare and contrast two pairs

of lovers, and in so doing, to point a moral to his tale. Exactly what that moral is, however, varies from critic to critic, depending on the view each takes of Erec's conduct and of Enide's role in the romance. For Mario Roques, Chrétien's aim was to suggest that love is not the whole of existence and that, ideally, lovers should be prepared to play their proper part in life.[45] For Nitze, Chrétien's purpose is to show that a man must have sovereignty in love[46] and a woman must submit 'to the domination of the stronger sex'.[47] But for Hoepffner, it was to complete the picture of married love which is extolled in this romance.[48]

Since no one of these views has commanded general assent, it would, I feel, be highly desirable to reopen the whole question of the significance of the *Joie de la Cort* adventure. Accordingly, the purpose of this study is to examine the matter afresh in the light of the preceding investigations into the motivation of Erec's second quest and into the part Enide plays in the romance.

On considering Chrétien's account of the *Joie de la Cort* adventure in its context, one realises that he does indeed use the conclusion of that episode to compare and contrast his two pairs of lovers. As the story of Mabonagrain and his mistress is unfolded, one comes to form a very clear picture of their relationship. And inevitably one is drawn into comparing it with the relationship that has been developing between Erec and Enide, especially when the conversation between Enide and her cousin focuses attention on the differences between them.

At first, one is aware only of the contrast between the two couples, for they differ markedly in three respects:

(a) They differ as regards the position of the female partner in the relationship. In the case of Mabonagrain and his mistress, the woman is the dominant partner. As was seen from vs 6032–9, her lover is obviously unwilling to offend her by any show of opposition to her wishes. Furthermore, it is plain that her pleasure is achieved, to some extent at least, at his expense. Mabonagrain's satisfaction at being released from the orchard certainly suggests that he was a fairly reluctant captive, as does his attempt to excuse his conduct to Erec and to represent himself as the victim of a rash promise:

> "Bien avez les hiaumes veüz
> de ces que j'ai vaincuz et morz;
> mes miens n'an est mie li torz,
> qui reison voldroit esgarder:
> de ce ne me poi ge garder,
> se ge ne volsisse estre fax
> et foi mantie et deslëax."        (vs 6058–64)

The reason for Mabonagrain's reluctance to comply with his mistress's wishes are not hard to divine. The example of Beroul's Tristan would suggest that he regretted being debarred from the company of his fellow-knights and from the normal pursuits of a warrior. These, we find are

two of the regrets which assail Tristan when the effects of the potion wear
off and he awakens to the cold realities of his position:

> "Ha! Dex, tant foiblement me vet!
> Or deüsse estre a cort a roi,
> et cent danzeaus avoques moi,
> qui servisent por armes prendre
> et a moi lor servise rendre.
> Aler deüse en autre(s) terre(s)
> soudoier et soudees querre(s)."    (Beroul, *Tristran* 2172–8)

With Erec and Enide, on the other hand, the man has a deep and tender
respect for the woman (as vs 5778–813 show), but is, nonetheless, the dominant partner in the relationship. The woman is prepared to follow his
lead – except where he is manifestly in the wrong – and is content to take
second place in his life, giving rather more in love than she receives.

(b) The couples differ in their attitude to marriage. For Mabonagrain
and his mistress, their relationship is a purely private matter, concerning
no one but their two selves, and entered into without the knowledge or
consent of the girl's family:

> "La feïmes noz covenanz
> antre nos deux, tex con nos sist.
>
> •    •    •    •    •
> si me plevi et fïança
> que toz jorz mes amis seroit
> et que il ça m'an amanroit;
>
> •    •    •    •
> si nos an venimes andui
> que nus ne le sot mes que nos."    (vs 6224–35)

In the case of Erec and Enide, on the other hand, we have a union entered
into with the full knowledge and consent of the girl's family ('Bele cosine,
il m'espousa, / si que mes peres bien le sot / et ma mere qui joie en ot'),
and approved both at the courts of Arthur and of Lac.

(c) Finally, the couples differ in their attitudes to their social obligations. Mabonagrain and his mistress live only unto themselves, entirely
cut off from the rest of the world. Their pleasure is achieved at the expense
of Evrain's court which is deprived of the fellowship and services of one
of its best knights. Accordingly, Mabonagrain's release from his obligations to his mistress is seen there as a release from bondage and as a
cause for universal satisfaction: the longed for *joie de la cort*:

> "Molt avez an grant joie mise
> la cort mon oncle et mes amis,
> c'or serai hors de ceanz mis;
> et por ce que joie an feront
> tuit cil qui a la cort vanront,
> Joie de la Cort l'apeloient
> cil qui la joie an atandoient."    (vs 6068–74)

With Erec and Enide, on the other hand, we have a couple who have both come to realise that they have obligations beyond their immediate pleasures, and who are fully prepared, now, to play their proper part in life and take their proper place in the world.

Although one is only aware at first of the differences between the two couples, further reflection shows that there are also striking resemblances between them. Indeed, in certain respects, the one is a mirror-image of what the other has been: the position of the lovers in the one relationship being the reverse of what the position of the other lovers used to be. Mabonagrain, for instance, is the exact counterpart of Enide. He suffers, as Enide did, from undue diffidence and deference in his dealings with his partner; like Enide, he is someone who must learn to assert himself. His mistress, on the other hand, is the counterpart of Erec's earlier self. Her withdrawal from Evrain's court into the enchanted orchard exactly parallels Erec's retiring from Arthur's court to his father's, to give himself up to amorous dalliance, an action no less regretted by Arthur (vs 2223–7) than the loss of his nephew was regretted by Evrain (vs 6068–70). Like Erec, the girl obviously has to learn that lovers can not turn their backs on the world and live solely for themselves, since there are obligations beyond their private interests which must be met. Like Erec again, she is someone who must also learn to treat her lover with more regard. In fact, comparing Erec and Enide with Mabonagrain and his *amie* is a way of comparing their present and their former selves, and a most effective means of indicating the progress that each has made as a result of their recent experiences.

Although Chrétien makes no explicit statement to guide his readers, there can be no doubt about the conclusion he expects them to draw from this comparison between his two pairs of lovers. In the first place, the releasing of Mabonagrain from his obligations to his mistress and the return of the couple to Evrain's court is presented as the cause for universal jubilation. Furthermore, it is a jubilation in which the man shares wholeheartedly and in which the girl finally acquiesces when the recognition of Enide as her cousin reconciles her to her lot:

> Ne puet müer que lors ne rie
> cele qui tant s'an esjoïst,
> einz que plus dire li oïst,
> que de son duel mes ne li chaut. (vs 6200–3)

In the second place, the girl is made to appear unattractively selfish and immature in her possessiveness[49] – this is particularly obvious when the cause of her tears and grief in vs 6164–5 is compared with the cause of Enide's grief and tears on the occasion of her quarrel with Erec (vs 2475–502), or when Erec decides to seek the *joie de la cort* (vs 5628–31; 5778–82).[50] Nothing, surely, could be clearer than Chrétien's intentions here. Plainly, we are being invited to see the relationship that has developed between Erec and Enide as infinitely superior to the one existing between Mabonagrain and his *amie*.

In using the *Joie de la Cort* episode to extol Erec and Enide in this way, Chrétien is using it to set a decidedly heretical view of ideal love before his courtly patrons. Though he agrees with them in seeing sexual love as a cause of joy and honour,[51] and, like them, rejects the ecclesiastical view that it is the cause of degradation and sin,[52] he takes issue with the courtly on two important matters:

(i) Where they were committed to the principle that love and marriage are incompatible,[53] he is suggesting that this is not necessarily the case, and that ideally the two should be reconciled, so that a woman is, as Enide claims to be (vs 4648–51), at once a mistress and a wife. The same point is made both in *Cligés* and *Yvain*, where the lovers marry when and as they can. Indeed, in *Cligés*, Chrétien is careful to stress that Fénice loses nothing by her marriage, since she continues to be treated as a lover:

> . . . s'amie a fame li donent,
> endeus ansanble les coronent.
> De s'amie a feite sa dame,
> car il l'apele amie et dame
> et por ce ne pert ele mie
> que il ne l'aint come s'amie
> et ele lui tot autresi
> con l'en doit amer son ami.          (*Cligés* vs 6631–8)

and in the same book, Guenevere can be found advocating marriage as the surest way of preserving and safeguarding love:

> "Or vos lo que ja ne querez
> force ne volanté d'amor.
> Par mariage et par enor
> vos antre aconpaigniez ansanble;
> ensi porra, si con moi sanble,
> vostre amors longuement durer."          (*Cligés* vs 2265–9)

(ii) Again, where the courtly demanded that women be treated with a reverence bordering, in extreme cases, on idolatry,[54] Chrétien is suggesting that it is enough that they should be treated with the respect due to equals. Since love is only part, not the whole of existence, they should not seek to dominate a man's whole life. A man must be free to follow his own avocations, and a woman be prepared to take second place in his life. And here one feels that Chrétien is making himself the champion of the rights of men, and not merely of women; recognising, as a man, their need to be enriched and not diminished by love.

In taking issue with the courtly on these two points and in stressing the need for lovers to realise that there is more to life than love, Chrétien was, I would suggest, putting forward a more practical ideal of love than the one his patrons had devised: one that took cognizance, as theirs did not, of the realities of life and of human nature. On the one hand, the balance he thought should be struck between the rights of the individual and the claims of society is one most likely to avoid any tragic clash between love and duty, and so ensure that love is an enrichment of life, not a disruptive and destructive power. Again, the balance he thought should be achieved between a woman's right to respect and a man's need to be a free agent and the dominant partner in their relationship, is one most likely to promote the best interests of both sexes in love and life.

In the circumstances it would seem that Chrétien's main purpose in making the adventure in the magic orchard end as it does, was to enable him to make an original contribution to the debate on ideal love which raged in courtly circles in the twelfth century. Though his patrons may not have approved of the moral he draws from his romance, they must at least have found it worthy of their interest and consideration.

Before closing this discussion of the ending Chrétien gives to the *Joie de la Cort* episode, it may perhaps be of interest to see how earlier interpretations of it compare with my own.

(1) By now it should, I hope, be plain that there are no grounds for claiming that Chrétien was solely concerned here to rationalise a folk-tale.

A re-reading of Gaston Paris' account of the episode leaves one with the distinct impression that a preoccupation with the sources of Chrétien's narrative had got between himself and the text. His observations and objections suggest that he was not considering the episode in its context and that the author's real intentions had escaped him.

(2) Myrrha Borodine's view that Chrétien's purpose was to contrast the selflessness of Enide with the selfish possessiveness of her cousin is fully confirmed by my findings. So too is her tentative suggestion that he may also be extolling married love as opposed to love outside marriage:

Ainsi le désintéressement si pur de la femme d'Erec est mis pleinement en lumière par l'égoïsme intense de l'amie de Mabonagrain.

Tandis qu'Enide s'oubliant elle-même est prête à sacrifier la joie et le repos de sa vie intime à celui qu'elle aime, sa cousine sacrifie au contraire celui qu'elle aime à son bonheur.

Déjà dans les propos qu'échangent les deux cousines, la pensée du poète est clairement visible. Enide s'efforce à consoler la pauvre demoiselle, et, après avoir reçu sa confession (sic) elle lui raconte à son tour l'histoire de son mariage avec Erec. On dirait presque que Chrétien oppose ici l'idée même du foyer à celle d'une libre union, fondée uniquement sur l'égoisme. Mais ce sont ces paroles d'Enide qui paraissent caractéristiques. Elle dit de son mari:

Il m'aimme mout et je lui plus          (v. 6306)

L'une répète la parole éternelle de la femme qui aime et qui se donne: "Prends tout, brise mon coeur, s'il le faut, mais sois heureux et digne de toi-même".

L'autre obéit à un instinct non moins profond, à la voix de la jalousie amoureuse de la femme: "Oublie tout et ne cherche ton bonheur que dans mes bras" (p. 74).

She makes no mention, however, of the parallel between Erec and Enide's cousin although this serves to emphasise the point that 'l'homme ne doit jamais sacrifier sa prouesse à son amour pour une femme' which she saw as the main issue in the romance (p. 76).

(3) At first there seems to be little amiss in Mario Roques' claim that the point illustrated in the *Joie de la Cort* episode is that 'l'amour le plus profond, le plus fécond en joies, n'est pas l'amour exclusif qui se subordonne toute la vie, mais celui qui tient compte de la vie, et se tient satisfait d'en avoir embelli tous les instants'.[55]

The rest of his comments in his review of Myrrha Borodine make it clear, however, that Roques was thinking only of Enide here and so was not fully aware of all that is involved. The fact is that he found himself unable to see Erec's *recreantise* as a dereliction of duty or to admit it to be a major issue in the romance.[56] For to him it seemed impossible to find a suitable explanation for Erec's treatment of Enide if he were guilty of such a dereliction – an objection which has proved to be invalid since it turns on the unwarranted assumption that no hero of a courtly romance could possibly behave as Erec does out of wounded pride:

> L'on veut voir dans *Erec* la mise en oeuvre de cette idée que "l'homme ne doit jamais sacrifier sa prouesse (ou les devoirs de sa vocation, quelle qu'elle soit) à son amour pour une femme", ou, selon la formule de G. Paris, "que la femme ne doit pas laisser son mari, par amour pour elle, négliger les devoirs, etc." (*Romania*, XX 165). Ce conflit admis entre la vocation de l'homme et son amour pour une femme, l'on se heurte à deux difficultés: 1° pourquoi Erec est-il gravement irrité contre Enide qui l'engage à suivre sa vocation glorieuse? 2° pourquoi Chrétien a-t-il ajouté à l'histoire d'Erec et d'Enide celle de Mabonagrain et de son amie, la tyrannique et malheureuse cousine d'Enide? Il se trouverait en effet que Chrétien réserve le plus malheureux sort au couple qui a su concilier l'amour exclusif et la prouesse obligatoire. L'on se débarasse de l'épisode de Mabonagrain en y voyant un hors d'oeuvre, ce qui n'est guère satisfaisant; et *l'on explique la colère d'Erec par une blessure d'amour-propre, qui ne saurait justifier les dangereuses épreuves auxquelles il soumet sa femme* (p. 379, my italics).[57]

Having rejected Borodine and Paris' definition of *recreantise*, Roques would seem to treat *chevalerie* as a mere sport, instead of the serious business it undoubtedly was in war, and to see *recreantise* as a mere 'loss of form', or as a renouncing of the pursuit of personal glory. Consequently, in discussing the use Chrétien makes of the *Joie de la Cort* episode, he speaks only of the contrast between the two young women and here mainly of the difference between Enide's realistic, not to say suburban acceptance of social conventions, and her cousin's romantic notions of elopements and clandestine unions. He does not see the parallel between Erec and the cousin who both turn their backs on the world and on their responsibilities to give themselves up to the pursuit of selfish pleasure. Nor again can he admit that the difference between the possessiveness of Mabonagrain's mistress and Enide's generous love lies in the fact that the one wishes to dominate her lover's entire life where the other is prepared to subordinate herself to her lover's career (as had been pointed out in the book he was reviewing):

> La chevalerie tient bien peu de place dans ce "drame psychologique" dont l'âme d'Erec est bien le théâtre: elle en est une circonstance, elle n'en est pas un élément. La leçon, s'il faut en tirer une, serait que l'amour le plus profond, le plus fécond en joies, n'est pas l'amour exclusif qui se subordonne toute la vie, mais celui qui tient compte de la vie et se tient satisfait d'en avoir embelli tous les instants.
>
> L'épisode de Mabonagrain s'accommode-t-il de cette interprétation? Sans aucun doute: ce n'est pas à l'idéal chevaleresque que doit céder l'amie de Mabonagrain, cet idéal devait s'accommoder parfaitement de la "prison" glorieuse où elle tenait le chevalier, toujours combattant, toujours triomphant; elle ne doit pas non plus renoncer à l'amour de Mabonagrain . . . mais elle doit renoncer à cette forme d'amour exclusif qui isolait le couple de la vie réelle. Il ne me semble pas que l'on ait toujours assez exactement marqué l'opposition, cependant bien indiquée par Chrétien, entre la sage Enide et sa romanesque cousine: celle-ci est liée à Mabonagrain par une affection de toute jeune fille (*Ancor estoie anfes assez*), leur amour déclaré est resté secret (6276-7), Mabonagrain a enlevé son amie, tous deux se sont enfuis, dit la jeune femme à Enide, "que nus ne le sot fors que nos" (6287) . . . il me semble que nous ne sommes pas trop loin ici de l'idéal amoureux de Magdelon-Polyxène. Que répond Enide? Son époux l'a choisie dans la maison de ses parents, au su et du gré de tous, bourgeoisement pourrais-je dire, sans "covenant" secret et sans "don" mystérieux, il l'aime et elle aime davantage encore ce "fils de roi" qui vint la prendre "povre et nue". Il est difficile d'opposer plus clairement le tendre et sage amour d'Enide, mêlé d'admiration et de reconnaissance et soucieuz des réalités de la vie, à l'exaltation romanesque, égoïste et exclusive, qui n'est pas l'amour parfait et il me paraît que cela précise et confirme la leçon du roman (pp. 380-1).

(4) I would agree in a general way with Hoepffner's contention that the love of Erec and Enide is extolled in the *Joie de la Cort* episode as 'l'image idéale de l'amour conjugal, qui, après s'être éprouvé en de dures épreuves communes, s'achève en une harmonie parfaite entre les deux époux' (p. 449).

We differ, however, over the nature of the love that is so extolled. This is only to be expected since we do not coincide in our views of the motivation of Erec's second quest or of Enide's role in it.[58] For his part, Hoepffner describes the bond between Erec and Enide as 'fait d'une part du dévouement total de la femme, toujours prête à se sacrifier pour son époux, fait d'autre part de l'amour protecteur du mari qui trouve dans ce sentiment même les sources profondes de son héroïsme chevaleresque' (p. 449). But as I see it, the love between Erec and Enide is much more a matter of a mutual desire, a mutual esteem and a mutual devotion. Moreover, in her own way and using her own weapons, Enide seems to me as actively protective in her love as Erec himself. Whilst the strength Erec claims to draw from her (vs 5806-9) stems as much from a desire to be worthy of her esteem as from the desire to protect and cherish her.

In discussing the significance of the *Joie de la Cort* episode, Hoepffner makes a further suggestion to which my findings give only partial support. He suggests that the ideal of married love extolled there by Chrétien was put forward by him as an alternative to the tragic love of Tristan and Iseut:

> Nous nous l'imaginons volontiers opposant à l'amour tragique et violent de Tristan et Iseut l'affection tendre et sereine d'Erec et d'Enide, à l'amour coupable et désordonné des amants de Cornouailles le bonheur calme et l'union honnête de ses jeunes époux. Peut-être trouve-t-on une trace de cette conception de l'amour conjugal dans le passage du roman où Enide raconte à sa cousine l'histoire de son mariage. C'est la description d'une honnête union bourgeoise: . . . Il est vrai qu'Enide oppose ainsi son mariage à l'union irrégulière de sa cousine qui vivait avec son ami, cachée dans le verger merveilleux, à l'insu de tous (*que nus ne le sot fors que nos*, v. 6278). Mais il est bien possible que Chrétien ait songé en même temps à l'autre exemple, fameux entre tous, de la passion déréglée, qui entraîne ses victimes aux crimes et à la mort, et qu'il ait voulu lui opposer, sans le dire, l'amour conjugal dans sa forme la plus pure, l'amour, qui après un trouble passager victorieusement surmonté, s'achève dans l'apaisement et dans la joie (p. 450).

The various attempts to 'civilise' the Tristan story certainly show that tragic, star-crossed passion was not felt to be a suitable ideal for courtly society. Furthermore, I would agree with Hoepffner that Chrétien seems to have been haunted by the tale of the Cornish lovers. But, as I see it, the doctrine advanced by Chrétien in *Erec* was not conceived, primarily, as an alternative to the romantic ideal of the Celtic legend, but as an amendment to the very different ideal which had already been devised – partly, perhaps, as a rejoinder to it – in courtly circles. Chrétien's own reply to the Tristan story was to come in his next romance, *Cligés*.

(5) Bezzola's rejection of the idea that Chrétien uses the *Joie de la Cort* adventure to advocate married love runs totally counter to my findings.

> C'est sur ce dialogue des deux cousines que certains critiques, comme nous l'avons dit, appuyent l'hypothèse selon laquelle le roman serait une exaltation du mariage parfait. Le couple de Mabonagrain et de son amie représenterait l'amour libre condamnable en face du couple marié destiné au bonheur, représenté par Erec et Enide. Cette interprétation est absolument insoutenable (p. 222).

There follows an alternative interpretation of the conversation between the two cousins which overlooks the point that the only honourable form an open association of lovers could take in the twelfth century, was in fact, marriage:

> Enide n'exalte pas le mariage en soi, mais elle insiste sur le fait que son amour s'est manifesté devant la communauté, qu'il a apporté la joie à ses parents et au comte de Lalut, son oncle et souverain, enfin qu'il l'a élevée de pauvre jeune fille inconnue aux honneurs de dame de la cour. (p. 222)

The reasons Bezzola gives for the stand he takes against Hoepffner are (a) that it is inconceivable that a twelfth-century writer should advocate so suburban an ideal as married love to courtly society; and (b) that for Chrétien to have done so in *Erec* would have been out of keeping with the line he takes in his other romances:

> La majorité des critiques modernes a cru reconnaître le sens du roman, son idée centrale dans "l'image idéale de l'amour conjugal qui, après s'être éprouvé en de dures épreuves communes, s'achève en une harmonie parfaite entre les deux époux". On a même voulu en voir l'opposé dans le couple du verger enchanté de la "Joie de la cour", Mabonagrain et son amie, représentant la liaison libre et par là immorale. Quelques passages du roman sont peut-être de nature à suggérer une interprétation de ce genre au lecteur moderne, habitué à voir traiter dans des romans sans nombre le problème du mariage. Mais cela n'était pas le cas pour la société courtoise dans la France du XIIe siècle. L'amour conjugal n'y jouait absolument aucun rôle. Depuis qu'on parlait d'amour, depuis qu'on chantait l'amour, c'est-à-dire depuis 1120 environ, on n'avait établi aucune connexion entre amour et mariage: bien au contraire, André le Chapelain, le grand théoricien de l'amour courtois, les déclarait incompatibles. . . . Si le roman d'Erec et Enide était une exaltation de l'amour conjugal, cette oeuvre occuperait vraiment une place tout à fait exceptionelle dans la littérature de l'époque (pp. 78–9).

> Cet hymne à l'amour conjugal ne serait pas moins étranger aux oeuvres de Chrétien lui-même, qui se serait complètement détaché de son idéal de jeune homme, en écrivant ensuite Le Roman de la Charrette, Cligès, Le Chevalier au Lion et le Conte du Graal (p. 79).

Neither argument, however, stands up to scrutiny. The first is not borne out by the evidence of the text. Rather than deny the facts, it would be better to accept them and to see Chrétien's heretical stand as an original contribution to the twelfth-century debate on ideal love. The second argument is not true either of *Cligés* or of *Yvain*. In any case, it involves two unwarranted assumptions. There is no justification for assuming that a man must, of necessity, be consistent in his views throughout his lifetime; nor does a writer necessarily express a personal view-point every time he sets pen to paper.

What else Bezzola has to say of the *Joie de la Cort* episode suggests that he has no very clear idea of the issues involved in it – or indeed of the issues involved in the romance as a whole:

> Ce dernier épisode était jugé superflu aussi bien par les critiques qui parlaient de la "faute d'Enide" que par ceux qui voyaient dans la suite d'aventures une punition de la *recreantise* d'Erec. Il ne l'est pas moins si l'on parle de "malentendu entre les époux" et de roman psychologique. Mais l'aventure de "la joie de la cour" est indispensable à Chrétien de Troyes, qui n'a jamais songé à punir ni Erec ni Enide, et à qui l'idée de malentendu est étrangère, puisqu'Erec a tout de suite donné raison à ses compagnons et à Enide qui ne faisait que rapporter leur opinion. Les paroles d'Erec sont décisives sur ce point:

> > "Dame, . . . droit en eüstes
> > et cil qui m'an blasment ont droit"

Ce dont le héros doute, c'est de sa vaillance, c'est de l'amour qui inspire cette vaillance et s'en nourrit en même temps. Et c'est cette vaillance, cet amour qu'il s'agit d'"essayer". Le doute portant sur ces deux aspects d'une même réalité est dissipé par la suite d'aventures, et l'aventure suprême où, pour la première fois, il ne s'agit plus seulement de réagir, soit à une agression, soit à un appel, naît de la certitude acquise en cours de route et exprimée par Erec lui-même immédiatement avant de l'affronter

> *Mes bien sachiez veraiment*
> *S'an moi n'avoit de hardemant*
> *Fors tant con vostre amors me baille,*
> *Ne doteroie je sanz faille*
> *Cors a cors nul home vivant.*

Les explications qu'Enide donne à la dame du verger la font sortir de son isolement, la font rentrer dans la société, comme la victoire d'Erec l'avait fait de Mabonagrain. Mabonagrain a révélé son nom qui symbolise non pas une personalité parfaite comme Erec, mais, comme patronyme, le lien qui le rattache à la société. Son amie sort encore moins de l'anonymat. Chrétien ne la nomme, ni ne parle de ses noces futures, maié de femme enchantée dans un jardin isolé du monde par magie, il la fait rentrer dans la communauté comme 'cousine d'Enide' (pp. 224–5).

(6) Lastly, my findings give only partial support to the view expressed by Nitze in 'Erec's treatment of Enide' that the *Joie de la Cort* episode serves to show that a man must have sovereignty in marriage – or in love – and a woman 'submit to the domination of the stronger sex':

> Crestien is contrasting one ideal of the love-relation: that in which the lover submits completely to his love, imposed by an imperious *amie* (Mabonagrain), with the other, more human ideal, in which the lover learns that he does not need thus to submit (Erec). . . . In short, against Mabonagrain, the slave of a selfish and exacting mistress, Crestien sets Erec, the examplar of self-respecting marriage of whom Enide has the right to say (vs 4689) that she is his *fame* as well as his *amie* (pp. 26–7).

Should there be any doubt as to the meaning of Nitze's final remark here, the explanation is provided later in the same article:

> To what extent can Erec's *fame* remain his *amie*, since Enide is both (see vs 4689)? To the extent of allowing Erec to rule when it is necessary (p. 32).

It is true that Erec is the dominant partner in his relationship with Enide, whilst Mabonagrain is the submissive partner in his relationship with her cousin. It is also true that Mabonagrain shows to his disadvantage against Erec. But I cannot agree with Nitze in seeing Erec as a man who has to learn to assert his authority over his wife. In making 'sovereignty' the main issue in *Erec*, Nitze shows himself to be too intent upon fitting the hero and the heroine into the pattern of a mortal cum fairy-mistress relationship to notice what is really involved in Chrétien's story.[59] As I have understood the romance, the two things that Erec has to learn are to respect his wife and to recognise that he has obligations towards society. Consequently, if a contrast is to be drawn between Erec and

Mabonagrain, they should not, I submit, be contrasted as a man who has learnt to assert his right to mastery in love and a man who has failed to do so; but as a man who has learnt to treat his partner with proper and becoming respect and a man who treats his partner with undue deference. In point of fact, of course, it would be more appropriate to call attention to the parallels which exist, on the one hand, between Mabonagrain and Enide (who both have to learn to assert themselves), and on the other, between Erec and Enide's cousin (who must both learn that there is more to life than their own selfish desires both as regards their respective lovers and as regards society).

This comparison between my findings and earlier interpretations of the significance of Mabonagrain's story shows, then, that none of them offers a completely satisfactory account of the moral which is pointed in it, since none of the previous investigators seems to have a complete or an entirely accurate picture of the issues involved in the romance.

Although one critic, at least, is prepared to admit that Chrétien uses the *Joie de la Cort* adventure to put forward an alternative to the sexual ethic which was being devised in the courtly circles of his day,[60] this is, I think, the first time that Chrétien has been presented as a champion of the rights of men. So far as I am aware, this is the first time that the ideal he extols there has been seen as an attempt, by a man, to correct the imbalance of a system devised solely in the interests of women, by catering also for the needs of men.

5    THE THEME OF CHRÉTIEN'S *EREC*: A FINAL DEFINITION

The investigations into the roles of Erec and Enide which have been carried out here suggest that the underlying theme of *Erec* might well be defined as the 'Enfances Erec et Enide'. It has been shown that the romance is concerned with their joint apprenticeship to marriage and to the duties they assume on the death of King Lac.

On the one hand, Erec and Enide are presented from the outset of the story as a perfect couple, ideally matched in every respect:

> Molt estoient igal et per
> de corteisie et de biauté
> et de grant deboneretê.
> Si estoient d'une meniere,
> d'unes mors et d'une matiere,
> que nus qui le voir volsist dire
> n'an poïst le meillor eslire
> ne le plus bel ne le plus sage.
> Molt estoient d'igal corage
> et molt avenoient ansanble;

li uns a l'autre son cuer anble;
onques deus si beles ymages
n'asanbla lois ne mariages.                    (vs 1484-96)

The quarrel which arises out of Erec's *recreantise* shows, however, that
they both have a failing which must be corrected if a truly satisfactory
relationship is to be established between them. Erec obviously lacks
consideration for his wife; Enide is unduly diffident about herself and
inclined to treat Erec with excessive deference. In both cases, the necessary
change in attitude is brought about by their joint quest. This reveals the
full extent of Enide's devotion and makes Erec aware of her courage and
good sense, so that he comes to treat her with a new tenderness and esteem.
In Enide's case, the quest drives her to act on her own initiative, and so
gives her a measure of self-confidence. Consequently, the second honeymoon which celebrates Erec's recovery is not just a return to their former
relationship, but marks the establishment of a deeper bond where understanding, confidence and esteem have been added to their original feelings
for one another.

Again, it is stressed from the outset that both Erec and Enide are well
qualified to succeed King Lac. The portrait Chrétien paints of Erec after
his triumph at Tenebroc shows that in looks, valour, address and bearing,
he has all the makings of a king:

Or fu Erec de tel renon
qu'an ne parloit se de lui non;
nus hom n'avoit si boene grace
qu'il sanbloit Ausalon de face
et de la lengue Salemon,
et de fierté sanbla lyon,
et de doner et de despandre
refu il parauz Alixandre.                      (vs 2207-14)

For her part, Enide is presented by her father as a fit consort for any
count or king:

"A dons soz ciel ne roi ne conte
qui eüst an ma fille honte,
qui tant par est bele a mervoille
qu'an ne puet trover sa paroille?
Molt est bele, mes mialz asez
vaut ses savoirs que sa biautez:
onques Dex ne fist rien tant saige
ne qui tant soit de franc coraige."            (vs 533-40)

But, once again, we discover from Erec's *recreantise* that both he and his
wife have a fault to correct before they are really fit to hold office. Erec
obviously has to learn that there are certain obligations which must be
given precedence over his personal desires; for her part, Enide is too
diffident to give Erec counsel when he requires it. In Erec's case, the

shock of Enide's revelations enables him to get his priorities right. In Enide's case, the quest helps to build up the confidence she will need if she is to act as Erec's consort with due dignity and assurance. Consequently, for both of them, the coronation at Nantes marks the end of an apprenticeship to office, and the opening of a new phase in their joint career.

The investigation into the significance of the conclusion to the *Joie de la Cort* adventure revealed a further factor which must be taken into consideration in determining the overall theme of *Erec*. It showed that the story of Mabonagrain and his mistress serves a double purpose. It provides a means of measuring the progress Erec and Enide have made as lovers and as the future successors of King Lac. It also enables Chrétien to present an alternative to the courtly ideal of love. He uses it to suggest that his hero and heroine have achieved a far more satisfactory relationship than the courtly couple he sets beside them. For he contrives to show that, unlike Mabonagrain and his *amie*, they have succeeded, on the one hand, in reconciling their personal inclinations with their social obligations, and, on the other, in striking a proper balance between a woman's right to be treated with respect and a man's need to follow his own avocations. The moral that we are left to draw from Mabonagrain's story is Chrétien's final 'comment' on the experiences of his hero and heroine. In the last analysis, then, it would seem appropriate to redefine the underlying theme of *Erec* as the study of a marriage which, from something that leaves much to be desired on both sides, develops into something that Chrétien holds out as an ideal love-relationship between a man and a woman.

In taking such a theme as the subject of *Erec*, Chrétien was fully justified in claiming that he had produced a work for all time. The problems it involves, both moral and psychological, arouse as much interest now as they did in Chrétien's day, and will continue to do so until human nature and the human condition are changed beyond all recognition.

## NOTES

1. M. Roques in his edition of Chrétien de Troyes, *Erec et Enide* (Paris, 1952), pp. xxii–xxiii.

2. An earlier version of this essay was first presented as a paper: 'Motivation in *Erec*: a reappraisal' at the Seventh Triennial Congress of the International Arthurian Society (Aberdeen, 1963), and later published as an article: 'Pourquoi Erec se décide-t-il à partir en voyage avec Enide?' in *Cahiers de Civilisation Médiévale* 7 (1964), pp. 179–85.

3. *Les Fragments du Tristan de Thomas*, edited by B. H. Wind (Geneva, 1960), Turin[1] vs 71–183.

4. 'Nouvelles Études sur la provenance du cycle arthurien: L'épisode des larmes d'Enide dans *Erec*', *Romania* 28 (1899), p. 335.

5. 'Why does Chrétien's Erec treat Enide so harshly?', *Romanic Review* 5 (1914), p. 115.

6. G. Paris, review of *Erec und Enide von Christian von Troyes*, hgg. von W. Foerster (Halle, 1890), *Romania* 20 (1891), pp. 163–4; Roques, review of Myrrha Borodine, *La femme et l'amour au XII<sup>e</sup> siècle d'après les poèmes de Chrétien de Troyes*, *Romania* 39 (1910), pp. 379–80; E. Hoepffner, ' "Matière et sens" dans le roman d'Erec et Enide', *Archivum Romanicum* 18 (1934), pp. 441–3.

7. W. A. Nitze, 'The Romance of Erec, Son of Lac', *Modern Philology* 11 (1914), pp. 445–9 and 'Erec's treatment of Enide', *Romanic Review* 10 (1919), pp. 26–7. This idea was later taken to extreme lengths by A. Adler in 'Sovereignty as the principle of unity in *Erec*', *P.M.L.A.* 60 (1945), pp. 917–36.

8. M. Borodine, *La femme et l'amour au XII<sup>e</sup> siècle d'après les poèmes de Chrétien de Troyes* (Paris, 1909), p. 45 (at the same time this critic also sees in Erec a need to test his wife's love, p. 49). See also B. M. Woodbridge, 'Chrétien's Erec as a Cornelian Hero', *Romanic Review* 6 (1915), pp. 440–2; G. Cohen, *Un grand romancier d'amour et d'aventure au XII<sup>e</sup> siècle. (Chrétien de Troyes et son oeuvre)*, (Paris, 1931), pp. 160–1.

9. R. R. Bezzola, *Le sens de l'aventure et de l'amour (Chrétien de Troyes)* (Paris, 1947), pp. 139–52.

10. Sheldon, pp. 123–6.

11. J. Frappier, *Chrétien de Troyes* (Paris, 1968), pp. 96–7. See also p. 98 which suggests that Erec's main preoccupation was to test Enide's love.

12. W. S. Woods, 'The plot structure in four romances of Chrestien de Troyes', *Studies in Philology* 50 (1953), p. 9.

13. Paris, review of *Erec und Enide*, p. 162.

14. Hoepffner, p. 443.

15. Paris, review of *Erec und Enide*, pp. 163–4.

16. Frappier, *Chrétien de Troyes*, p. 98.

17. Nitze, 'Erec's treatment of Enide', pp. 31–2 (my italics).

18. Hoepffner, p. 443. See also Borodine, pp. 67, 68.

19. Borodine, pp. 58–9. The line references given by her refer to the Foerster edition.

20. Chrétien de Troyes, *Cligés*, edited by A. Micha, vs 3836–7.

21. See: *Cligés* vs 4103–28 (note especially vs 4110–1: 'Nequedant ne li dit pas tote / la verité si en apert'); *Lais*, edited by A. Ewert (Oxford, 1952), 'Equitan' vs 65–88; *Tristan*, edited by Wind, Sneyd¹ vs 1–232.

22. *Les caractères ou les moeurs de ce siècle*, edited by R. Barthes, Club des Libraires de France (Paris, 1964), Du coeur, p. 156.

23. Roques, review of Myrrha Borodine, p. 379.

24. Hoepffner, pp. 441–2. The line references given by him refer to the Foerster edition.

25. Woods, see above, p. 3.

26. W. W. Comfort's translation in *Chrétien de Troyes: Arthurian Romances*, Everyman's Library 698 (London, 1958), p. 67. A similar rendering is given by Borodine: 'Erec ne peut rien lui reprocher après l'avoir bien éprouvée en toutes choses et n'avoir rien trouvé en elle que grand amour pour lui'. ('Chrétien de Troyes: Erec et Enide' in *Poèmes et Récits de la Vieille France* IV (Paris, 1924). In Woodbridge (p. 440) this passage is cited as evidence that Erec has been testing his wife, and the 'li' of its last line is changed, significantly, to 'lui'. Earlier W. Foerster had found 'vers li' nonsensical and had suggested that 'en li' or 'vers lui' would make better sense here (*Christian von Troyes: Erec and Enide* (Halle, 1890), note on vs 5138).

27. Godefroy (XI, p. 550) gives 'apprécier'. For a survey of the various meanings of the word in Chrétien see Appendix 1 ('Esprover' and its uses in 'Chrétien de Troyes'). It is interesting to note that A. R. Press (whose objection to my interpretation of Erec's behaviour turns on the uses of 'esprover' in Old French) admits

that the word can mean 'évaluer la qualité de (quelqu'un)', but does not see that this is a rather different operation from deliberately subjecting someone to a test. Nor does he seem to realise that the facts on which an assessment is based may as well be acquired fortuitously as deliberately. See his article: 'Le Comportement d'Erec envers Enide dans le roman de Chrétien de Troyes', *Romania* 90, p. 538, note 1. See also p. 532, note 1.

28. A point recognised by Nitze in 'Erec's treatment of Enide', p. 29 ('. . . we are not concerned here with the *result* of Erec's action, but with its cause. . . . The real question is whether the test-idea is the well-spring of his action, the impulse . . . upon which he "abruptly gives (Enide) the order to prepare at once to ride".'). See also p. 30 of the same article.

29. Sheldon, p. 122 (my italics). For a similar stand see Hoepffner, p. 441; Woods, p. 9.

30. Paris, review of *Erec und Enide*, p. 164.

31. Roques, review of Myrrha Borodine, p. 379. For similar views see Sheldon, p. 115; Hoepffner, p. 441.

32. 'The Romance of Erec, Son of Lac', p. 448.

33. A point recognised by Borodine, p. 76. 'Adouci par l'influence bienfaisante de l'amour et de la souffrance, le fier chevalier retourne pour toujours à sa vocation. Et l'idée maîtresse du roman se dégage d'elle-même comme un fruit mûr, se détachant de la branche: l'homme ne doit jamais sacrifier sa prouesse à son amour pour une femme.' This view is vigorously rejected by Roques in his review of her book (pp. 379–81).

34. On this point my stand is midway between that of Paris and that of Nitze. For Paris, Enide's is the dominant role: 'Elle est le vrai centre de ce petit drame, qui a pour sujet la rupture momentanée de son bonheur conjugal, rétabli finalement avec plus de plénitude et de solidité . . .' (review of *Erec und Enide*, p. 162). For Nitze, Enide's role is secondary to Erec's: 'For me, as well as for the poet (D'Erec, le fil Lac, est li contes, vs 19), the theme of the story throughout is Erec . . .' (Erec's treatment of Enide', pp. 27–8).

35. Hoepffner, pp. 444–5 (my italics). The idea that Enide is guilty of doubting Erec's valour is also shared by Woodbridge (p. 440); Roques (*Erec*, p. xvii); and Frappier (*Chrétien de Troyes*, p. 98). For W. Küchler, Enide is guilty both of listening to gossip and of pride in criticising Erec (see Moshé Lazar, *Amour Courtois et Fin' Amors dans la littérature du XII<sup>e</sup> siècle* (Paris, 1964), p. 203).

36. Here I agree with Nitze who speaks of Enide's alarm at her 'woman's presumption' ('Erec's treatment of Enide', pp. 29–30). On the other hand, I take issue with Bezzola who claims that she is held back by the fear of putting an end to her happiness (p. 154). In so doing, Bezzola overlooks vs 2492–502, which show that Enide's distress at being the cause of Erec's disgrace is due solely to her concern for him, and vs 2465–8, which show her very real fear of angering him.

37. A point recognised by Sheldon, pp. 117–8, 126.

38. See vs 1252–85 (Erec's rebuff to the count who insists on offering him hospitality after the Sparrow-hawk contest); vs 2692–737 (his refusal to heed his father's warnings against setting off on a quest unattended); vs 5367–431 (his refusal to be dissuaded by Guivret from visiting Evrain's court); vs 5544–620 (his refusal to be deterred by King Evrain from seeking the *Joie de la Cort*).

39. Frappier, 'Chrétien de Troyes' in *Arthurian Literature in the Middle Ages*, edited by R. S. Loomis (Oxford, 1959), p. 170.

40. Paris, review of *Erec und Enide*, p. 162. The view of Enide as the wife who gives proof of her love is shared by Hoepffner (pp. 442–3), Roques (*Erec*, pp. xvii–xviii), and Frappier (*Chrétien de Troyes*, pp. 96, 98). The view of Enide as the wife who gives proof of her respect is put forward by Nitze ('Erec's treatment of Enide', pp. 31–2).

41. Cohen, p. 159 (my italics).

42. Borodine, p. 75.

43. Review of *Erec und Enide*, p. 156.

44. E. Philipot, 'Un épisode d'Erec et Enide; La Joie de la Cour. Mabon l'enchanteur', *Romania* 25 (1896), pp. 262–3; F. Whitehead, '*The Joie de la Cour* episode in *Erec* and its bearing on Chrétien's ideas on love', B.B.I.A.S. 21 (1969), pp. 142–3.

45. Roques, review of Myrrha Borodine, pp. 379–81.

46. Nitze, 'Erec's treatment of Enide', pp. 26–7.

47. Nitze, 'The Romance of Erec, Son of Lac', p. 448.

48. Hoepffner, pp. 447–9.

49. A point overlooked by Whitehead, p. 143 ('But no moral blame is attached explicitly to the knight or the lady: *both are presented in an attractive light* (my italics). Part folk-tale, part a story of two faithful lovers, the innocent victims of an "evil custom", the story is not meant to have a *moral* or *social* significance'.

50. For a full discussion of this point see Hoepffner, pp. 448–9.

51. See for example Andreas Capellanus, *The Art of Courtly Love*, translated by J. J. Parry (New York, 1959), p. 58 ('. . . all courtesy comes from the plentiful stream of Love and to this generous lord should be credited the beginning of all good deeds and the carrying out to the end of every good . . .'); p. 88 ('. . . all men are clearly agreed and the rule of Love shows us that neither woman nor man in this world can be considered happy or well-bred, nor can he do anything good, unless love inspires him.')

52. Some idea of the stand taken by the Church can be obtained from Andreas Capellanus' chapter on the rejection of love (pp. 187–212). The following comments are typical: '. . . we know beyond a doubt that God Himself is the fountainhead and origin of chastity and of modesty, and from Scripture we know that the Devil is really the author of love and lechery. And so, because of their sources, we are bound forever to observe modesty and chastity and to shun lechery completely . . .' (pp. 194–5).

53. See Andreas Capellanus, pp. 106–7, for the letter sent by the Countess of Champagne to the couple enquiring 'whether love can have any place between husband and wife?' Note particularly: 'We declare and we hold as firmly established that love cannot exert its powers between two people who are married to each other.'

54. This is plainly the case with Chrétien's Lancelot: '. . . puis vint au lit la reïne, / si l'aore et se li ancline, / car an nul cors saint ne croit tant' (*Charrete*, edited by Roques (Paris, 1958), vs 4651–3. See also vs 4716–8.

55. Review of Myrrha Borodine, p. 380.

56. See Paris, review of *Erec und Enide*, pp. 162–3.

57. The idea that *recreantise* is an important issue in *Erec* is again rejected by Roques in *Erec*, pp. xxiii–xxiv.

58. See Hoepffner, pp. 440–7. In particular Hoepffner denies that *recreantise* is an issue in *Erec* (pp. 446–7).

59. See: 'The Romance of Erec, Son of Lac', pp. 468–70, 472–3.

60. Frappier, *Chrétien de Troyes*, p. 100: 'On peut dire encore que Chrétien a été dans son premier roman arthurien un apologiste du mariage d'amour, ce qui ne manquait pas d'originalité au regard tant des conceptions courtoises que de la réalité contemporaine.'

# The Structure of *Erec*[1]

THERE has been as much divergence of opinion over the structure of *Erec* as over the question of its underlying theme. At least five interpretations of its general organisation have been put forward.

According to Gaston Paris, the work consists of three major components, which have no connection whatsoever with one another, and the concluding description of Erec's coronation:

> *Erec* est un roman fort décousu, comprenant au moins trois parties qui n'ont entre elles aucun lien intime (on pourrait en ajouter une quatrième; celle-là de pur placage, la description du couronnement d'Erec à Nantes, [v. 6452–6878]): 1° mariage d'Erec et d'Enide [v. 27–1796], plus le passage de raccord [v. 1797–2427]; 2° brouille, aventures et réconciliation des époux [v. 2428–5211], plus le morceau de raccord [v. 5212–5318] et la conclusion de l'épisode [v. 6359–6451]; 3° l'aventure de la "joie de la cour" [v. 5319–6358]. La première est un petit roman fort agréable, quoique déparé par quelques-unes des absurdités ordinaires des roman bretons. . . . Cette introduction ne tient en rien à la suite, non plus que l'épisode de la "joie de la cour", . . . , ne tient à ce qui le précède.[2]

For W. A. Nitze, *Erec* is tripartite. Each section contains the account of one of the hero's major exploits, and all three are bound together as parts of a greater whole by the underlying theme which runs through the romance. This view is outlined very briefly, and in passing only, in two articles which appeared in 1914 and 1954 respectively:

> To sum up, it is probable that Crestien de Troyes strove to put into appropriate form an episodic tale about Erec and his imperious *amie*. In conformity with his clerical training he gave the story the benefit of his *sans*. That is, he adorned the narrative with allusions and descriptions suited to the taste of [his] readers. . . . But, above all, he read into his text a controlling purpose or theme, so that Part 1, the Sparrow-hawk Adventure, became an introduction to Part 2, the sloth and madness of the hero, and both were set in contrast to Part 3, the *Joie de la cour*; the various episodes thus acquiring definite meaning in the career of the legendary Erec.[3]

> This [uxoriousness] is the pivot upon which Chrétien's romance turns, the details of which I forebear to repeat here except to note that it falls into three parts: (1) the winning of Enide, (2) Erec's redemption and the testing of Enide, and (3) the contrast of the pair with Mabonagrain and Enide's nameless cousin – an "adventure" which the poet aptly calls (vs 5465) *La Joie de la Cort* and which is not the 'récit absurde' and 'incohérent' that Gaston Paris

(*Romania* XX (1891), 154) thought it, nor a frameless adjunct as Foerster (*Erec*, 3rd ed., p. xx) maintained, but an integral part of the *matiere* on which Chrétien drew and which by his lyrical reiteration of the word *joie* (vs 681, 1310, 2039, 2372, 6330, 6462, 6581, 6701) binds together the apparently disjointed plot.[4]

In Hoepffner we have a double interpretation of the organisation of *Erec*. On the one hand, this critic ascribes three main structural components to the romance:

> Dans le roman d'*Erec et Enide* on distingue nettement trois parties: une vaste introduction qui raconte comment Erec fit la conquête de sa femme; une partie centrale, la partie essentielle de l'oeuvre, où sont narrées les diverses aventures que les époux subissent en commun jusqu'au moment où réconciliés, ils reprennent le chemin du retour; enfin, tout à la fin, l'épisode étrange de la *Joie de la Cort*, qui semble à première vue ne former qu'un hors-d'oeuvre étranger au roman et dont celui-ci pourrait aisément se passer.[5]

On the other hand, it would seem that, thematically, the romance falls for him into two sections: an introductory account of the winning of Enide, and the romance of Erec and Enide proper, which starts with their wedding and ends with their coronation:

> ... Foerster attribuait encore ... les descriptions du mariage, du tournoi et de la réception d'Erec dans son pays, à ce qu'il considère comme la première partie du poème. Il a tort. ... Ces tableaux ne sont pas, dans l'idée du poète, la conclusion des aventures précédentes, mais au contraire, l'introduction au roman proprement dit. Avec la grande description finale du couronnement d'Erec, elles forment un cadre magnifique aux aventures des deux époux. (p. 434)

A division of the romance into two thematic sections is also to be found in R. R. Bezzola:

> ... on distingue dans tous les romans de Chrétien une nette bipartition. Dans *Erec et Enide*, la première partie comprend la conquête d'Enide; la deuxième débute par les noces d'Erec et d'Enide ...; elle est remplie par une suite d'aventures et se termine par le couronnement.[6]

In the opinion of J. Frappier, *Erec* is composed of three, very unequal, components. These consist of two series of adventures (those involved in the winning of Enide, and those befalling the couple when they set off together 'en aventure'), which are linked together by the – relatively short – account of a psychological crisis arising out of the one and leading to the other:

> Structure en trois temps, à la fois souple et savante. C'est d'abord l'apparition d'un chevalier d'élite et une aventure d'amour au dénouement heureux; puis une crise psychologique donne un nouvel élan au récit; la troisième partie, de beaucoup la plus ample, fait s'évanouir d'épisode en épisode le drame intérieur, rétablit un bonheur menacé, s'enrichit d'une aventure prodigieuse entre toutes, qui accroît encore le prestige du héros dans sa quête de la perfection.[7]

This view of the structure of *Erec* is very similar to that of T. B. W. Reid and J. P. Collas. These critics differ from Frappier only in seeing the wedding of Erec and Enide as an essential part of the story of the winning of Enide.[8] This means that the second component of the romance is considerably reduced, so that J. P. Collas is led to insist that *Erec*, like *Yvain*, is essentially a bipartite work, consisting, as it does for him, of two major sections joined by a mere bridging passage:

> . . . we must dismiss all idea of any tripartite structure in any valid sense of the term. The third section is far too long, the second far too short. We seem to have two major sections linked by a very minor one of little more than 300 lines (p. 84).

Since there is so little agreement among critics over the structure of *Erec*, it would seem in order to reopen the whole question. The purpose of the present study, therefore, is to examine the romance afresh and to do so in the light of the preceding investigations into its overall theme.

At first sight, one might be tempted to dismiss the story of Erec and Enide as an uninterrupted succession of battles and festivities. A closer perusal of the text reveals the existence of certain obvious breaks in the narrative, and one finds that the romance is composed of nine well-defined episodes – three of major and six of minor importance structurally – which cover the main events in the lives of the hero and heroine.

*Episode I* (*vs 1–1796*) is a component of major importance (1796) lines, which could be detached from the rest of the romance to stand as an independent tale. It deals with the quest Erec undertakes to avenge an insult to himself and to Guenevere, and which leads to the winning of Enide. The story of Erec's quest is skilfully combined with an account of Arthur's hunting of the White Stag. For the incident leading to Erec's expedition arises out of the hunt, whilst the outcome of the hunt is decided by that of the quest. In the one case, Erec and the Queen meet with Yder and his churlish dwarf whilst riding out to watch the hunt. In the other, the bride Erec brings back with him is unanimously declared the lady best entitled to the kiss that Arthur must bestow to mark his success in the chase; thus settling a problem which had threatened to disrupt the court:

> Quant li rois antant qu'a toz plest,
> or ne leira qu'il ne la best;
> beisiee l'a come cortois,
> veant toz ses barons, li rois,
> et si li dist: "Ma dolce amie,
> m'amor vos doing sanz vilenie;
> sanz malvestié et sanz folage,
> vos amerai de boen corage."
> Li rois, par itele avanture,
> randi l'usage et la droiture
> qu'a sa cort devoit li blans cers:
> ici fenist li premiers vers.          (vs 1785–96)

With the coalescence of its two themes at this point, the first section of the romance is brought to a natural and a satisfactory close – a fact underlined by the author's comment in vs 1796: 'ici fenist li premiers vers'.

*Episode 2 (vs 1797–1864)* is a mere bridging passage (68 lines). It prolongs the story of Erec's first quest beyond vs 1796 by an account of Erec's generosity in fulfilling the promises made to Enide's parents in vs 1306–30.

*Episode 3 (vs 1865–2214)* is a component of minor importance (350 lines). Again, it is a natural sequel to the first episode, since it is a descriptive sequence covering the wedding of Erec and Enide. Here Chrétien gives a detailed list of the wedding guests, and a full account of the hospitality provided by Arthur. The episode ends with a lively report of the tournament held in honour of the occasion, in which Erec distinguishes himself above all the knights at Arthur's court.

*Episode 4 (vs 2215–2468)* is a minor component (254 lines). It describes Erec's withdrawal into private life at his father's court. After an account of the joyous welcome the couple receive at Carnant, and the thanksgiving service they attend there, Chrétien describes the reception that first Erec and then Enide meets with at Lac's court, and then turns to Erec's growing preoccupation with his wife and so to his *recreantise*.

*Episode 5 (vs 2469–4900)*, like Episode 1, is, structurally, a component of major importance (2432 lines) which could stand on its own as an independent tale. It is the account of the quest Erec forces Enide to undertake with him when she faces him with the fact of his sloth. This episode, like the first, has a very definite unity. As the preceding investigation into the meaning of *Erec* showed, the various adventures in which the couple find themselves involved are contained within the story of their estrangement and reconciliation. The occasion which leads to the expedition is the quarrel which forces Enide to blurt out her condemnation of Erec's *recreantise*; the purpose behind it is Erec's resentful determination to vindicate himself; but the unexpected result of his adventures is his discovery of Enide's love and worth. This so disarms him, that he is left to look for an occasion which will allow him to make peace with his wife whilst preserving his dignity; and this chance eventually comes with the rescuing of Enide from the clutches of Count Oringles.

Without this unifying theme to give it shape and significance, the story of Erec's second quest would be the mere *roman à tiroirs* that is found in *Gereint*. As it is, each encounter has its appointed place and marks a definite step towards the reconciliation of the lovers and the establishing of a more satisfactory relationship between them.

*Episode 6 (vs 4901–5211)* is a minor component (311 lines). It tells of the rescuing of Erec and Enide by Guivret, and of Erec's convalescence at Pointurie. It ends with an account of the second honeymoon that celebrates Erec's recovery and sets a seal upon the reconciliation of the lovers:

Or fu Erec toz forz et sains,
or fu gariz et respassez,
or fu Enyde liee assez,
or ot sa joie et son delit.
Ansanble jurent an un lit,
et li uns l'autre acole et beise:
riens nule n'est qui tant lor pleise.
Tant ont eü mal et enui,
il por li et ele por lui,
c'or ont feite lor penitance.
Li uns ancontre l'autre tance
comant il li puise pleisir:
del sorplus me doi bien teisir.
Or ont lor dolor obliee
et lor grant amor afermee,
que petit mes lor an sovient.          (vs 5196–211)

*Episode 7 (vs 5212–6451)* is the third major structural component of the romance (1240 lines). It likewise could stand on its own as an independent tale; for, contained within the framework of an account of Erec's return to Arthur and to public life, is the story of his last major exploit. This is his quest for the *Joie de la Cort*, which he undertakes when his journey brings him to King Evrain's domains.

*Episode 8 (vs 6452–6500)*, like Episode 2, is a mere bridging passage (49 lines). As an account of the death of King Lac, it serves as a natural introduction to the last episode of the romance.

*Episode 9 (vs 6501–6878)* is a minor episode (378 lines). A descriptive passage, like Episode 3, it gives details of the regalia, the festivities and the ceremonial involved in the coronation which brings the 'enfances Erec et Enide' to a triumphant close.

On considering how the nine episodes which compose *Erec* are related to one another, one finds that they group themselves into three well-defined series.

The first three episodes are linked by the fact that the second and third provides the sequel to the story told in the first. Both are concerned with the fulfilment of a promise made in the course of Erec's first quest. In Episode 2, Erec carries out his promise to provide for Enide's parents; in Episode 3, he honours his pledge to make Enide his wife (vs 659–65; 1309–11). Together, Episodes 1–3 form a thematic whole: the story of the winning of Enide.

The next three episodes are connected by the fact that the fourth and sixth respectively provide an introduction and a conclusion to the story told in the fifth. It is Erec's withdrawal into private life, recorded in Episode 4, which leads to the quarrel that results in Erec's second quest; whilst Erec's convalescence and second honeymoon, described in Episode 6, rounds off the account of the expedition with Enide. Episodes 4–6, therefore, are to be treated as a thematic whole: the story of the estrangement and reconciliation of Erec and Enide.

The last three episodes of *Erec*, in their turn, constitute a connected series. But here the link between the seventh episode and the two which follow it is not immediately apparent. At first it seems that the death of Lac breaks completely with the events which precede it and opens a new phase in the lives of Erec and Enide. On second thoughts, however, one realises that the coronation at Nantes is the fulfilment of the promise contained in Erec's return to Arthur. For at Nantes, he finally assumes the responsibilities he showed he was fit to take up by going back to public life. From this point of view, then, Episodes 7–9 can be taken as a thematic whole: the story of Erec's return to duty, his return to court.

If one now consults the accompanying diagram where the results of the foregoing analysis of *Erec* are presented in schematic form, it will be seen that, structurally, the romance is organised as a triptych which is remarkable for its symmetry. On the one hand, the diagram shows that the romance contains three main components that are of roughly comparable size. On the other, one finds that the structural pattern of the first component (viz: major narrative unit + bridging passage + descriptive sequence) is exactly reflected in that of the third, whilst the central component has a definite symmetry of its own:

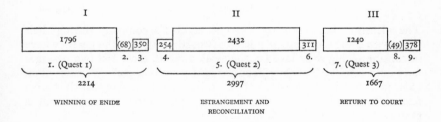

One must, however, beware of exaggerating the formal perfection of the romance, since the ratio of its three main components is, roughly, $2:3:1\frac{1}{2}$ instead of the $2:3:2$ required for an ideal balancing of parts in a triptych.

It only remains now to complete this study of the organisation of *Erec* by considering the significance of the threefold division which has been found there.

Since each member of the triptych contains the account of one of Erec's major exploits, one might, at first, be tempted to see the romance as a trilogy of adventure stories which are linked by the fact that the end of the first is the starting point of the second, and the end of the second, the starting point of the third. On the one hand, the marriage which concludes the account of Erec's first quest leads to his *recreantise*, which results in his second expedition. On the other hand, the reconciliation which rounds off the story of the second quest leads to Erec's return to Arthur's court, and this involves him in his third great adventure. A closer examination of the text reveals, however, that the links between the three main sections of the romance are far closer than this. It shows that Parts I and III of *Erec* provide the introduction and the conclusion to the story of estrangement and reconciliation that runs through Part II – thus disproving Gaston Paris' claim that the three main sections of the work 'n'ont entre elles aucun lien intime'.

On studying the account of Erec's first quest and the marriage that follows it, one finds that it has been used to set the scene for the crisis which comes in vs 2430–579.

(1) Chrétien stresses the very great physical attraction that exists between the lovers and which explains Erec's *recreantise*. Enide's beauty is described in detail (vs 411–41), and the impact it has on Erec at their first meeting is dramatically conveyed. Clearly, it is the *coup de foudre*:

> Issue fu de l'ovreor;
> quant ele le chevalier voit,
> que onques mes veü n'avoit,
> un petit arriere s'estut:
> por ce qu'ele ne le quenut,
> vergoigne en ot et si rogi.
> *Erec d'autre part s'esbahi,*
> *quant an li si grant biauté vit.*                    (vs 442–9)

The pleasure the couple take in one another's company during their journey to court is described at length (vs 1466–96); as is the joy they have in consummating their love (vs 2027–54). Indeed, these last two passages have been censured for their 'réalisme naïf et un peu cru'[9] by critics of an older generation who were too offended by them to realise that they are a necessary preparation for Erec's lapse into uxoriousness and not a gratuitous pandering to the salacious.

(2) The reader is prepared for the diffidence which drives Enide to deal so tactlessly with Erec when the moment of crisis comes. As we have already seen, Chrétien particularly emphasises the disparity in fortune between Erec and Enide's father,[10] and what he shows of Enide at her father's house or at Arthur's court stresses her modesty and her docile acceptance of authority.[11]

(3) Lastly, Chrétien prepares the reader for the violence of Erec's reactions. On the one hand, the disregard for Enide's feelings which leads Erec to press so brutally for an explanation of her 'Amis, con mar i fus' (vs 2503–35) is betrayed at the very outset of their relationship by his failure to consult her wishes over the marriage (vs 631–80) and by his insistence that she appear at court in her ragged gown (vs 1331–58). On the other hand, Erec's rejection of the hospitality he is offered after the victory over Yder shows something of his imperious nature which makes it difficult for him to accept guidance from anyone, still less a charge of *recreantise*:

... "Sire, s'il vos pleisoit,
bien devrïez et par reison
vostre ostel prandre an ma meison,
quant vos estes filz Lac le roi;
se vos prenïez mon conroi,
vos me ferïez grant enor,
car je vos tieng por mon seignor.
Biax sire, la vostre merci,
de remenoir o moi vos pri."
Erec respont: "Ne vos enuit,
ne lesserai mon oste enuit,
qui molt m'a grant enor mostree,
quant il sa fille m'a donee.
Et qu'an dites vos, sire, dons?
Don n'est biax et riches cist dons?
– Oïl, biax sire, fet li cuens,
cist dons si est et biax et buens;

.    .    .

certes molt en ai lié le cuer
(sachiez que sa mere est ma suer),
quant vos ma niece avoir deigniez.
Ancor vos pri que vos veigniez
o moi herbergier enuit mes."
*Erec respont: "Lessiez m'an pes:*
*nel feroie an nule meniere."*
*Cil voit n'i a mestier proiere*
*et dist: "Sire, a vostre pleisir.*
Or nos an poons bien teisir,
mes gié et mi chevalier tuit
serons avoec vos ceste nuit
par solaz et par conpaignie."                    (vs 1254–58)

Erec's words to the Queen as he presents Enide to her are a further indication of his masterful nature, his tendency to heed no one, but to impose his own will on others – even the highest in the land. They strongly suggest a fixed resolve in him that the court shall sanction his choice of a bride in spite of her poverty:

... "Je vos amain,
dame, ma pucele et m'amie
de povres garnemanz garnie;
si com ele me fu donee,
ensi la vos ai amenee.
D'un povre vavasor est fille:
povretez mainz homes aville;
ses peres est frans et cortois,
mes d'avoir a molt petit pois;
et molt gentix dame est sa mere,
qu'ele a un gentil conte a frere.
Ne por biauté ne por linage
ne quier je pas le mariage
de la dameisele esposer.
Povretez li a fet user

> ce blanc chainse tant que as cotes
> an sont andeus les manches rotes.
> Et ne por quant, se moi pleüst,
> boenes robes asez eüst,
> c'une pucele, sa cosine,
> li volt doner robe d'ermine,
> de dras de soie, veire ou grise;
> mes ne volsisse an nule guise
> que d'autre robe fust vestue
> tant que vos l'eüssiez veüe."          (vs 1534–58)

On turning to Part III of *Erec*, one finds there are two respects in which it serves as a conclusion to the story of the lovers' quarrel. In the first place, it is used to illustrate the effect that their recent experiences have had on Erec and Enide – with the result that the romance proves, after all, to be a story of their apprenticeship to marriage and to public office, which ends, fittingly enough, with the account of their joint coronation.

(1) By stressing Erec's desire to return to Arthur (vs 5217–34), his eagerness to undertake the quest for the 'joie de la cort' (vs 5367–425; 5543–620), and his self-restraint at the time of his father's death (vs 6466–75), Chrétien makes it very clear that his hero is a thoroughly reformed character who realises that duty must take precedence over private inclination.

(2) By describing Erec's attempt to comfort his wife before riding off into the enchanted orchard (vs 5777–819), Chrétien likewise shows that Erec has acquired a regard for Enide that was so conspicuously lacking in him at the time of their quarrel.

(3) By using the end of the adventure in the orchard to set beside them a couple who are a reflection of their former selves, Chrétien provides us with a means of gauging the progress achieved by his hero and heroine.[12]

In the second place, Chrétien exploits Part III of *Erec* to point a moral which provides the final clue to the overall theme of the romance. As we have seen, the contrast between the two pairs of lovers in the *Joie de la Cort* episode invites the reader to conclude that the relationship achieved between Erec and Enide is more likely to meet the requirements of everyday life and to promote the best interests of both partners than any courtly association. This is a conclusion which leaves us to gather that, in the last analysis, *Erec* should not be seen as the story of the 'enfances Erec et Enide' but rather as the study of a marriage which develops before our eyes into something that Chrétien can hold up as an ideal love relationship.

From this discussion of the thematic links which hold together the three main sections of *Erec*, it should by now be clear that the romance is to be seen as a triptych when it is read with an eye to the adventures it records; but as a subject logically organised into a beginning, middle and end when it is read with an eye to its overall theme. In the one case, the imbalance of its parts may appear regrettable; in the other, it seems a matter of very little importance.

If my analysis of *Erec* is compared with the findings of other critics, it will be seen to confirm the views on the general organisation of the work put forward by Nitze.

In the first place, the work is indeed tripartite in the way envisaged by Nitze (and also by Paris and Hoepffner). It does consist of three major components, which do each contain the account of one of the hero's main exploits.

In the second place, a 'controlling theme' does run through the text as Nitze claims. So that the three main components of the work are related to one another as parts of a greater whole – in spite of Paris' denials. Had Nitze described the relationships between the three parts of *Erec* in any detail, however, it is unlikely that his account of them would have borne much resemblance to the one given here. My views on the 'controlling theme' in *Erec* differ as widely from his as they do from those of other critics.

Where the demarcation of the constituent episodes in *Erec* is concerned, it will be found that my findings tally more nearly with Gaston Paris' than with those of any other critic. We agree over the ending of Erec's first adventure (vs 1796); over the ending of the second major component (vs 5211); and over the limits of the narrative containing the account of his last great exploit (vs 5212–6451). The main point of difference between us is that Paris does not distinguish (any more than the other critics do) between the account of the wedding (which in my eyes forms the natural conclusion to the story of the Winning of Enide) and the account of Erec's withdrawal to Lac's court (which, as a retreat into private life, forms the natural introduction to the story of the lovers' estrangement and reconciliation). Instead, he takes the two episodes together as the first of his 'passages de raccord'.[13] Consequently, the story of Erec's second adventure starts for him at vs 2428, whereas I see it as starting at vs 2215, the beginning of the account of the withdrawal to Lac's court. A second point of difference between Paris and myself is that he does not treat vs 5212–6451 as a single compound episode. Instead, he separates the story of the *Joie de la Cort* adventure from the narrative containing it and which he sees as a further 'morceau de raccord'.

Although only one of the divisions noted here has been specifically indicated by Chrétien, the rest correspond to equally obvious and natural breaks in the narrative – with the sole exception of the division between the fourth and fifth episodes (the account of the withdrawal to Lac's court and the account of Erec's second quest). This is shown as coming between vs 2468 and vs 2469. It could come just as well between vs 2428–9 and vs 2430–2:

> El rëaume ne an l'empire
> n'ot dame de si boenes mors.
>
> ———————
>
> Mes tant l'ama Erec d'amors,
> que d'armes mes ne li chaloit,
> ne a tornoiemant n'aloit.

For here we have an instance of the way Chrétien sometimes avoids an abrupt transition between episodes by dovetailing them into one another. Similar examples will be found later in *Cligés*.

A comparison between my analysis of *Erec* and the findings of other critics also shows that it calls attention to two features in the romance which have passed unnoticed until now. In the first place, it brings out the unity (in the sense of cohesiveness and self-containedness) of the fifth and the seventh episodes, which is no less remarkable than the unity Frappier rightly attributes to the *premier vers*: 'Le prélude – *le premier vers* – petit roman idyllique . . . forme un tout'.[14] In the case of the fifth episode, this unity has been achieved by using a psychological theme to give shape and significance to episodic material: a device used again in *Erec* to bind its three main parts together. In the case of the seventh episode, unity is achieved by including one adventure within the framework of another: a device that Chrétien was also to use in *Yvain*.

The second point in *Erec* to which my analysis has called attention is the truly remarkable symmetry of the work, which gives it a unity of form hitherto unsuspected.

This unity of form, together with the unity conferred by its overall theme, may well explain what Chrétien had in mind in describing *Erec* as the *molt bele conjointure* that he had produced from a *conte d'aventure*:

> Por ce dist Crestïens de Troies
> que reisons est que totevoies
> doit chascuns panser et antandre
> a bien dire et a bien aprandre;
> et tret d'un conte d'avanture
> une molt bele conjointure
> par qu'an puet prover et savoir
> que cil ne fet mie savoir
> qui s'escïence n'abandone
> tant con Dex la grasce l'an done:
> d'Erec, le fil Lac, est li contes,
> que devant rois et devant contes
> depecier et corronpre suelent
> cil qui de conter vivre vuelent.          (vs 9–22)

Surely, what Chrétien is claiming here with this insistence on the need to 'bien dire et bien aprandre', and with this scathing criticism of his less conscientious – or less able – *confrères*, is that he has taken the formless mass of a mere adventure story and fashioned it into a well-organised whole that has both meaning and shape.

# NOTES

1. An earlier version of this essay was given as a paper in October 1965 at the Burn Conference for Departments of French in the Scottish Universities, and later published in *M.L.R.* 62 (1967), pp. 608–19.

2. Review of *Erec und Enide*, pp. 158–9. The line references in the original text refer to Foerster's edition of *Erec*.

3. 'The Romance of Erec, Son of Lac', p. 488.

4. 'Erec and the Joy of the Court', *Speculum* 29 (1954), p. 692. Nitze's line references refer to the Foerster edition of *Erec*.

5. ' "Matière et sens" dans le roman d'Erec et Enide', p. 433.

6. *Le sens de l'aventure et de l'amour (Chrétien de Troyes)*, p. 81.

7. *Chrétien de Troyes*, p. 90. See also pp. 87–90. A similar view of the structure of *Erec* appears in the 1957 edition of this book (pp. 85–92). A rather different one, however, will be found in the analysis of *Erec* which appears in *Arthurian Literature in the Middle Ages*, edited by R. S. Loomis (Oxford, 1959), pp. 165–7. Here Frappier divides the work, like Nitze, into: 1, the *premier vers*; 2, the joint quest of Erec and his wife (ending at vs 4900); 3, the *Joie de la Cort* adventure and the Coronation.

8. Reid, in his edition of Chrestien de Troyes, *Yvain* (Manchester, 1948), p. xi; Collas, in 'The Romantic Hero of the Twelfth Century', in *Medieval Miscellany Presented to Eugène Vinaver*, edited by F. Whitehead, A. H. Diverres and F. E. Sutcliffe (Manchester, 1965), pp. 80–4.

9. Borodine, *La femme et l'amour au XII^e siècle*, p. 35.

10. See above, pp. 29–30.

11. See above, pp. 28–29.

12. See above, p. 46.

13. See above, p. 60. In the case of Reid (*Yvain*, p. xi) and Collas ('The Romantic Hero', pp. 83–4) the withdrawal to Lac's court is included in the first section of the work which ends for them at vs 2429. For Frappier (*Chrétien de Troyes*, pp. 87–8), the first part of *Erec* ends at vs 1796 so that the wedding, the withdrawal to Lac's court and the quarrel must constitute the 'crise psychologique' which leads to the adventures related in his third section of the romance. As for Bezzola and Hoepffner, we have already seen (p. 61) that for them the second part of the romance opens with the wedding of Erec and Enide.

14. Frappier, *Chrétien de Troyes*, p. 87.

# The Question of Yvain's Redemption[1]

IT has been claimed that the story behind the exploits performed by Yvain after his estrangement from Laudine is that of his attempt to rehabilitate himself in his own eyes and in hers by a series of evermore heroic endeavours:

> La première partie d'*Yvain* était le récit audacieux d'un amour conquis par une valeur exceptionnelle, perdu par l'impardonnable légèreté d'un chevalier oublieux . . .
>
> La seconde partie sera le récit d'une rédemption, acceptée pour la réparation de cet oubli à force d'entreprises toujours nouvelles et plus hardiment dangereuses et peut-être en progrès de générosité: . . . Tout cet effort continu d'Yvain pour les malheureux constitue une oeuvre voulue de haute charité et de supérieure rédemption.
>
> Or Yvain, après son retour à la raison, n'a pas un moment cessé de penser à son bonheur enfui, . . . La question était de savoir quand il pourrait avoir l'audace de demander à sa dame un pardon qu'elle avait assez le droit de lui refuser.
>
> Au terme de ses succès en bonnes oeuvres, justifié par l'indécision même de sa bataille avec Gauvain, chevalier sans pair, il peut se croire digne de pardon, étant bien décidé à mourir s'il ne l'obtient pas. Alors il se trouve amené à reprendre les choses au début de ses rapports avec la dame de la Fontaine, en lui forçant la main au sujet de la tempête, et en venant, avec l'aide de Lunete, se jeter à ses pieds. C'est ainsi que Lancelot hésite longtemps devant l'apparent dédain de Guenièvre, et prend le courage de parler librement à celle qu'il aime quand il se sent assez grandi et excusé par tant de traverses et de dangers affrontés pour elle. Mais Yvain ne demandera pas son pardon à une reconnaissance personnelle, il veut l'obtenir par la preuve, si longuement donnée, d'une valeur morale qui domine et efface un manque d'attention amoureuse, plus blâmable que vraiment déshonorant et destructeur d'amour.
>
> L'amour de Lancelot allait sortir vainqueur par sa persistante soumission à la légitime volonté de Guenièvre; l'amour d'Yvain triomphe grâce à un effort conscient et continu de sentiment chrétien et de perfectionnement humain.[2]

The role attributed here to Yvain seems a suitably edifying one for the hero of a courtly romance. It is not surprising, therefore, that this view of Yvain as a man who redeems himself is widely shared, and in particular by those who feel there must be some point and purpose behind his various adventures.[3] Indeed, one commentator specifically states that it offers so reasonable an explanation for Yvain's adventures as to be the obvious one:

Some scholars have gone so far as to declare that in the last half of the poem Chrétien was spinning out episodes merely for the pleasure of telling a tale. But it would be very surprising indeed if the poet who composed the first part of the poem with such admirable clarity had strung out adventures endlessly and to no point in the second part. He must have had in mind a plan in the light of which the series of adventures would make sense: Yvain obviously could not have gone directly back to the fountain when Lunete snatched Laudine's ring from his hand ... and *forced* Laudine to take him back. No matter how much of a storm he raised, Laudine could not have taken him back as husband and defender of the fountain before he made some sort of amends. ... But if the adventures are not pointless, they must have had a purpose. It would be reasonable to expect that the series of episodes would provide Yvain with a means of redeeming himself and that they would prepare the way for his return to Laudine's castle. It is obvious, at least so far as Chrétien's version of *Yvain* is concerned, that the second part of the story contains a careful rebuilding of Yvain's moral character and his reputation.[4]

But however reasonable and fitting it may seem that a courtly hero should make due reparation for any wrong done by him, the fact remains that there are no grounds in Chrétien's story for ascribing such a rôle to Yvain.

(1) There is no justification for claiming that Yvain's exploits form 'une oeuvre *voulue* de haute charité et de supérieure rédemption', or for saying, as another critic does, that their sole purpose is to obtain 'le pardon de sa femme'.[5] None of Yvain's adventures is specifically undertaken by him as a means of redemption. With the exception of the fight at Pesme-Avanture, which is forced upon him, Yvain is responding in each case to a call for help. And in each case his response comes either as the immediate reaction of a generous man whose own sufferings have probably made him all the more ready to alleviate the distress of others, or as that of a loyal friend, returning services rendered:

(a) The defence of the lady of Noroison (vs 3142–313) is the return for curing Yvain of his madness which her maid had led her to hope for:

> "Car li eüst or Des randu
> le san au miauz, qu'il eüst onques,
> et puis si li pleüst adonques,
> qu'il remassist an vostre aïe!
> Car trop vos a mal anvaïe
> li cuens Aliers, qui vos guerroie.
> La guerre de vos deus verroie
> a vostre grant enor finee,
> se Des si buene destinee
> vos donoit, qu'il le remeïst
> an son san, si s'antremeïst
> de vos eidier a cest besoing."
> La dame dist: "Or n'aiiez soing!
> Que certes, se il ne s'an fuit,
> a l'aïe de De, ce cuit,
> li osterons nos de la teste
> tote la rage et la tanpeste." (vs 2934–50)

(b) The defence of the lion is prompted by the sympathy Yvain feels for a noble animal when he discovers the cause of the 'cri mout dolereus et haut' that had attracted his attention:

> ... il oï anmi le gaut
> un cri mout dolereus et haut,
> si s'adreça lors vers le cri
> cele part, ou il l'ot oï.
> Et quant il parvint cele part,
> vit un lion an un essart
> et un serpant, qui le tenoit
>
> · · · · · ·
>
> A lui meïsme se consoille,
> au quel des deus il eidera.
> Lors dit, qu'au lion secorra;
> qu'a venimeus et a felon
> ne doit an feire se mal non.
>
> Eidier li voldra il adés;
> *que pitiez l'an semont et prie,*
> *qu'il face secors et aïe*
> *a la beste jantil et franche.*                    (vs 3343–75)

(c) The defence of Lunete is prompted by the loyalty he feels for a staunch friend whose life is in danger because of himself:

> "Troi sont, qui traïtre me claimment."
> "Et qui sont cil, qui tant vos aimment,
> don li uns si hardiz seroit,
> qu'a trois conbatre s'oseroit,
> por vos sauver et garantir?"
> "Je le vos dirai sanz mantir:
> li uns est mes sire Gauvains,
> et li autre mes sire Yvains,
> por cui demain serai a tort
> livree a martire de mort."
> "Por cui?" fet il, "qu'avez vos dit?"
> "Sire! se Damedés m'aït,
> por le fil au roi Uriien."
> "Or vos ai antandue bien,
> mes vos n'i morroiz ja sanz lui.
> Gié meïsmes cil Yvains sui,
> por cui vos estes an esfroi;
> et vos estes cele, ce croi,
> qui an la sale me gardastes,
> ma vie et mon cors me sauvastes
>
> · · · · · ·
>
> Morz i eüsse esté ou pris,
> se ne fust vostre buene aïe.            (vs 3619–43)
>
> ... "Ja De ne place,
> que l'an por moi nul mal vos face!
> Tant que je vive, n'i morroiz!
> Demain atandre me porroiz

apareillié lonc ma puissance,
de metre an vostre delivrance
mon cors, si con je le doi feire."  (vs 3721–7)

(d) The defence of Gauvain's relatives is prompted by compassion and
by the love he bears Gauvain:

". . . sis fiz chevaliers avoie,
plus biaus el monde ne savoie;
ses a toz sis li jaianz pris.
Veant moi a les deus ocis,
et demain ocirra les quatre,
se je ne truis, qui s'ost conbatre
a lui por mes fiz delivrer,
ou se je ne li vuel livrer
ma fille; et dit, quant il l'avra,
as plus vils garçons, qu'il savra
an sa meison, et as plus orz
la liverra por lor deporz;

. . . . . .

Mes sire Yvains onques ne fine
de sospirer, quant ce antant;
de la pitié, que il l'an prant,
li respont: "Biaus douz sire chiers!
Je m'an metroie volantiers
an l'avanture et el peril,
se li jaianz et vostre fil
venoient demain a tel ore,
que n'i face trop grant demore;
que je serai aillors que ci
demain a ore de midi,
si con je l'ai acreanté."  (vs 3863–951)

Et la pucele, qui s'esmaie
comance mout fort a plorer,
si li prie de demorer.
Come destroite et angoisseuse
por la reïne glorïeuse
del ciel et des anges li prie
et por De, qu'il ne s'an aut mie,
ainz atande ancore un petit,
et por son oncle, dont il dit,
que il conoist et aimme et prise.
Lors l'an est mout granz pitiez prise,
quant il ot, qu'ele se reclaimme
de par l'ome, que il plus aimme,
et de par la dame des ciaus,
et de par De, qui est li miaus
et la douçors de piëté.
D'angoisse a un sospir gité;
que por le reaume de Tarse
ne voldroit, que cele fust arse,
que il avoit asseüree.

. . . . . .

> Neporquant ancor ne se muet,
> einçois demore et si atant,
> tant que li jaianz vint batant.          (vs 4060–90)

(e) The fight at Pesme-Avanture is a matter of obligation not of choice for Yvain:

> Mes sire Yvains aprés la messe
> oï novele felenesse,
> quant il cuida, qu'il s'an deüst
> aler, que riens ne li neüst;
> mes ne pot mie estre a son chois.
> Quant il dist: "Sire! je m'an vois,
> s'il vos plest, a vostre congié",
> "Amis! ancor nel vos doing gié",
> fet li sire de la meison;
> "Je nel puis feire par reison;
> qu'an cest chastel a establie
> une mout fiere deablie,
> que il me covient maintenir.
> Je vos ferai ja ci venir
> deus miens serjanz mout granz et forz:
> ancontre aus deus, soit droiz ou torz,
> vos covandra voz armes prandre".          (vs 5457–73)

> "Donc m'i covient il tote voie
> conbatre maleoit gre mien;
> mes je m'an sofrisse mout bien
> et volantiers, ce vos otroi.
> La bataille, ce poise moi,
> ferai, quant ne puet remenoir."          (vs 5506–11)

(f) The defence of the disinherited sister is undertaken out of compassion:

> "Miaudre de moi a vos m'anvoie,
> plus jantils fame et plus vaillanz.
> Mes se ele est a vos faillanz,
> donc l'a vostre renons traïe;
> qu'ele n'atant d'aillors aïe.
> Par vos cuide ma dameisele
> tote desresnier sa querele,
> qu'une soe suer deserete;
> ne viaut, qu'autre s'an antremete.
> Nus ne li puet feire cuidier,
> que autre li poïst eidier.
>           .     .     .     .     .
> Or me respondez, s'il vos plest,
> se vos venir i oseroiz
> ou se vos an reposeroiz!"
> "Nenil," fet il, "de reposer
> ne se puet nus hon aloser,
> ne je ne reposerai mie,
> ainz vos siurai, ma douce amie!
> volantiers la, ou vos pleira.

> Et se de moi grant afeire a
> cele, por cui vos me querez,
> ja ne vos an desesperez,
> que je tot mon pooir n'an face.
> Or me doint Des eür et grace,
> que je par buene avanture
> puisse desresnier sa droiture!"        (vs 5072–106)

(2) Again, there is no justification for the claim that Yvain feels himself redeemed and 'digne du pardon' when he at last decides to approach Laudine after the battle with Gauvain. There is no evidence in Chrétien's text to show that 'la réconciliation des époux avait pour cause première la conviction, chez Yvain, de son mérite non seulement regagné, mais accru'.[6] How far Yvain really is from feeling that his merits will plead his case can be gauged from the fact that the only way he sees open to him for persuading his wife to make her peace with him is a resort to main force:

> Mes sire Yvains, qui sanz retor
> avoit son cuer mis an amor,
> vit bien, que durer ne porroit,
> mes por amor an fin morroit,
> se sa dame n'avoit merci
> de lui; qu'il se moroit por li.
> Et pansa, qu'il se partiroit
> toz seus de cort et si iroit
> a sa fontainne guerroiier,
> et s'i feroit tant foudroiier
> et tant vanter et tant plovoir,
> *que par force et par estovoir*
> *li covandroit feire a lui pes,*
> ou il ne fineroit ja mes
> de la fontainne tormanter
> et de plovoir et de vanter.        (vs 6511–26)

In other words, when he sets off for the fountain, Yvain has as little hope of being found worthy of pardon as he had after the fight to defend Lunete against the seneschal and his sons. On that occasion, he was so despairing of being taken back into favour that he let the opportunity for a reconciliation go by. In spite of Laudine's obvious admiration for him, and in spite of her condemnation of the lady who could bar her door against a knight of his calibre (vs 4580–98), he refused her offer of hospitality and kept his identity concealed (vs 4599–634), merely trusting himself to beg Lunete to put in a good word for him if a chance to do so ever presented itself:

> Atant s'an part a grant angoisse,
> si n'i a nul, qui le conoisse
> fors que Lunete solemant,
>
>         .   .   .   .   .
>
> et il li prie tote voie
> que ja par li ne soit seü,

> quel chanpion ele a eü.
>
> .    .    .    .    .    .    .
>
> *Apres ce li repria cil,*
> *que de lui li ressovenist,*
> *et vers sa dame li tenist*
> *buen leu, s'ele an venoit an eise.*                      (vs 4635–47)

But the best proof of Yvain's lack of confidence in his chances of being found worthy of pardon is the comment Chrétien makes when Lunete brings Yvain the news that Laudine has committed herself to a reconciliation. This, we are told, is something he had never expected to hear:

> "... j'ai ma dame a ce menee,
> s'ele parjurer ne se viaut,
> que tot aussi come ele siaut,
> iert vostre dame et vos ses sire;
> par verité le vos os dire".
> *Mes sire Yvains formant s'esjot*
> *de la novele, que il ot,*
> *qu'il ne cuidoit ja mes oïr.*                      (vs 6684–91)

(3) Lastly, there are no grounds for claiming that it is the cumulative effect of Yvain's achievements which redeems him in Laudine's eyes:

> ... Yvain ne demandera pas son pardon à une reconnaissance personnelle, il veut l'obtenir par la preuve si longuement donnée, d'une valeur morale qui domine et efface un manque d'attention amoureuse, ...
>
> L'amour de Lancelot allait sortir vainqueur par sa persistante soumission à la légitime volonté de Guenièvre; l'amour d'Yvain triomphe grâce à un effort conscient et continu de sentiment chrétien et de perfectionnement humain.

When she pardons him, Laudine is in fact unaware of Yvain's last two victories.[7] Indeed, Lunete's whole stratagem for reconciling the lovers turns on Laudine's ignorance of the identity of the Knight of the Lion, and this, as we know, was revealed at the end of the duel with Gauvain. Where Laudine is concerned, the defence of Lunete is enough in itself to ensure Yvain's pardon:

(a) It brings to her notice the prowess and the plight of the Knight of the Lion (vs 4580–629). This means that it is simple enough for Lunete to suggest that he might well deal with the mischief-maker at the fountain if Laudine promised to intercede for him with his lady (vs 6602–14). And it is equally natural for Laudine to agree to this plan (vs 6615–21), little realising that she is committing herself to a reconciliation with her own husband.

(b) Laudine likewise commits herself to pardoning Yvain by the comment she makes, after the battle, on the lady of the Knight of the Lion. For she will stand self-condemned as thoroughly uncourtly, 'mie ... tres cortoise' if she holds out against a knight of his distinction:

"Ne taing mie por tres cortoise
la dame, qui mal cuer vos porte.
Ne deüst pas veer sa porte
a chevalier de vostre pris,
se trop n'eüst vers li mespris."                    (vs 4594–8)

(c) Finally, the lasting peace that is eventually established between the lovers – if we are to believe Chrétien (vs 6811–3) – is probably due in large measure to Yvain's behaviour after the trial. His failure to press an obvious advantage at that time, and his utter acceptance of his lady's displeasure (vs 4599–600), must be the best proof that Laudine could have of the sincerity of his repentance, or of the promises he makes for the future in vs 6782–89:

"Conparé ai mon fol savoir
et je le dui bien conparer.
Folie me fist demorer,
si m'an rant coupable et forfet.
Et mout grant hardemant ai fet,
quant devant vos osai venir;
mes s'or me volez retenir,
ja mes ne vos mesferai rien."                    (vs 6782–89)

A study of the text shows, then, that there are no grounds for interpreting the second part of *Yvain* as the story of the hero's attempt to earn his pardon, that is, as the 'récit d'une rédemption, acceptée pour la réparation de cet oubli à force d'entreprises toujours nouvelles ...'. Indeed, the difficulties in making the theory of Yvain's deliberate rehabilitation square with the facts of Chrétien's story have led one critic to abandon all hope of making any sense of the romance at the literal level:

In the *Yvain* nothing is said about recovering Laudine's affections or his earlier status. Interestingly enough, in this romance Yvain realizes, before being told, that he has erred. Since the device for making Laudine finally relent was available to Yvain before his adventures it would appear probable that Chrestien's failure to use this device must be due to Yvain's not having earned the right to it through penance. It is also of interest that Yvain starts on his adventures while mad and therefore his first steps of rehabilitation are unconscious. *The inevitable conclusion, hence, is that the motivation for the Yvain is also ambiguous and hardly comprehensible on the plot level alone. One must look for a higher interpretation which will explain away these vague plot elements and will reconcile these apparent discrepancies and reveal the full meaning of the romance.*[8]

This conclusion, however, is unduly pessimistic. An examination of *Yvain* reveals that there is a rather different but perfectly logical explanation for the hero's behaviour, and a rather different but entirely coherent story behind the events in which he finds himself involved after his estrangement from his wife.

In the first place, the indications are that it is Yvain's desire to get away from other people and be alone with his misery which drives him to adopt a wandering life when he has been cured of his madness at Noroison. We know, for instance, that his first reaction to the news of his disgrace was to flee from the court to be alone with his grief. This is specifically stated by Chrétien:

> ... ses enuiz tot adés croist:
> quanquë il ot, tot li ancroist,
> et quanque il voit, tot li enuie.
> *Mis se voldroit estre a la fuie*
> *toz seus an si sauvage terre,*
> *que l'an ne le seüst, ou querre,*
> *n'ome ne fame n'i eüst,*
> *ne nus de lui rien ne seüst*
> *ne plus, que s'il fust an abisme.*
> Ne het tant rien con lui meïsme,
> ne ne set, a cui se confort
> de lui, qu'il meïsmes a mort;
> mes ainz voldra le san changier,
> que il ne se puisse vangier
> de lui, qui joie s'est tolue.
> D'antre les barons se remue;
> qu'il crient antre aus issir del san
> et de ce ne se gardoit l'an,
> si l'an leissierent seul aler,
> *Bien sevent, que de lor parler*
> *ne de lor siecle n'a il soing.*        (vs 2781–801)

It seems reasonable enough to suppose that the self-same desire for solitude sends Yvain wandering over the face of the earth when he is restored to health and sanity.[9] At all events, we do know that he is pursued into his self-imposed exile by the other feelings which assailed him after the denunciation of his faithlessness. His reactions on coming across the fountain a second time show that grief and self-disgust are as strong as ever in him. The fresh reminder of his loss almost drives him out of his mind a second time and causes him to faint:

> ... par po ne se forsena
> mes sire Yvains autre foiiee,
> quant la fontainne ot aprochiee
> et le perron et la chapele.
> Mil foiz las et dolanz s'apele
> et chiet pasmez, tant fu dolanz.        (vs 3492–7)

When he regains consciousness, his thoughts turn to suicide as an extreme form of self-mortification,[10] until he is diverted from this course by Lunete and her plight:

> Au revenir mout fort se blasme
> de l'an, que trespassé avoit,
> por quoi sa dame le haoit,

et dit: "Que fet, que ne se tue
cist las, qui joie s'est tolue?
Que faz je, las! que ne m'oci?
Comant puis je demorer ci
et veoir les choses ma dame?
An mon cors por qu'areste l'ame?
Que fet ame an si dolant cors?

.   .   .   .   .

Haïr et blasmer et despire
me doi voir mout et je si faz.
Qui pert la joie et le solaz
par son mesfet et par son tort,
mout se doit bien haïr de mort.
Haïr et ocirre se doit.
Et gié, tant con nus ne me voit,
por quoi m'esparng? que ne me tu?"          (vs 3528–47)

To turn now to Yvain's reasons for hesitating so long to approach
Laudine, here the text shows that he is held back by the conviction that
his offence is beyond pardon – and not by any feeling that he must first
rehabilitate himself. As we have seen, Yvain's decision to resort to main
force as the only means of compelling his wife to come to terms with him
shows that he is ridden, to the very last, by the fear that he is beyond all
forgiveness. It is proof that he still has as little faith in being able to plead
his case successfully as he had at the end of Lunete's trial. And, as we have
seen, Chrétien himself states that Yvain had never expected Laudine to
consider receiving him back into favour:

Mes sire Yvains formant s'esjot
de la novele que il ot,
qu'il ne cuidoit ja mes oïr.          (vs 6689–91)

This view of Yvain as a man crippled by guilt and despair will no doubt
be contested by those who feel with Roques that he is only guilty of a
minor fault, 'plus blâmable que vraiment déshonorant et destructeur
d'amour', or who think that he comes perilously near the henpecked
husband of comedy. But such critics forget that they are looking at Yvain
from a twentieth-century standpoint and not from the standpoint of the
public for whom Chrétien was writing.

In the first place, Yvain was in fact guilty of two major crimes in the
eyes of courtly society. On the one hand, he had sacrificed love to vain
glory: and we know from the example of Lancelot that the ideal lover was
supposed to sacrifice himself to the wellbeing – and even the whim – of the
beloved.[11] On the other hand, Yvain had broken his promise to Laudine;
and we can judge from the case of Mabonagrain in *Erec* how serious an
offence this was thought to be. For once that knight had committed
himself to remaining with his mistress in her orchard, he felt constrained
to do so, however much it irked him and whatever the price might be:

Ma dameisele, qui siet la
tantost de ma foi m'apela
et dist que plevi li avoie
que ja mes de ceanz n'istroie,
tant que chevaliers i venist
qui par armes me conqueïst.
Reisons fu que je remainsisse,
ainz que ma fïance mantisse,
ja ne l'eüsse je plevi.

. . . . .

Et ge feïsse mesprison,
se de rien nule me fainsisse
que trestoz ces ne conqueïsse
vers cui ge eüsse puissance:
vilainne fust tex delivrance.
Bien vos puis dire et acointier
que je n'ai nul ami si chier
vers cui je m'an fainsisse pas;
onques mes d'armes ne fui las,
ne de conbatre recreüz.
Bien avez les hiaumes vëuz
de ces que j'ai vaincuz et morz;
mes miens n'an est mie li torz,
qui reison voldroit esgarder,
de ce ne me poi ge garder,
se ge ne volsisse estre fax
et foi mantie et deslëax.

(*Erec* vs 6023–64)

In other words, where Yvain has been seen by modern critics as merely guilty of 'un manque d'attention amoureuse', he had in fact put himself beyond the pale of courtly society. In the circumstances, the despair which first drives him mad and then pursues him into his exile is as understandable as it is justified.

Again, it should be remembered that there would be nothing exaggerated or unbecoming for the courtly in the diffidence Yvain feels for Laudine. As Chrétien's comment on the paradoxical timidity of Cligés shows, such diffidence was seen as the essential condition for love:

Et qui a Amor se comande
son mestre et son seignor an feit:
S'est droiz qu'an remanbrance l'eit
et qu'il le serve et qu'il l'enort,
s'il vialt bien estre de sa cort,
Amors sanz criemme et sanz peor
est feus ardanz et sanz chalor,
jorz sanz soloil, cire sanz miel,
estez sanz flor, yvers sanz giel,
ciax sans lune, livres sanz letre.
Et s'a neant le volez metre,
que la ou criemme se dessoivre,
n'i fet Amors a ramantoivre.
Qui amer vialt, crienbre l'estuet,
ou autrement amer ne puet;

> mes seul celi qu'il aimme dot
> et por li soit hardiz par tot.
> Donc ne fausse ne mesprant mie
> Cligés, s'il redote s'amie.          (*Cligés* vs 3842–60)

When one comes to consider why Yvain finally decides to approach Laudine, the text shows that it is because the sheer force of circumstances drives him to realise that no other course is open to him. The fact is that the duel with Gauvain puts a stop to his wanderings, since it ends with his making his identity known (vs 6215–291) and this leads to his return to court (vs 6447–509). Once there, he is obliged to face the facts of his position, and, finding that he can procrastinate no longer, he screws up the courage to approach Laudine. As Chrétien says, he is brought to realise that he must either be reconciled to her or die of misery:

> Mes sire Yvains, qui sanz retor
> avoit son cuer mis an amor,
> vit bien, que durer ne porroit,
> mes por amor an fin morroit,
> se sa dame n'avoit merci
> de lui; qu'il se moroit por li.          (vs 6511–16)

And so he determines to make his despairing bid for a reconciliation by the only means he sees open to him – a recourse to main force:

> et pansa, qu'il se partiroit
> toz seus de cort et si iroit
> a sa fontainne guerroiier,
> et s'i feroit tant foudroier
>
> .    .    .    .    .
>
> que par force et par estovoir
> li covandroit feire a lui pes,
> ou il ne fineroit ja mes
> de la fontainne tormanter.          (vs 6517–25)

On the strength of the evidence we have been considering, I would suggest that the story behind Yvain's adventures as the Knight of the Lion can best be defined as that of a man who cannot bring himself to approach the wife he knows he has grievously offended, until despair proves stronger than the shame which has been holding him back.

Although Yvain emerges so plainly from a close study of the romance as a man ridden by remorse and despair, only three critics seem to have been prepared to see him in this light:

Gustave Cohen:
> Guéri par les onguents féeriques, il erre néanmoins d'aventure en aventure, désespéré, n'osant même pas révéler son identité à Laudine quand il se trouve en sa présence, après le duel judiciaire qu'il soutient pour sauver Lunete. Il faudra toute la ruse de celle-ci . . . pour faire rentrer en grâce, auprès de sa femme, l'époux repentant. . . .[12]

Faith Lyons:

> ... par sa crise de folie et par sa tentative de suicide il témoigne de l'état de désespoir où il se trouve après l'oubli, causé par sa légèreté. (p. 373)

> Quand Yvain cherche à rejoindre Laudine c'est que la séparation le fait souffrir au-delà des limites de l'endurance. C'est le désespoir qui le fait braver Laudine.... (p. 376)

J. P. Collas:

> Yvain ... is not consciously, at l. 2804, advancing into the unknown. He is merely fleeing from Arthur's court in quest of solitude to hide his shame and remorse. ... Yvain's remorse drives him to insanity, and when he recovers his senses all memory has gone. He awakes one day, ashamed only of his physical nakedness, and without the least idea of its cause (ll. 3016–19). Yet unwittingly he is already involved in his first adventure. ...

> The reader is prepared to see him pass like Erec in linear progression from adventure to adventure until the end of the romance. Chrétien improves the 'quest' ... by giving it another pattern. Cast off by Laudine, *with no hope of reconciliation*, Yvain will remain attached, as if by chance, to the place and personages of the *lai* of his marriage, since his odyssey will never move far from the magic spring. Thus, while retaining the genetic notion of an aimless quest as the essential feature of romance ... Chrétien succeeds in superimposing a pattern which appears to transcend the disruption necessarily produced by the passage from *lai* to romance.[13]

The majority of critics have been reluctant to admit that the hero of a medieval romance can be driven by so negative a motive as despair to take the decisive step in his career, and that even then he should need the good offices of a friend to make the move a profitable one. This reluctance would seem to stem from the assumption, which appears to be general, that a courtly hero should be the master of his own destiny. It is surely this assumption that lies behind such statements as 'il résolut d'être l'artisan de son bonheur',[14] or 'se jugeant digne du pardon, il précipite le dénouement par un acte de volonté'.[15] It is most certainly on these grounds that one critic was led to conclude that the most reasonable and, therefore, the obvious explanation for Yvain's exploits is that he is determined to redeem himself[16] and that another was driven to despair of making any sense of the romance at the literal level when the theory of Yvain's deliberate rehabilitation failed to square with the facts of Chrétien's narrative.[17] Finally, it is the same conviction that a hero ought to be in control of events which makes Cohen account it a weakness in the romance that chance should play so large a part in determining those in which Yvain finds himself involved:

> Ce qu'on peut objecter encore à ces aventures accessoires greffées sur la principale, c'est qu'elles sont toujours déterminées par le hasard, conduit par la fantaisie du conteur, et que rarement elles sont amenées par le caractère du protagoniste.[18]

But for all this assumption appears to be widely held, there is no more justification for it than there was for assuming that a courtly hero must at all times be a worthy figure, totally devoid of any human weaknesses or foibles. Yvain's exploits as the Knight of the Lion are none the less heroic for being prompted by generosity or loyalty rather than a grim determination to make amends for his past lapse. Due reparation is made for the wrong he does, even though his mental anguish and the physical pain he endures are not self-inflicted as a deliberate penance. As for the moral to be drawn from his experiences, this is a suitably edifying one – at least in courtly eyes. For they serve to demonstrate that one cannot sacrifice love to vain glory with impunity, or lightly set aside a promise to one's lady, be she mistress or wife.

# NOTES

1. First presented as a paper, 'The Theme of Rehabilitation in Chrétien's *Yvain*' at the Ninth Triennial Congress of the International Arthurian Society (Cardiff, 1969). The line references in this and the following essay refer to Reid's edition of *Yvain*.

2. M. Roques, in his edition of Chrétien de Troyes, *Le Chevalier au lion* (*Yvain*) (Paris, 1960), pp. xi–xiii. See also p. viii.

3. See: A. Adler, 'Sovereignty in Chrétien's *Yvain*', *P.M.L.A.* 62 (1947), p. 281; J. Harris, 'The Rôle of the Lion in Chrétien de Troyes' *Yvain*', *P.M.L.A.* 64 (1949), pp. 1144, 1147, 1161, 1163; W. S. Woods, 'The Plot Structure in Four Romances of Chrestien de Troyes', p. 11; J. Frappier, *Chrétien de Troyes*, p. 154, and again, *Étude sur Yvain, ou le Chevalier au lion* (Paris, 1969), pp. 293–4 where he reaffirms support for Roques' view against F. Lyons; M. Lazar, *Amour Courtois et "Fin' Amors" dans la littérature du XIIᵉ siècle* (Paris, 1964), p. 250; L. Maranini (see Frappier, *Étude sur Yvain*, pp. 290–1); J. J. Duggan, 'Yvain's Good Name. The unity of Chrétien de Troyes' "Chevalier au Lion"', *Orbis Litterarum* 24 (1969), pp. 115, 116, 122, 128.

4. Harris, p. 1144. See also Woods, pp. 10–11.

5. Lazar, p. 250.

6. Frappier, *Étude sur Yvain*, p. 293.

7. A point recognised by F. Lyons ('Sentiment et rhétorique dans l'*Yvain*', *Romania* 83 (1962), pp. 375–6), but she goes too far in suggesting that none of the exploits performed by Yvain give him any hold over Laudine ('aucun droit sur le coeur de la dame, du moins dans la scène de réconciliation', p. 376).

8. Woods, p. 11 (my italics).

9. In somewhat similar circumstances, Erec likewise finds the society of friends and acquaintances unendurable. Until he has put an end to the estrangement between himself and Enide, he is unwilling to accept any offer of hospitality however dire his need: he turns down Guivret's invitation and he refuses to spend more than one night at Arthur's camp when Gauvain traps him into going there (see *Erec* vs 4088–4273).

10. A point recognised by Lyons: '. . . par sa tentative de suicide il témoigne de l'état de désespoir où il se trouve après l'oubli causé par sa légèreté.' (p. 373).

11. See the discussion of the theme of Lancelot's ride in the cart in the essay on the structure of the *Charrete*, pp. 134–5.

12. G. Cohen, *Un grand romancier d'amour et d'aventure au XIIᵉ siècle. Chrétien de Troyes et son oeuvre* (Paris, 1931), p. 355.

13. J. P. Collas, 'The Romantic Hero of the Twelfth Century', pp. 88–9 (my italics).

14. Frappier, *Étude sur Yvain*, p. 56.

15. Frappier, *Chrétien de Troyes*, p. 154. See also p. 124 where this critic speaks of Chrétien's 'prédilection pour les personnages qui agissent en vertu d'un choix délibéré'.

16. Harris, see above p. 73.

17. Woods, see above p. 79.

18. Cohen, p. 354. See also Collas (p. 88): 'Had Chrétien been writing a novel he would no doubt have endowed Yvain with courage to seek atonement, a means of redemption, forgiveness at the end'.

I. Yvain Slays Ascalon and Yvain Presented to Laudine. Detail of an embroidery; c. 1325. Freiburg in Breisgau, Augustinermuseum.

II. Lancelot on the Swordbridge. From a capital in the church of St Pierre in Caen; 1350–1400.

# The Structure of *Yvain*[1]

OPINION is much divided over the structure of Chrétien's *Yvain*: so much so, indeed, for J. P. Collas to maintain that, at first sight, the descriptions which three eminent critics have given of the romance "would hardly seem to bear upon the same work".[2]

There would appear to be two main schools of thought: that of Professors Bezzola and Roques on the one hand and that of Professors Reid and Frappier on the other. For Bezzola and Roques, *Yvain* is bipartite. Section 1 deals with the events which lead first to the marriage of Yvain and Laudine, and then to their estrangement. Section 2 deals with the events which culminate in their reconciliation:

> ... on distingue dans tous les romans de Chrétien une nette bipartition. ... Dans la première partie du Chevalier au Lion, Yvain conquiert et perd l'amour de Laudine et finit dans la démence, dans la deuxième, il est guéri et, après une longue suite d'aventures, réalise la conquête définitive de sa dame.[3]
>
> La première partie d'*Yvain* était le récit audacieux d'un amour conquis par une valeur exceptionnelle, perdu par l'impardonable légèreté d'un chevalier oublieux, pénétré d'un sentiment intense, mais peut-être sans profondeur suffisante.
> La seconde partie sera le récit d'une rédemption, acceptée pour la réparation de cet oubli à force d'entreprises toujours nouvelles et plus hardiment dangereuses et peut-être en progrès de générosité.[4]

For Reid and Frappier, and also for Collas, who accepts their interpretation of the romance,[5] *Yvain* is tripartite. Section 1 deals with the events leading to the marriage of Yvain and Laudine. Section 2, a mere bridging passage, is the account of the crisis in their relationship. Section 3, the longest in the romance, deals with the events that end with the reconciliation of Yvain and his wife:

> *Yvain* est, avec *Erec*, le roman le mieux construit de Chrétien; de l'un à l'autre le parallélisme de la "conjointure" est frappant; le plan, dont les lignes générales sont très caractéristiques, s'articule en trois parties:
> (1) Une longue exposition situe le début du récit à la cour du roi Arthur, introduit le héros et raconte l'aventure au cours de laquelle il rencontre, aime et épouse une femme très belle. L'aventure mène à un mariage d'amour vite conclu et célébré par des fêtes brillantes auxquelles participe la cour d'Arthur. Cette exposition ... constitue à elle seule un poème indépendant; dans l'*Yvain* elle occupe un peu plus du tiers de l'ensemble (vs 1–2475).

(2) Une crise fait rebondir l'action; un malentendu . . . trouble le bonheur des époux. Ce drame psychologique pose aussi un problème d'ordre moral et social. Il surgit soudain et il est noué rapidement. (dans l'*Yvain* vers 2476–2795)

(3) Le héros accomplit la reconquête de son bonheur et accroît son mérite en prenant une conscience plus vive de ses devoirs et de sa mission de chevalier; les aventures qu'il traverse et les exploits qu'il réalise se succèdent selon une progression destinée à illustrer sa volonté continue de se dépasser lui-même, sans que cet ordre ascendant soit d'une rigeur absolue, car le développement d'un conte n'est pas comparable à un mécanisme d'horlogerie. L'une des aventures est plus chargée que les autres de mystère et de fantastique; elle se passe dans un pays qui semble bien appartenir à un "autre monde". A la fin du roman, le héros et l'héroïne, réconciliés, goûtent la joie d'un amour réciproque et confiant. . . .[6]

Romances of adventure are necessarily episodic in structure, and often formless. Among those of Chrestien, however, at least *Erec*, *Cligés* and *Yvain* are built up on a definite and characteristic plan; and in *Erec* and *Yvain* the plan is in its main lines identical. Both these poems comprise (I) by way of exposition, a narrative which, beginning at King Arthur's court, introduces the hero, relates the adventures through which he wins his bride, and is rounded off with an account of Court festivities in such a way that it could almost stand alone as an independent poem; then (II), rather briefly and casually introduced, a crisis in the relations between husband and wife, which creates a conflict and states a moral problem; finally (III) a series of progressively more formidable adventures, leading ultimately to the resolution of the conflict and the reconciliation of the hero and heroine; but the conclusion of the story is postponed by the insertion into the series of adventures of (IV) an elaborate episode, complete in itself, which is not essential to the plot, but serves to display the prowess of the hero and to introduce fantastic or supernatural elements.[7]

In addition to these interpretations of Yvain others have been put forward from time to time.[8] There would, therefore, seem to be as clear a case for making a fresh analysis of the structure of this romance as there was for re-opening the question of the structure of *Erec*. Accordingly, the purpose of this essay is to examine Yvain anew, and to do so along the lines of the preceding investigation into the organisation of *Erec*, that is, by analysing it into its basic components and then seeing how they are related to one another.

On examining Yvain, one finds that the narrative can be broken down into seven main components each of which has a recognisable unity thematically. These episodes are of varying length (ranging from around 300 lines to various multiples of that sum), and indeed one of them contains two components which are themselves of major importance structurally.

*Episode 1* (vs 1–580). This is a minor episode of 580 lines. It is the story of Calogrenant's visit to the magic fountain in Broceliande as told by himself to his fellow knights.

*Episode 2* (vs 581–2169). This is a major episode in the romance (1589 lines) and could stand as an independent tale in its own right. It is an account of Yvain's visit to the magic fountain. It tells how he went to Broceliande and overcame the defender of the fountain; how he pursued the dying knight into his castle and there came to meet, and, eventually, to marry, the man's widow, Laudine, with the assistance of her lady-in-waiting, Lunete.

*Episode 3 (vs 2170–2475)*. This is a minor episode of 306 lines. It is an account of the visit that Arthur pays in his turn to Broceliande. It tells how Arthur came to the fountain with his knights; how Yvain, as its new defender, overcame Arthur's champion, Kay, and how he invited the king and his retinue back to his castle for a week of feasting and festivities.

*Episode 4 (vs 2476–2780)*. This again is a minor episode of 305 lines. It is the story of the estrangement of Yvain and his wife, Laudine. It tells how Yvain obtained her permission to return to Britain for a limited period with King Arthur; how he overstayed his leave, and how he eventually received word from Laudine that she had cast him off for ever.

This episode, which follows directly on from the preceding one, is divided from it by a well marked break in the time sequence. Having told us in the opening sentence, vs 2476–8, that the King decided after a week at Laudine's castle to bring his visit to an end, Chrétien then goes back in time. He turns to consider the events of the previous seven days, which led to Yvain's being given leave to return to Arthur's court, and to his setting off with the King in vs 2615:

> 2476 Quant li rois ot fet son sejor,
> tant qu'il n'i vost plus arester,
> si refist son oirre aprester.
>
> ———
>
> 2479 Mes il avoient la semainne
> trestuit proiié et mise painne
> au plus, qu'il s'an porent pener,
> que il an poïssent mener
> mon seignor Yvain avuec aus.
>
> .    .    .    .    .
>
> 2547 La dame an a a consoil treite,
> qui del congié pas ne se gueite,
> si li dist: "Ma tres chiere dame!
> vos, qui estes mes cuers et m'ame,
> mes biens, ma joie et ma santez,
> une chose me creantez
> por vostre enor et por la moie!"
> La dame tantost li otroie,
> qui ne set, qu'il viaut demander,
> et dit: "Biaus sire! comander
> me poez, quanque buen vos iert."
> Maintenant congié li requiert
> mes sire Yvains, de convoiier
> le roi et d'aler tornoiier,
> que l'an ne l'apiaut recreant.
> Et ele dit: "Je vos creant

le congié jusqu'a un termine;

· · · · ·

Ore a mes sire Yvains congié,

———————

2615    s'ont mout ploré au congié prandre.
Et li rois ne vost plus atandre
por rien, qu'an dire li seüst,
ainz li tarda, qu'an lor eüst
tost les palefroiz amenez

*Episode 5 (vs 2781–3340)*. This is a minor episode of 560 lines. It is the story of Yvain's madness, and tells how he went out of his mind with grief on hearing that he had been cast off by Laudine; how he lived like a wild man in the woods until he was discovered and restored to health by the lady of Noroison, and how he repaid her by defeating her enemy count Alier.

*Episode 6 (vs 3341–6509)*. This is a very long episode, almost half the total length of the romance (3169 lines), and is itself composed of three episodes, two of which are of major importance. It is the story of Yvain's self-imposed exile which follows on his restoration to health at Noroison, and which lasts until he finally screws up the courage to seek a reconciliation with his wife. The three episodes contained in it recount the various adventures that befall Yvain during his wanderings:

*Episode 6a (vs 3341–3484)*. This is a very short episode, a half episode in fact (144 lines). It tells of the rescue of the lion, who becomes Yvain's faithful companion and from whom he takes the name of the 'Chevalier au Lion' that he chooses to be known by during his time of exile.

*Episode 6b (vs 3485–4699)*. This is a major episode (1215 lines) and is important enough to be able to stand as an independent narrative in its own right. It is the account of the first two exploits that Yvain performs with the aid of his lion: (a) the defence of Lunete, who has been charged with treason for the part she played in arranging the marriage between her mistress and Yvain, and (b) the deliverance of Gauvain's niece and nephews from the clutches of the giant Harpin. These two adventures are linked by the fact that the one is contained within the other: it is whilst he is taking shelter for the night with them to prepare for Lunete's trial that Yvain becomes involved in the affairs of Gauvain's relatives.

*Episode 6c (vs 4700–6509)*. This again is a major episode (1810 lines), and again, it is important enough to be able to stand as an independent narrative in its own right. It is the story of the last two exploits performed by Yvain as the Knight of the Lion: (a) his championing of the younger daughter of the lord of Noire Espine against her sister and Gauvain, and (b) his deliverance of the captives in the castle of Pesme-Avanture. As in the previous episode, the two adventures are linked by the fact that the one is contained within the other. For it is whilst Yvain is on the way to defend the cause of the disinherited sister that he and his party come to the castle of Pesme-Avanture.

It should be noted that although Yvain's involvement in the affairs of the two sisters follows immediately upon his recovery from the wounds he received in defending Lunete, Chrétien has been at great pains to separate episodes 6b and 6c by a second break in the time sequence of his romance. In the first sentence of episode 6c (vs 4700–02) Chrétien brings Yvain to the point of leaving the house where he and the lion have been recuperating after their previous exploits. He then goes back in time for some 349 lines to describe the quarrel between the two sisters which leads in vs 5052 to Yvain's being overtaken by the emissary of the younger sister before he has got very far on his way:

4700   Jorz i sejorna ne sai quanz,
        tant que il et ses lions furent
        gari et que raler s'an durent.

---

4703   Mes dedanz ce fu avenu,
        que a la Mort ot plet tenu
        li sire de la Noire Espine,
        si prist a lui tel anhatine
        la Morz, que morir le covint.
        Aprés sa mort einsi avint
        de deus filles, que il avoit,
        que l'ainznee dist, qu'ele avroit
        trestote la terre a delivre
        toz les jorz, qu'ele avroit a vivre,
        que ja sa suer n'i partiroit.

.    .    .    .

5038   Einsi galope par les tes
        con par la voie igal et plainne,
        tant qu'ele voit celui, qui mainne
        le lion an sa conpaignie.
        Lors a joie et dit: "Des, aïe!
        Or voi ce, que tant ai chacié,
        mout l'ai bien seü et tracié.

.    .    .    .

        Einsi parlant s'est tant hastee,
        que toz ses palefroiz tressue,

---

5052   si l'ataint et si le salue.
        Et cil li respont aussi tost:
        "Des vos gart, bele! . . . "

At first sight it may not be very apparent that the various adventures which befall Yvain as the Knight of the Lion do, in fact, form a single episode in his life. A closer examination reveals, however, that Chrétien has been at some pains to link them together. In two cases, as we have seen, he has contrived to combine two adventures into a single compound episode by containing one within the other. In their turn, these compound episodes are bound together, paradoxically enough, by the very passage

which serves to mark the division between them. For vs 4703–5051 which
separate Episodes 6b and 6c are used by Chrétien to elaborate a whole
system of co-incidental links which connect the fight with Gauvain with
the defence of Lunete and the encounter with Harpin:

(i) In vs 4737–4820 Chrétien is careful to stress that it is Yvain's
earlier involvement in the affairs of Gauvain's relatives that leads to his
championing the cause of the younger daughter of the lord of Noire
Espine. It is because the girl arrives at court in time to hear Gauvain being
told of the part the Knight of the Lion played in rescuing his sister's
family, that she decides to turn to him in her distress.

(ii) In vs 4898–5031 he is at even greater pains to show that it is through
the various people concerned in Yvain's previous exploits that the emissary
of the younger daughter eventually succeeds in tracking him down.[9] First
we find that she has had the great good luck to alight at the castle belonging
to Gauvain's kinsmen. From there she is directed to Laudine's domains
where she meets with Lunete. Lunete sets her on the road which Yvain
took when he left to get his wounds attended to. Following this road, she
arrives at the house where Yvain and the lion have been staying, and here
she is shown the road by which they have just left. So that in vs 5052
she at last overtakes Yvain, and the story of his final adventure, at least
in so far as he himself is concerned, begins.

*Episode 7 (vs 6510–6818).* This is a minor episode of 309 lines. It is the
story of the reconciliation of Yvain and Laudine. It tells how Yvain was
finally driven to try to make peace with his wife, and how Lunete contrived
in the end to bring them together.

When we come to consider how the seven main components of Yvain
are related to one another, we find in the first place that the three initial
episodes form a carefully-knit series:

(a) Episodes 2 and 3 are linked by a causal connection to Episode 1.
The telling of Calogrenant's story leads directly both to Yvain's mission
and to Arthur's. On the one hand, it prompts Yvain to offer to avenge his
cousin (a resolve that is only strengthened by Kay's sneering accusation of
pot-valiance in vs 590–611):

> "Par mon chief!" dist mes sire Yvains,
> "vos estes mes cosins germains,
> si nos devons mout antramer;
> mes de ce vos puis fol clamer,
> quant vos le m'avez tant celé.
> Se je vos ai 'fol' apelé,
> je vos pri qu'il ne vos an poist;
> car, *se je puis et il me loist,*
> *j'irai vostre honte vangier.*"          (vs 581–9)

On the other hand, the account the Queen gives Arthur of Calogrenant's
adventures fills him with a desire to see the wonders of the fountain for
himself:

Que que il parloient einsi,
li rois fors de la chanbre issi,
ou il ot fet longue demore;

.     .     .     .     .

Delez la reïne s'assist,
et la reïne maintenant
les noveles Calogrenant
li reconta tot mot a mot;
que bien et bel conter li sot.
Li rois les oï volantiers
et fist trois seiremanz antiers
l'ame Uterpandragon son pere,
et la son fil et la sa mere,
qu'il iroit veoir la fontainne,
ja ainz ne passeroit quinzainne,
et la tanpeste et la mervoille,
si que il i vandra la voille
mon seignor saint Jehan Batiste,
et s'i prandra la nuit son giste,
et dit que avuec lui iront
tuit cil, qui aler i voldront.              (vs 649–72)

(b) Episodes 2 and 3, moreover, are linked by the fact that Arthur's projected expedition has a two-fold influence on the fortunes of Yvain. It precipitates his visit to the fountain, and it brings Laudine to consent to marriage with him.

(i) Yvain knows that unless he forestalls the others and arrives at the fountain first, he will lose all chance of making good his offer to avenge Calogrenant. Either Kay or Gauvain will be granted the privilege of challenging the defender of the fountain before him:

De ce, que li rois devisa,
tote la corz miauz l'an prisa;
car mout i voloient aler
li baron et li bacheler.
Mes qui qu'an soit liez et joianz,
mes sire Yvains an fu dolanz,
qu'il i cuidoit aler toz seus,
s'an fu dolanz et angoisseus
del roi, qui aler i devoit.
Por ce solemant li grevoit,
qu'il savoit bien, que la bataille
avroit mes sire Kes sanz faille
ainz que il, – s'il la requeroit,
ja veee ne li seroit, –
ou mes sire Gauvains meïmes
espoir la demanderoit primes.
Se nus de cez deus la requiert,
ja contredite ne li iert.
Mes il ne les atandra mie,
qu'il n'a soing de lor conpaignie,
einçois ira toz seus son vuel
ou a sa joie ou a son duel                  (vs 673–94)

(ii) The threat of Arthur's imminent arrival is put forward by Lunete as a reason for Laudine to stop grieving over her husband and to turn her mind to the question of finding a replacement for him:

> . . . "Dame! mout me mervoil,
> que folemant vos voi ovrer.
> Dame! cuidiez vos recovrer
> vostre seignor por feire duel?"
>
> . . . . .
>
> "Mes or dites, si ne vos griet:
> vostre terre qui deffandra,
> quant li rois Artus i vandra,
> qui doit venir l'autre semainne
> au perron et a la fontainne?
> Vos an avez eü message
> de la Dameisele Sauvage,
> qui letres vos an anvea.
> Ahi! con bien les anplea!
> Vos deüssiez or consoil prandre
> de vostre fontainne deffandre,
> et vos ne finez de plorer!
> N'i eüssiez que demorer,
> s'il vos pleüst, ma dame chiere!
> Que certes une chanberiere
> ne valent tuit, bien le savez,
> li chevalier, que vos avez.
>
> . . . . .
>
> Et li rois vient a si grant ost,
> qu'il seisira tot sanz deffanse."     (vs 1598–1637)

On Lunete's advice (vs 1845–68), the threat of Arthur's visit is later used by Laudine herself to persuade her people to consent to her hasty marriage – with the result, so confidently predicted by Lunete, that they all beg her to avail herself of the services of the champion who has so opportunely presented himself (vs 2081–2108).

(c) A further link between the first three episodes of *Yvain* is provided by the narrative theme of the quarrel between Yvain and Kay which runs through them.

The quarrel breaks out when Yvain offers to avenge Calogrenant and is immediately accused of being a drunken braggart by Kay:

> "Bien pert qu'il est aprés mangier,"
> fet Kes, qui teire ne se pot.
> "Plus a paroles an plain pot
> de vin, qu'an un mui de cervoise.
> L'an dit que chaz saous s'anvoise.
> Aprés mangier sanz remuër
> va chascuns Noradin tuër,
> et vos iroiz vangier Forré!
>
> . . . . .
>
> Or tost, por De, mes sire Yvain!
> Movroiz vos anuit ou demain?
>
> . . . . .

Et je vos pri, comant qu'il soit,
n'an alez pas sanz noz congiez;
et se vos anquenuit songiez
mauvés songe, si remanez!''                    (vs 590–611)

Although he holds his own in the verbal exchanges which follow Kay's
gibes (vs 612–48), it is clearly the prospect of the taunts that he will have
to endure, unless he gives Kay the lie, which drives Yvain to slip off on his
own when he learns of Arthur's plans to visit the fountain. It is certainly
the fear of Kay's mockery should he return to court empty-handed,
without tangible proof of his success, that makes Yvain pursue his opponent
into his castle, and later fills him with such misgivings as he watches the
funeral procession go by and, with it, all hope of securing the 'ansaingnes
veraies' that he needs:

... cil del chacier s'esvertue;
qu'il crient sa painne avoir perdue,
se mort ou vif ne le detient;
que des ranposnes li sovient,
que mes sire Kes li ot dites.
N'iert pas de la promesse quites,
que son cosin avoit promise,
ne creüz n'iert an nule guise,
s'ansaingnes veraies n'an porte.              (vs 891–9)

... cil remaint,
qui ne set, comant se demaint.
Del cors, qu'il voit que l'an anfuet,
li poise, quant avoir n'an puet
aucune chose, qu'il an port
tesmoing, qu'il l'a conquis et mort,
que mostrer puisse an aparant.
S'il n'an a tesmoing et garant,
donc est il honiz an travers.
Tant par est Kes fel et pervers,
plains de ranposnes et d'enui,
que ja mes ne garroit a lui;
toz jorz mes l'iroit afitant
et gas et ranposnes gitant,
aussi come il fist l'autre jor.
Celes ranposnes a sejor
li sont el cuer batanz et fresches            (vs 1339–55)

The theme of the quarrel is taken up again at the beginning of the third
episode, when Kay notices that Yvain is not among the knights at the
fountain, and sneeringly calls attention to the fact until he is silenced by
Gauvain:

"Ahi! qu'est ore devenuz
Yvains, quant il n'est ça venuz,
qui se vanta aprés mangier,
qu'il iroit son cosin vangier?
Bien pert, que ce fu aprés vin.

Foïz s'an est, je le devin;
qu'il n'i osast venir por l'uel.
Mout se vanta de grant orguel.
Mout est hardiz, qui vanter s'ose
de ce dont autre ne l'alose,
ne n'a tesmoing de sa loange,
se ce n'est par fausse losange.
Mout a antre mauvés et preu;

.    .    .

2207    Einsi mes sire Kes parloit,
et mes sire Gauvains disoit:
"Merci, mes sire Kes, merci!
Se mes sire Yvains n'est or ci,
ne savez, quel essoine il a.
Onques voir tant ne s'avilla,
qu'il deïst de vos vilenie
tant come il a fet corteisie."
"Sire!", fet Kes, "et je m'an tes.
Ne m'an orroiz parler hui mes,
des que je voi, qu'il vos enuie."          (vs 2179–217)

The end of the quarrel comes shortly afterwards, when Kay is granted the
privilege of acting as Arthur's champion (vs 2228–38) and Yvain, as the
new defender of the fountain, has the satisfaction first of unhorsing
the man, and then of completing his mortification by revealing that it is his
much maligned self who has done so – to the satisfaction of the entire
court:

Kes . . . si monte.
S'or li puet feire un po de honte
mes sire Yvains, liez an sera
et mout volantiers li fera;
que bien le reconoist as armes.

.    .    .

2254    Mes sire Yvains cop si puissant
li dona, que par son la sele
a fet Kes la torneboele,
et li hiaumes an terre fiert.
Plus d'enui feire ne li quiert
mes sire Yvains, einçois desçant
a la terre et le cheval prant;
s'an fu mout bel a tes i ot,
et fu assez, qui dire sot:
"Ahi, ahi! come or gisiez
vos, qui les autres despisiez!
Et neporquant s'est il bien droiz,
qu'an le vos pardoint ceste foiz
por ce qu'ains mes ne vos avint."
Antre tant devant le roi vint
mes sire Yvains, . . .

.    .    .

Lors s'est mes sire Yvains nomez,
s'an fu Kes de honte assomez

et maz et morz et desconfiz,
qu'il dist, qu'il s'an estoit foïz.
Et li autre mout lié an sont,
qui de s'enor grant joie font.                    (vs 2239–84)

With the duel between Kay and Yvain the three narrative themes which
stem from the telling of Calogrenant's tale (the quarrel between Kay and
Yvain; Yvain's quest for vengeance; Arthur's visit to the fountain) come
together and fuse. The celebrations which follow at Laudine's castle
(vs 2302–2475) mark the personal victory of Yvain over Kay; the successful
accomplishment of a mission by one of Arthur's knights; and the welcome
arrival of an honoured guest.

If Episode 3 provides a triumphant conclusion to the story of the
quarrel between Yvain and Kay, the prelude to it is contained in Episode 1.
This opens with a quarrel which flares up when Calogrenant rises to greet
the Queen, who has slipped in among the knights to listen to the story
that he is telling them, and Kay immediately rounds on him for wishing
to show up his fellows as unmannerly boors:

Et Kes, qui mout fu ranposneus,
fel et poignanz et afiteus,
li dist: "Par De, Calogrenant!
Mout vos voi or preu et saillant,
et certes mout m'est bel, que vos
estes li plus cortois de nos;
et bien sai, que vos le cuidiez,
tant estes vos de san vuidiez;
s'est droiz que ma dame le cuit,
que vos aiiez plus que nos tuit
de corteisie et de proesce.
Ja le leissames por peresce,
espoir, que nos ne nos levames,
ou por ce, que nos ne deignames!
Par ma foi! sire, non feïmes,
mes por ce, que nos ne veïmes
ma dame, ainz fustes vos levez."            (vs 69–85)

This outburst and the exchanges between the Queen, Kay and Calogrenant (vs 86–141) which follow it seem, at first, to be a rather pointless
preface to Calogrenant's story. But when they are seen in the context of
the next two episodes, it becomes clear that they serve to prepare us for
Kay's savage attack upon Yvain and for Yvain's reaction to it. The
preliminary skirmish between Kay, Calogrenant and the Queen gives a
very complete picture of Kay's vitriolic spite.

By stressing the causal connections between Episodes 1 to 3, and by
providing an additional link in the form of a common secondary theme,
Chrétien has, then, achieved a remarkable degree of cohesion between
the first three components of *Yvain*. If these episodes are now considered
together, it is found that they amount to rather more than a close-knit

series of self-contained narrative-units. They clearly form a thematic whole: the story of the Winning of the Lady of the Fountain. Episode I provides a natural introduction to the story told in the second and most important episode. In its turn, Episode 3 functions equally clearly as a conclusion to that story; for here all the narrative themes which stem from the account of Calogrenant's adventures are brought together and rounded off.

To turn now to the remaining episodes of *Yvain*, we find that these also form a connected series where Episode 4 leads directly to Episodes 5 and 6, and Episode 6 leads, in its turn, to Episode 7.

(a) Episodes 4 and 5 are connected by the fact that Yvain's madness is caused by his estrangement from Laudine. This is made plain in the opening section of Episode 5 where Chrétien is careful to call attention to Yvain's reaction to the news brought by Laudine's messenger. Vs 2790–95 show Yvain overwhelmed by grief, shame and self-disgust to find himself cast off by his wife:

> Ne het tant rien con lui meïsme,
> ne ne set, a cui se confort
> de lui, qu'il meïsmes a mort;
> mes ainz voldra le san changier,
> que il ne se puisse vangier
> de lui, qui joie s'est tolue.

His immediate impulse is to rush away from his fellows and from all who know him, to be alone with his misery and his guilt:

> . . . ses enuiz tot adés croist:
> quanquë il ot, tot li ancroist,
> et quanque il voit, tot li enuie.
> Mis se voldroit estre a la fuie
> toz seus an si sauvage terre,
> que l'an ne le seüst, ou querre,
> n'ome ne fame n'i eüst,
> ne nus de lui rien ne seüst
> ne plus, que s'il fust an abisme.
>
> D'antre les barons se remue;
> qu'il crient antre aus issir del san.
> Et de ce ne se gardoit l'an,
> si l'an leissierent seul aler.
> Bien sevent, que de lor parler
> ne de lor siecle n'a il soing.      (vs 2781–801)

But, before long, his feelings overcome him completely and drive him out of his mind:

> Et il va tant que il fu loing
> des tantes et des paveillons.
> Lors li monta uns torbeillons
> el chief si granz, que il forsane.      (vs 2802–5)

(b) Episodes 4 and 6 are connected by the fact that the self-imposed exile, which follows Yvain's restoration to health and sanity at Noroison, stems, like his madness, from his estrangement from Laudine. The motive which sends him wandering over the face of the earth is clearly the self-same desire to be alone with his misery that drove him from Arthur's court, when the news of his disgrace was first broken to him (vs 2781–801). For, as has already been shown, his reactions on coming across the fountain again (vs 3492–62) reveal that he is pursued in his exile by the grief and the self-hate which swept over him as he listened to Laudine's denunciation of his faithlessness. His failure to exploit the excellent opportunity for a reconciliation that presents itself after his victory over Lunete's enemies (vs 4583–634) makes it plain that he is ridden by the conviction that his offence is beyond all pardoning. And this conviction, as can be seen from vs 6684–91, remains with him until Lunete brings him news that Laudine has committed herself to receiving him back into favour:

> ". . . j'ai ma dame a ce menee,
> s'ele parjurer ne se viaut,
> que tot aussi come ele siaut,
> iert vostre dame et vos ses sire;
> par verité le vos os dire."
> Mes sire Yvains formant s'esjot
> de la novele, que il ot,
> qu'il ne cuidoit ja mes oïr.

(c) Episodes 6 and 7 are connected by the fact that the reconciliation of Yvain and his wife arises directly out of the exploits he performs during his self-imposed exile:

(i) It is Yvain's championing of the cause of the younger daughter of the lord of Noire Espine which leads to his despairing attempt to force Laudine to make her peace with him. The duel ends with Yvain making his identity known when he learns that his opponent has been none other than Gauvain (vs 6226–67):

> Tantost con mes sire Yvains l'ot,
> si s'esbaïst et espert toz,
> par mautalant et par corroz
> flatist a la terre s'espee,
>
> .    .    .    .    .
>
> Et dit: "Ha, las! Quel mescheance!
> Par trop leide mesconoissance
> ceste bataille feite avomes,
> qu'antreconeü ne nos somes;
> que ja, se je vos coneüsse,
> a vos conbatuz ne me fusse,
> ainz me clamasse recreant
> devant le cop, ce vos creant."
> "Comant?" fet mes sire Gauvains,

"Qui estes vos?" – "Je sui Yvains,
qui plus vos aim qu'ome del monde"    (vs 6268–85)

This means that Yvain remains at court after the fight to have his wounds attended to (vs 6447–54; 6498–509). His return to court puts an end to his wanderings and drives him to face up to the need to approach Laudine. As the beginning of Episode 7 shows, he comes to realise that he must at all costs put an end to their estrangement, so that he finally resolves on the desperate course of using the fountain to force her to take him back into favour – a desperate course, since this resort to *force majeure* shows how little faith he has in his own cause, how utterly despairing he is of being forgiven:

> Mes sire Yvains, qui sanz retor
> avoit son cuer mis an amor,
> vit bien, que durer ne porroit,
> mes por amor an fin morroit,
> se sa dame n'avoit merci
> de lui; qu'il se moroit por li.
> Et pansa, qu'il se partiroit
> toz seus de cort et si iroit
> a sa fontainne guerroiier,
> et s'i feroit tant foudroiier
> et tant vanter et tant plovoir,
> que par force et par estovoir
> li covandroit feire a lui pes,
> ou il ne fineroit ja mes
> de la fontainne tormanter
> et de plovoir et de vanter.    (vs 6511–26)

(ii) As has already been shown, Yvain's fight against Lunete's enemies (a) leads Laudine to commit herself to pardoning her husband if she is not to stand self-condemned as thoroughly uncourtly by refusing to listen to a knight of his distinction (vs 4594–8); and (b), provides Lunete with the means of effecting a reconciliation between the lovers when the storm Yvain raises at the fountain drives Laudine to ask her for advice (vs 6540–635).

Like the first series, the second series of episodes in *Yvain* forms a thematic whole: and the story of the estrangement and reconciliation of Yvain and Laudine. Taken together, Episodes 4 to 7 tell the tale of a man who offends his wife so deeply as to be cast off by her. The shock of this first drives him mad. Then, when he is cured of his madness, the enormity of his offence so overwhelms him that he cannot bring himself to approach her, but is driven by grief and shame into a life of homeless wandering until circumstances force him to face up to the task of trying to make his peace with her. In taking the theme of a quarrel to give shape and significance to episodic material Chrétien is employing the device already used by him to good effect in *Erec*. But in *Yvain* the theme is less well developed than in the earlier romance and serves more obviously as a frame to contain the accounts of the hero's various exploits. For whereas each adventure in Erec's second quest is a definite step towards the reconciliation of the lovers, two of Yvain's major exploits (the fight with Harpin and the adventure at Pesme-Avanture) do not affect the relations between Laudine and himself in any way. They are merely bound to the two adventures which do contribute towards their reconciliation by purely co-incidental ties. To compensate, perhaps, for the relative weakness of the underlying theme in this part of the romance, Chrétien uses the figure of Gauvain as an additional element of cohesion. For, throughout the story of the lovers' quarrel, Yvain's fortunes are linked with those of his friend:

(i) In Episode 4, it is Gauvain who shames him into leaving his bride to return with the king and go a-tourneying (vs 2484–543); and it is Gauvain who later leads him into overstaying his leave (vs 2667–78).

(ii) In Episode 6b, it is because Gauvain is away from court looking for the queen that the tasks of defending Lunete and of rescuing his relations from Harpin falls to Yvain in his stead (vs 3698–715; 3905–39).

(iii) In Episode 6c, it is through Gauvain, as we have seen, that Yvain becomes involved in the dispute between the two sisters, and it is against Gauvain that he has to defend the younger sister's cause (vs 5872–6364).

(iv) Finally, in Episode 7, it is through Gauvain that Yvain is eventually brought to seek a reconciliation with his wife. As we know, it was on finding that he had been fighting his best friend that Yvain came to make his identity known. This led to his return to court, and once there, he was driven to see that the task of approaching Laudine could be shirked no longer.

On examination, then, *Yvain* proves to be thematically bipartite. The preceding analysis has shown that it is organised into two self-contained narratives of unequal length: 'The Winning of Laudine' (2475 lines) and 'The Estrangement and Reconciliation of the Lovers' (4343 lines: almost twice as long as the other). These two stories are connected by the fact that the conclusion of the one is the starting point of the other: Arthur's visit to the fountain leading directly to Yvain's departure for Britain on a year's leave of absence. At the same time, the division between the two narratives is clearly indicated by the break in the time sequence which occurs at the beginning of Episode 4 between vs 2478 and vs 2615 and proves to be as effective a way of punctuating a romance as the statement 'ici fenist li premiers vers' employed in vs 1796 of *Erec*.

It only remains now to consider the function of the second break in the time sequence of the romance which comes between vs 4702 and vs 5052, and separates Episodes 6b and 6c. This, perhaps, can best be done by consulting the following diagram which represents the general organisation of *Yvain*. This shows quite clearly that the presence of the second break means that the romance is divided into three roughly equal sections, each containing the account of a major incident in the hero's career: his visit to the fountain; his defence of Lunete (which is combined with the fight against Harpin); and the duel with Gauvain (which is combined with the adavnture at Pesme-Avanture.

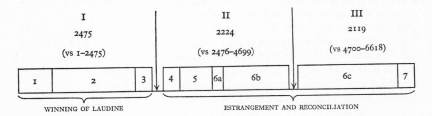

In other words, we now find that if *Yvain* is thematically bipartite, it is structurally a tripartite work, organised for the purposes of narration into three roughly equal instalments. This tripartition provides yet another point of similarity between *Yvain* and *Erec,* but once again it proves to be a similarity with a difference.

On comparing the results of this analysis of *Yvain* with the findings of other critics, it will be found that my views tally for the most part with those of Reid where the division of the work into its basic episodes is concerned. As regards the relationship of these episodes to one another, however, what is said here is mostly new:

1. The only major point on which Reid's account of the chief components of *Yvain* differs from mine is that he does not reduce the story of the winning of Laudine to its constituent parts, whereas he does do this with the two compound episodes which are here called 6b and 6c. The two minor points on which we differ are that (a) the story of the estrangement ends for him at vs 2773 (where I feel that it should end at vs 2780 with the departure of Laudine's messenger), and (b), the story of the duel with Gauvain begins for him at vs 4703 (where I see vs 4700-2 as the opening sentence of Episode 6c, just as vs 2476-8 forms the opening sentence of Episode 4).[10]

2. As regards the organisation of the first part of *Yvain* (which is here examined in detail for the first time), my findings justify Harris' admiration for the 'admirable clarity' of its composition[11] and confirm Frappier's statement that '... la première partie formait un tout pourvu de son unité'.[12] On the other hand, I cannot accept the interpretation of the Kay-Yvain quarrel put forward in a recent article which presents Yvain as a man who undergoes a very necessary spiritual transformation in the second part of the romance.[13] Here it is argued that Yvain's reaction to Calogrenant's story and Kay's retort to it are proof of the brash presumption that has to be cured in Yvain:

> Yvain reacts to the story of his cousin Calogrenant's adventure by calling him a fool, adding immediately that he should not resent the insult because Yvain will avenge his shameful defeat. Keu mocks Yvain for this attitude, *and rightly*

*so: he has shown himself to be impolite, proud and presumptuous.* Yvain refuses to reply, however, alleging that in doing so he would only be a dog gnashing his teeth before the snarls of other dogs (vs 648). This seemingly praiseworthy restraint on his part is in reality a clumsy insult to Queen Guenievre, who has already deigned to answer Keu (vv 619–629) and is therefore implicitly likened to a snapping dog. *Yvain's characteristics in this first scene are fool-hardiness and a certain rudeness, and these traits will dominate his conduct during the first half of the romance* (pp. 112–13: my italics).

This somewhat surprising interpretation of vs 581–648 is supported by an equally unlikely interpretation of Yvain's motives for (a) arriving at the fountain before Arthur (here vs 689–90, which explain the order of precedence at the court, are conveniently overlooked); and (b) pursuing Esclados into his castle:

> When King Arthur declares his intention of going to the fountain, Yvain, instead of accompanying his sovereign, secretly vows to arrive there before him and leaves the court stealthily (Chrétien insists on this, repeating it in vv 719, 741 and 724–743). There is only one motive for this surreptitious behaviour: jealousy of Keu, who he thinks, will surely be granted the right to do battle with the fountain's defender if he asks it: and if not Keu, then Gauvain (vv 682–688). *Apparently it does not enter his mind to request the privilege for himself* (p. 113: my italics).

> Even after he has successfully defended himself by wounding Esclados, Yvain pursues him, and Chrétien tells us then that his motive for doing so is pride:

> > qu'il crient sa poinne avoir perdue
> > se mort ou vif ne le retient,
> > que des ranpones li sovient
> > que mes sire Kex li ot dites.
> > N'est pas de la promesse quites
> > que son cosin avoit promise,
> > ne creüz n'iert an nule guise
> > s'anseignes veraies n'an porte.

> > (892–899; cf. also 1351–1357)

> This pride has two aspects: Yvain fears above all Keu's mockery, or at least this is the first reason that comes into his mind. Only then does he think of the somewhat presumptuous promise made to Calogrenant, *but even then in recalling it he is preoccupied with being believed by his cousin rather than with the personal satisfaction of knowing he has accomplished his duty.* It is significant that this ill-motivated pursuit of Esclados, and not the fact of mortally wounding him at the fountain, is what leads Yvain into the castle where he will eventually meet and marry Laudine. There he is caught in a trap between the gate of the castle wall and the door leading to the interior courtyard, a trap constructed like one set to catch a rat when he comes bent on mischief, as Chrétien tells us in a comparison which is less than flattering for his hero (vv 913–920).

> Yvain, then, can be said to enter into marriage as the result of a series of incidents in which his conduct is impetuous and, at times, morally unjustified (pp. 113–4: my italics).

When these commentaries are set against Chrétien's text, it is plain that the whole case for seeing Yvain as a man guilty of 'rather un-Christian behaviour' which rightly arouses 'divine discontent' (p. 115) is based on a distortion of the facts selected for discussion, and a suppression of others.

(i) Yvain's offer to avenge Calogrenant is in fact dictated by a generous and entirely proper impulse to uphold family honour. If he calls his cousin a fool for keeping the matter of his disgrace from him, what he says next shows that the remark is no more offensive than it usually is when used in similar circumstances; certainly no offence is intended:

> "Se je vos ai 'fol' apelé
> je vos pri qu'il ne vos an poist;
> car, se je puis et il me loist,
> j'irai vostre honte vangier."          (vs 586–8)

(ii) The account of the skirmish between Calogrenant and Kay, which is not mentioned, makes it perfectly clear that Kay's remarks to Yvain are dictated by pure spite, and are no justified rebuke.

(iii) The claim that it is improper pride which drives Yvain to pursue Esclados is patently absurd. Vs 1341–55 (1345–59 in the Roques edition of *Yvain*) make it abundantly clear that the 'anseignes veraies' are meant for Kay, not Calogrenant. Yvain's purpose in trying to secure them is to provide himself with the means of giving Kay the lie, of proving that he is no drunken braggart. That he is motivated here by self-respect and entirely proper pride is obvious from the account of the final confrontation between Yvain and Kay (of which no mention is made in this article). From this it is clear enough that the reader is expected to share the view of Arthur's knight that Yvain's victory is a satisfactory triumph of common decency over spite.

3. My examination of the links between Episodes 4 to 7 confirms Cohen's views on the role of Episode 4 (the Estrangement of the Lovers). Where other critics include this episode in the first part of the romance or treat it as a bridging-passage between its two main sections, Cohen's plan of *Yvain* shows it as an integral part of the account of Yvain's second series of adventures, which forms the third of the four divisions he recognises in the romance:

> 1° La Cour d'Arthur, récit de Calogrenant;
> 2° L'aventure d'Yvain et la conquête de la dame Laudine, à l'aide de la servante Lunete;
> 3° Départ d'Yvain à l'instigation de Gauvain, oubli du terme fixé, folie et aventures du héros ... dont la rencontre du lion ... la victoire sur le géant, le duel contre les trois *losengiers* pour sauver Laudine (sic), la délivrance des Pucelles, le duel contre Gauvain pour la déshéritée;
> 4° Réconciliation de l'époux-amant et de sa dame par l'astuce de Laudine (sic).[14]

On the other hand, I cannot agree with Cohen in treating the reconciliation of the lovers as a separate incident. For me it is an integral part of the story of Yvain's second series of adventures, and exactly balances the account of the lovers' quarrel which gives rise to them. His reason for isolating it as his fourth main division of the romance is, undoubtedly, his failure to see the bearing that the duel with Gauvain has on Yvain's decision to return to Laudine. This is what is suggested by the fact that the one flaw Cohen finds in the composition of *Yvain* is 'la multiplication des aventures, dont le lien avec le sujet principal n'apparaît pas toujours avec la même netteté que dans le sauvetage de Lunete...' (p. 354). A similar failure to see the connection between Yvain's bid for a reconciliation and the duel described in Episode 6c probably explains why Reid maintains that this episode 'is not essential to the plot', and why he later adds that its structural significance 'is uncertain, except in so far as it is evidently intended to form a pendant and counterpoise to the introductory section' (*Yvain* p. xiii).

4. As for the theme that lies behind Yvain's second series of adventures, my findings in this and in the previous essay show that there are no grounds for seeing it as the story of Yvain's attempt to redeem himself. Nor again can I agree with those who claim that the romance can only make sense at an allegorical level when they find it impossible to make this interpretation of Yvain's role square with the facts of Chrétien's text:

> The inevitable conclusion, hence, is that the motivation for the *Yvain* is also ambiguous and hardly comprehensible on the plot level alone. One must look for a higher interpretation which will explain away these vague plot elements and will reconcile these apparent discrepancies and reveal the true meaning of the romance.[15]

Although the possibilities of providing an allegorical interpretation of *Yvain* have been explored, with interesting results, by certain critics,[16] I hope the present essay has proved their basic premise (that no sense can be made of the work at the literal level) to be completely unjustified.

5. As regards the means employed by Chrétien to give cohesion to his account of Yvain's adventures as the Knight of the Lion, my findings confirm Frappier's comments on his use of *entrelacement* in the two compound episodes (6b and 6c).[17] They also confirm Reason's observations on the way the account of the travels of the younger sister's emissary serves to connect Yvain's fight with Gauvain with the first two exploits he performs as the Knight of the Lion.[18] My investigations show, however, that Chrétien's use of coincidental links is far more extensive and more varied than either of these critics has imagined. They also show that it is on such ties that Chrétien mainly relies to combine his four adventures into a single 'super' episode – a fact which has not been appreciated before.

Hitherto, those who have been unwilling to dismiss this section of *Yvain* as a succession of loosely connected adventures have postulated, as an additional thematic link between them, a progression in the magnitude of Yvain's exploits and sacrifices:

> La seconde partie (d'*Yvain*) sera le récit d'une rédemption, acceptée pour la réparation de cet oubli à force d'entreprises toujours nouvelles *et plus hardiment dangereuses* et peut-être en progrès de générosité: services à la dame de Norison . . . lutte avec le serpent pour sauver le lion, combat disproportionné contre les ennemis de Lunete; le premier épisode au château de Norison étant d'une courtoisie chevaleresque assez banale et après tout simple reconnaissance de la guérison réussie, le second marquant l'effort pour le lion contre le reptile, service, mais aussi récompense, de la confiance accordée par le noble animal, le troisième, plus dangereux, juste paiement de services rendus par Lunete. Le quatrième, celui d'Harpin de la Montagne, plus difficile encore par la force de l'adversaire, rehaussait Yvain dans l'échelle des valeurs, et dans l'estime de tous, puisqu'il sauvait du deuil et du déshonneur la famille du plus noble des chevaliers, Gauvain; enfin le cinquième triomphe d'Yvain, au château de Pesme-Aventure, apporte le salut, non pas seulement à un être ou à quelques personnes, mais à trois cents malheureuses, en même temps qu'il marque le dédain d'Yvain pour toutes les richesses que lui eût assurées leur abominable exploiteur, avec la main et la beauté de son héritière.[19]

The case set out here reads convincingly enough, and most critics have subscribed to the view that there is a gradation in Yvain's exploits. But reference to Chrétien's text suggests that there is little justification for doing so.

(i) Is there really any progression in the magnitude of Yvain's achievements as the Knight of the Lion? If they are taken at their face value there is surely little to choose between a fight with a giant, a fight against three mortal opponents, and a fight against two demons. In each case the odds seem equally, if differently, weighted against the hero. In each case he only prevails with the help of the lion, who makes the combat a more equal one (as Chrétien himself points out on one occasion, namely, in vs 4533). As for the fight against Gauvain, this could, from one point of view, be seen as an anti-climax, since it is an equal fight between two men. From another point of view, it can, of course, be taken as Yvain's greatest triumph, since it proves him to be the match of the greatest warrior in the world. Even if Yvain's exploits are assessed, as has been attempted, in terms of what they cost him in mental and physical suffering, it is still not possible to make out a convincing case for their gradation. It is, for instance, naïve, to claim of his last fight that 'truly Yvain fought under the greatest possible tension, both physical and psychological' on the grounds that he fought – unwittingly – against Gauvain and 'at the Court of King Arthur, before an audience that was accustomed to witnessing and well able to evaluate deeds of valour'.[20] Yvain's most exacting exploit is undoubtedly the defence of Lunete. There he is under the greatest possible strain, since he is fighting in the presence of his wife (a strain that Chrétien sees fit to underline in vs 4344–56), and since, personally, so much is at stake for him: the life of a staunch friend impeached for treason on his account.

(ii) At first the claim that there is progression in the importance of Yvain's achievements might seem a safer one. But again, the case that has just been stated for it is not borne out by Chrétien's text. The fight with Harpin precedes and does not follow the deliverance of Lunete. This means that Yvain's signal service to the family of the most distinguished knight in the world does not follow the repayment of his debt to a mere lady-in-waiting. Again, the triumph at Pesme-Avanture (correctly described as his fifth adventure) is not Yvain's culminating victory: it is followed by the duel with Gauvain, which merely assures the well-being of a single person after the deliverance of three hundred unfortunates. Lastly, Yvain can hardly be congratulated for spurning the wealth and the wife offered to him at Pesme-Avanture; his heart has always been entirely committed to Laudine, and in any case he was not, as a married man, in any position to accept a second bride.[21]

As so much ingenuity has to be expended to prove its existence, it is hardly surprising that one critic finds it necessary to caution us against looking for too much rigour in the gradation of Yvain's adventures:

> ... les aventures qu'il traverse et les exploits qu'il réalise se succèdent selon une progression destinée à illustrer sa volonté continue de se dépasser lui-même, sans que cet ordre ascendant soit d'une rigeur absolue, car le développement d'un conte n'est pas comparable à un mécanisme d'horlogerie.[22]

This statement does not seem very far removed from the admission that there is no gradation at all in Yvain's adventures, at least on the literal level. On the allegorical level, of course, a much more plausible case can be made for speaking of progression in Yvain's exploits and in his rehabilitation. For here all things are possible, since, in accordance with the best medieval tradition, one is no longer restricted to the bald facts of a text.

6. Finally, a comparison between my analysis of *Yvain* and the findings of other critics shows that it calls attention to a feature that has hitherto passed unnoticed, the use Chrétien makes of breaks in the time sequence to punctuate his romance. The existence of the first of these breaks has not been commented on before. The second was noted by Harris who did not, however, recognise its structural significance.[23]

My investigation into the organisation of *Yvain* is now complete. It shows that neither of the two views of the structure of that romance quoted at the beginning of this essay is wholly right or wholly wrong.

From one standpoint, the work is definitely bipartite. But the division does not come where Bezzola and Roques say it does. It is in fact marked by the first break in the time sequence which occurs at the very beginning of the account of the estrangement, and divides the work into two unequal but thematically self-contained units: the story of the winning of Laudine, and the story of the lover's estrangement and reconciliation.

From another standpoint, the work is definitely tripartite. But again, not quite as Reid, Frappier and Collas see it. The first section is most certainly the story of the winning of Laudine. The second, however, is not, as they claim, the account of the estrangement. This is no bridging-passage, but the introduction to Yvain's second series of adventures (as indeed is indicated by the difficulty one has in deciding where Episode 4 ends and 5 begins;[24] in every other case, the episodes are clearly delimited in this romance). The middle section of *Yvain* is in fact comparable in size with the first and the third. It consists of the first half of the story of the lovers' quarrel, which is divided by the break in its time sequence into two roughly equal parts – largely, one suspects, for the convenience of a narrator.

This analysis also shows the dangers of assuming that any one of Chrétien's works can be interpreted along the lines of another. Although the desire to give form and meaning to episodic material remains constant in him, the means he adopts to achieve this end are never quite the same. Where there are similarities, they are usually similarities with a conscious difference. For with Chrétien, it is variation, not repetition, that is the rule.

# NOTES

1. First published in *M.L.R.* 65 (1970), pp. 523–40, and here reprinted, in revised form, by permission of the Modern Humanities Research Association and of the editors.
2. 'The Romantic Hero of the Twelfth Century', in *Medieval Miscellany Presented to Eugène Vinaver*, p. 81.
3. R. R. Bezzola, *Le sens de l'aventure et de l'amour*, pp. 81–2.
4. M. Roques in his edition of Chrétien de Troyes, *Le Chevalier au lion* (*Yvain*), p. xi.
5. 'The Romantic Hero', pp. 83–4. Note particularly the statement 'we seem to have two major sections linked by a very minor one of little more than 300 lines'.
6. J. Frappier, *Le roman breton: Yvain ou le Chevalier au lion* (Paris, 1952), pp. 8–9.
7. T. B. W. Reid in his edition of Chrestien de Troyes, *Yvain* (Manchester, 1948), p. xi.
8. For the views of Voretzsch, Foerster, Cohen, Kellerman, Woods, and Reason see J. H. Reason, *An Inquiry into the Structural Style and Originality of Chrestien's Yvain* (Washington D.C., 1958), pp. 10–14. See also C. A. Robson, 'The Technique of Medieval Symmetrical Composition in Medieval Narrative Poetry', in *Studies in Medieval French Presented to A. Ewert*, edited by E. A. Francis (Oxford, 1961), pp. 38–9; S. Hofer, 'Les Romans du Graal dans la littérature des XIIe et XIIIe siècles', in *Colloques internationaux du Centre National de la Recherche scientifique*, vol III (Paris, 1956), pp. 16–18.
9. A point noted by Reason, p. 13.
10. Reid, pp. xi–xiii.
11. J. Harris, 'The Rôle of the Lion in Chrétien de Troyes' *Yvain*', p. 1144.
12. Frappier, *Chrétien de Troyes* (Paris, 1968), p. 154.

13. J. J. Duggan, 'Yvain's Good Name: The unity of Chrétien de Troyes' "Chevalier au Lion" '.

14. G. Cohen, *Un grand romancier d'amour et d'aventure au XII^e siècle, Chrétien de Troyes et son oeuvre*, p. 354.

15. W. S. Woods, 'The Plot Structure in Four Romances of Chrestien de Troyes', p. 11.

16. See for example: Harris, pp. 1143–63; A. Adler, 'Sovereignty in Chrétien's *Yvain*', *P.M.L.A.* 62 (1947), 281–305; A. T. Hatto, 'Der Aventiure Meine' in Hartmann's *Iwein*' in *Mediaeval German Studies presented to Frederick Norman* (London, 1965), 94–103. Much of this applies to Chrétien's *Yvain* (see p. 102, note 13).

17. Frappier, *Le roman breton*: '*Yvain*', pp. 29–30 (and again in *Étude sur Yvain ou le Chevalier au lion* (Paris, 1969), pp. 63–4.

18. Reason, p. 13.

19. Roques, *Le chevalier au lion* (*Yvain*), pp. xi–xii (my italics).

20. Reason, pp. 39–40.

21. An equally unconvincing case for seeing gradation in the services rendered by Yvain is made out by Reason (pp. 40–1), who is reduced to suggesting, among other and similar arguments, that the life of poverty and suffering facing the disinherited sister 'may have been more unbearable for her than it was for the three hundred damsels' on the grounds that 'if we grant that one who is reduced to poverty and suffering through the covetousness of her sister has greater need of help than the three hundred damsels, then there is established a relatively clear gradation in the need of the six individuals for whom Yvain fought during his period of reparation'.

22. Frappier, *Le roman breton*: '*Yvain*', p. 9.

23. Harris, p. 1154: 'The death of the Sire de la Noire Espine is the starting point of the final and crowning adventure. In order to bring it off, Chrétien has to abandon the main thread of the story for the time being and make a new start.'

24. For Reid (p. xii) the account of the crisis in the marriage ends at vs 2773; for Frappier (*Le roman breton*: '*Yvain*', p. 9) it ends at vs 2795; for Collas (p. 84) at vs 2803 (i.e. vs 2801 in the Reid edition). Of these three suggestions, that of Reid is the most satisfactory since it allows (a) the story of the estrangement to come to a conclusion with the casting off of Yvain; (b) the story of Yvain's madness to start with an adequate introduction in the account of the effect of Laudine's denunciation on Yvain.

# The Structure of the *Charrete*

THE structure of the *Charrete* is a question that critics have long neglected. An initial study of the work by Gaston Paris provided a paraphrase of its contents, an outline of the plot, a passing reference to the fact that it is bipartite and a vehement condemnation of the many features in it which made it seem illogical and incoherent to him.[1] His charges of incoherence and obscurity were countered to some extent by Foerster, who maintained that in many cases Chrétien's apparent lapses were deliberately perpetrated to achieve and maintain suspense.[2] But the general impression of the *Charrete* as an unsatisfactory composition was confirmed by Foerster's conclusion that the romance was abandoned by Chrétien before it was completed because of the distaste he felt for the subject.[3] Since Paris and Foerster, the majority of critics have been content to dismiss the romance out of hand as ill-constructed and incomplete,[4] whilst the few who have felt more favourably disposed towards it have not examined its structure in any detail.[5] So it is not surprising to find that in the introduction to his edition of the *Charrete* Mario Roques contents himself with summarising its contents after an opening which suggests that he had renounced all hope of making sense of its general structure:

> Une analyse précise du roman est rendue difficile par la multiplicité des épisodes, leur manque de lien logique et par l'anonymat ou le manque de personalité définie de nombreux personnages. . . .[6]

This long-standing omission has now been rectified in Kelly's recent study of the romance[7] which contains a minute analysis of its organisation. As a result of his investigation, Kelly has been led to claim for the romance a tripartite structure remarkable for its symmetry. For he finds that the structural pattern of its third component reflects that of the first, whilst the central component is symmetrically constructed around an episode which is also the core of the whole romance:

> I have shown that the poem is built upon a symmetrical pattern, with the scene in which Lancelot and Guenevere confess and analyse their love as the core. This episode is found in the centre of the central structural division (B) of the plot which describes the events that took place in Bath. Embracing the central division are the two divisions describing Lancelot's quest (A) and Lancelot's imprisonment (C); they contribute to the symmetry of the plan by their respective positions directly before and after the central division as well

as by the similarity of their internal tripartite structure. The opening and closing Arthurian scenes complete the symmetrical arrangement while serving as nouement and dénouement to the plot. The structural symmetry of the *Charrette* can best be seen in the following figurative representation of the results of my analysis:

I. Opening Arthurian Scene

II. Division A: Lancelot's quest

    A. Part 1. Gawain
        Ford scene
    B. Part 2. Maiden
    C. Part 3. Two companions

III. Division [B] Lancelot at Bath
    A. Arrival of Lancelot
    B. First interrupted combat with Meleagant
    C. Guenevere refuses Lancelot's service

I'. Closing Arthurian Scene

II'. Division C: Lancelot's imprisonment
    A'. Part 1. Liberation of Lancelot
    B'. Part 2. Meleagant's challenge
    C'. Part 3. Tournament

    A'. Departure of Lancelot
    B'. Second interrupted combat with Meleagant
    C'. Guenevere rewards Lancelot's service

    D. Core: Search for Gawain
    Lancelot and Guenevere confess their love (p. 184)

Once one has grasped how to read Kelly's diagram, his demonstration of the symmetrical construction of the *Charrete* seems impressive enough. But a closer scrutiny shows that it contains several debatable features which suggest that it has been achieved by sacrificing the logic of Chrétien's narrative. The most obvious example is the inclusion of the Departure of Lancelot (vs 5044–358)[8] in Division B, where it is shown as balancing the Arrival of Lancelot. In point of fact, this passage forms the introduction to the account of Lancelot's imprisonment, since it relates how he comes to be abducted, and is then left behind in Gorre when the Queen and the other captives are hoodwinked into returning to Logres without him. By rights, it should be included in Division C. But this would throw out Kelly's entire scheme, for it would destroy both the symmetry of his Division B and the correspondence between his Divisions A and C.

It seems, therefore, that there is room for a further investigation into the structure of the *Charrete*. Accordingly, I propose in the present essay to examine the work afresh, and to proceed, as in the cases of *Erec* and *Yvain*, by breaking it down into its basic components and then seeing how they are related to one another.

Like *Erec*, the *Charrete* is an adventure story with an underlying theme. On the one hand, it is a straightforward account of Lancelot's rescuing of Guenevere from the land of Gorre. As such, it opens with the abduction of the Queen from Arthur's court and closes with her final deliverance from her abductor when he is killed in the last of the three battles that are fought over her. On the other hand, the *Charrete* is also a study of a human relationship, namely, the love relationship which is established between Lancelot and the Queen in the course of his quest. Although the second aspect of the romance is undoubtedly more interesting than the first, it is with an analysis of the work as an adventure story that an investigation into its structure must begin.

As the story of the rescuing of Guenevere, the *Charrete* breaks down into six principal episodes which cover the main stages of Lancelot's quest. Apart from the first, which is just under 700 lines, and the second, which proves to be a 'double-episode', these components are of comparable size, each averaging 1000 lines.

*Episode 1 (vs 30–709: 680 lines)* is an account of the initial search for information about the fate of the Queen which ends with Lancelot's being directed to the sword-bridge that gives access to her abductor's stronghold.

It tells how Guenevere came to be handed over, at Kay's request, to a stranger who appeared one day at Arthur's court; how Gauvain set off in pursuit of them; how he was soon joined in the search by a second knight who later (vs 3660) proves to be Lancelot; how Lancelot willingly risked his reputation by agreeing to ride in a cart like a common criminal in order to get news of the Queen (a price Gauvain refused to pay when he overtook the cart); how the two knights were entertained at the castle to which Lancelot was driven; and how, the next day, they eventually met a damsel at a crossroads who told them that the Queen's abductor was called Meleagant; that he was taking her to the land of Gorre where many of Arthur's subjects were already held captive by him; and that the only two ways of reaching his stronghold were a waterbridge (which Gauvain decided to look for), and a more perilous swordbridge (which it fell to Lancelot to seek).

*Episode 2 (vs 710–3002: 2293 lines)* is an account of Lancelot's journey to the swordbridge. It is the longest episode in the romance, being composed of two elements which are both comparable in size with its other episodes.

*Episode 2a (vs 710–2010: 1301 lines)* is the account of the first stage in Lancelot's journey to the swordbridge: his passage through Logres. Here Chrétien is concerned with two adventures that befall him on his way: (a) an encounter with the guardian of a ford into which his horse carries him whilst he is deep in thoughts of the Queen; and (b) an encounter with a seductive damsel who offers him hospitality for the night and insists the next day on accompanying him for part of his way.

*Episode 2b (vs 2011–3002: 992 lines)* is an account of the second stage in the journey to the swordbridge, namely: Lancelot's passage through the land of Gorre.

It tells how Lancelot was entertained by a former subject of Arthur's, then a prisoner in Gorre; how, on the following day, he became involved in a general uprising of the captives who had been roused to rebellion by the news that their liberator had arrived; and how, on the last evening of his journey, he was challenged to fight by a man who taunted him with his presumption in thinking to cross the swordbridge after being paraded in a cart like a criminal.

*Episode 3 (vs 3003–3923: 921 lines)* is the story of Lancelot's first fight with Meleagant which wins for the Queen her provisional liberty.

It tells how Lancelot reached his enemy's stronghold by crossing the swordbridge; how this feat was very differently viewed by Meleagant and by his father, King Bademaguz, who welcomed Lancelot to his city as an honoured guest; how the next day, in spite of the King's efforts to persuade his son to hand the Queen over to Lancelot without a fight, the two men fought to decide her fate; and how, on the request of the King, the battle was halted on the understanding that it should be resumed at a later date at Arthur's court, and that, meanwhile, the Queen and her fellow captives should be free to return to Logres.

*Episode 4 (vs 3924–5043: 1120 lines)* is the story of the reward Lancelot received from the Queen for his service and devotion.

It tells how Guenevere rebuffed Lancelot when he was led into her presence after his victory over Meleagant; how the news that he had been killed whilst searching for Gauvain led her to repent the heartlessness of her conduct and also to realise that she fully returned his love; how her reception of Lancelot at their next meeting emboldened him to ask for the more private interview at which their love was finally consummated; and how, as a result, Lancelot had to defend the Queen and Kay against Meleagant who had concluded from the bloodstains on the Queen's bed that she and the seneschal had been committing adultery.

*Episode 5 (vs 5044–6146: 1103 lines)* is the story of Meleagant's abduction of Lancelot. It tells how Lancelot was kidnapped as he set out a second time to look for Gauvain; how he came to be left behind in Gorre when the Queen, Gauvain and the other captives were led into returning to Logres without him; how he obtained permission from his jailer's wife to attend the tournament held in Logres shortly after the return of the Queen; and how, on his return to prison, Meleagant had him shut up in a tower from which he would not be likely to escape a second time.

*Episode 6 (vs 6147–7097: 951 lines)* is the story of the last fight between Lancelot and Meleagant which finally removed the threat to the Queen.

It tells how Meleagant went to Arthur's court knowing that Lancelot was safely out of the way in prison; how it was agreed that he should fight Gauvain if Lancelot failed to appear in Logres within the year; how his subsequent boastings at his father's court aroused the suspicions of his sister who was prompted to go out and look for Lancelot; and how she managed to rescue him so that he was able to arrive in Logres in time to fight and, at last, to kill Meleagant.

Turning now to the question of the relationships between the six principal episodes of the *Charrete*, we find that they combine to form three larger units which constitute the three major structural components of the romance.

Section I of the *Charrete*, its first major structural component, is composed of Episodes 1 and 2 which together form the story of Lancelot's pursuit of the Queen to her abductor's stronghold. In addition to the obvious thematic connection between them, a causal link also joins the two episodes. It is the information received by Lancelot and Gauvain from the maiden they meet at the end of Episode 1 which leads to Lancelot's journey to the swordbridge.

At first sight, this account of the pursuit seems to lack cohesion and coherence, especially if it is approached with the first part of *Erec* or *Yvain* in mind. There is no secondary narrative theme to bind its parts together by acting as a connecting element (like the Kay–Yvain quarrel in Part I of *Yvain*), or as a containing element (like the hunting of the White Stag in Episode 1 of *Erec*). As often as not, there is no causal connection between successive incidents within the episodes. In Episode 1, the maiden whom Lancelot and Gauvain meet at the cross-roads has nothing to do with the carter or the hostess they encountered on the previous day; in Episode 2a, the guardian of the ford is entirely unconnected with the seductive damsel; in Episode 2b, the man who challenges Lancelot to single combat on the last evening of his journey appears out of the blue, as does the damsel who sues for his head. This lack of cohesion in the account of the pursuit proves, however, to be more apparent than real. The various incidents in it are linked together by the fact that each contributes to the picture of Lancelot[9] and his mission which is gradually built up as the tale of the journey to Bade unfolds. At the beginning, we are very much in the dark about the fate of the Queen and about the knight who joins Gauvain in the search for her. All we learn of Guenevere's abductor in the opening scene of the romance is that he holds many of Arthur's subjects captive in his land and is prepared to set them free if any one of Arthur's knights can successfully defend the Queen against him. And all we learn in the next scene about the man who comes rushing to her rescue is that he is filled with a far greater sense of urgency than the rest of the court.

Thereafter, however, each incident is designed to throw fresh light upon the magnitude and nature of the task ahead of Lancelot, or to call attention to those qualities in him which will enable him to succeed in his mission. The incident with the cart shows that the unknown knight is moved by such devotion for the Queen that he is prepared to sacrifice his standing in the world, not merely his life, in her service. Exactly what his sacrifice entails is brought out by the reception he gets at the castle to which he is driven, whilst his composure in the face of dangers both natural and supernatural is demonstrated by his reactions to the perils of the enchanted bed he chooses to sleep in there. As for the last incident in Episode 1, the meeting with the damsel at the cross-roads, this provides, as we know, the name and destination of Guenevere's abductor; and it is here that we first learn of the perilous bridge that Lancelot must cross if he is to reach his enemy's stronghold. In Episode 2a, the encounter with the guardian of the ford is an occasion for illustrating Lancelot's strength, his skill at arms and his magnanimity. The encounter with the seductive damsel which follows shows, from Lancelot's utter indifference to her considerable charms, how utterly the Queen dominates him. The finding of the Queen's comb whilst he is riding with the seductive damsel is an occasion for illustrating the quasi-religious veneration Lancelot feels for Guenevere. The incident at the chapel proclaims him to be the predestined liberator of the Queen and her fellow captives, as well as displaying his superhuman strength when he raises the lid of a tomb which it would normally take ten men to lift. In their turn, the adventures which befall Lancelot in Episode 2b serve to illustrate his prowess and his powers of leadership, to underline the extent and the nature of the sacrifice he made in riding in a cart, and to prepare us for the perils awaiting him at the swordbridge. All in all, by the time his journey has come to an end, the figure of Lancelot has been brought very sharply into focus and we have a fairly clear idea of what he must face before he can challenge Meleagant to do battle for the Queen.

Passing now to Episodes 3 and 4, we find that, in their turn, these are connected by a causal and a thematic link to form Section II of the *Charrete*, its second major component.

Here again, the conclusion of the one episode is the starting point of the other. Lancelot's victory over Meleagant leads to his interview with Guenevere which is to cause her the bitter remorse that eventually results in their becoming lovers.

Thematically, the two episodes constitute a well-defined whole, with Episode 4 providing a natural conclusion to the story of Lancelot's first fight to secure the deliverance of the Queen. It is after all only fitting that his outstanding services to her should receive appropriate recognition from Guenevere, and, in the eyes of the public for whom the *Charrete* was written, the gift of her love is the most appropriate form such recognition can take. This is a point which certain critics have tended to overlook. In their horror at Guenevere's betrayal of Arthur, they seem to forget that adultery is prescribed as the essential condition for love in a letter ascribed to the Countess Marie herself in the *De Amore*[10] (a treatise which expounds many of the ideas on love extolled in the *Charrete*), or that love, adulterous as it needs must be, is described throughout that work as the most ennobling experience it is given to man to know.

"To the prudent and noble woman A. and the illustrious and famous Count G., M., Countess of Champagne, sends greeting.

. . . . . . . We declare and we hold as firmly established that love cannot exert its powers between two people who are married to each other. For lovers give each other everything freely, under no compulsion of necessity, but married people are in duty bound to give in to each other's desires and deny themselves to each other in nothing. . . . And we say the same thing for still another reason, which is that a precept of love tells us that no woman, even if she is married, can be crowned with the reward of the King of Love unless she is seen to be enlisted in the service of Love himself outside the bounds of wedlock. . . ." (pp. 106–7)

All men are clearly agreed and the rule of Love shows us that neither woman nor man in this world can be considered happy or well-bred, nor can he do anything good, unless love inspires him. Wherefore you must needs conclude that loving is a good thing and a desirable one. Therefore if a person of either sex desires to be considered good or praiseworthy in the world, he or she is bound to love (p. 88).

When we come to look at the last two episodes of the *Charrete*, Episodes 5 and 6, we find they form Section III of the romance, its third major component. For they too are connected by a causal and a thematic link.

In the first place, it is the confidence that Meleagant derives from knowing that Lancelot is safely out of his way which is the cause of his undoing. It leads to his insolent boasting at Bade, and this drives his father to make the remarks which prompt his sister to go out to look for Lancelot:

> ". . . nule rien an toi ne voi
> fors seulemant forssan et rage.
> Je conuis molt bien ton corage
> qui ancor grant mal te fera;
> et dahait qui ja cuidera
> que Lanceloz, li bien apris,
> qui de toz fors de toi a pris,
> s'an soit por ta crieme foïz;
> mes espoir qu'il est anfoïz
> ou an tel prison anserrez,
> don li huis est si fort serrez
> qu'il n'an puet issir sanz congié.
>                 .    .    .    ."
> A tant Bademaguz se test;
> mes quan qu'il ot dit et conté
> ot antendu et escouté
> une soe fille pucele;
>
>          .    .    .    .
> qui n'est pas liee quant an conte
> tex noveles de Lancelot.
> Bien aparçoit qu'an le celot,
> quant an n'an set ne vant ne voie.
> "Ja Dex, fet ele, ne me voie
> quant je ja mes reposerai
> jusque tant que je an savrai
> novele certainne et veraie."          (vs 6354–87)

In the second place, the two episodes clearly form a thematic whole where Episode 5 provides the natural preface to the account of Lancelot's final battle to secure the deliverance of the Queen. For the abduction of Lancelot is a logical, if unprincipled, attempt on the part of Meleagant to secure victory in the coming contest by making sure that the one man likely to defeat him will be in no position to take the field.

A study of the relationships between the six principal episodes of the *Charrete* reveals furthermore that Episodes 3 and 6 are connected by a causal link. For the duel fought at Arthur's court between Meleagant and Lancelot arises out of the decision to halt the first duel they fought at Bade. Although Lancelot stops fighting immediately he hears the Queen agree to Bademaguz' request to be spared the sight of his son's death, Meleagant can only be brought to do so on condition that a second contest be held at a future date in Logres:

> La parole oï Lanceloz:
> ne puis que li darrïens moz
> de la boche li fu colez,
> puis qu'ele ot dit: "Quant vos volez
> que il se taigne, jel voel bien",
> puis Lanceloz, por nule rien,
> nel tochast, ne ne se meüst,
> se il ocirre le deüst.
> Il nel toche ne ne se muet;
> et cil fiert lui tant com il puet,
> d'ire et de honte forssenez,
> quant ot qu'il est a ce menez
> que il covient por lui proier.
> Et li rois, por lui chastïer,
> est jus de la tor avalez;
> an la bataille an est alez
> et dist a son fil maintenant:
> "Comant? Est or ce avenant,
> qu'il ne te toche et tu le fiers?"

> .    .    .    .    .

> 3875    Tant li dit et tant le chastie
> que pes et acorde ont bastie.
> La pes est tex que cil li rant
> la reïne, par tel covant
> que Lanceloz, sans nule aloigne,
> quele ore que cil l'an semoigne,
> des le jor que semont l'avra,
> au chief de l'an se conbatra
> a Melïagant de rechief.    (vs 3805–83)

The fact that Episodes 3 and 6 are connected in this fashion means, of course, that the two components containing them, Sections II and III, are joined by a causal link. Sections II and III are also connected by a thematic bond. Together, they make up the story of the rescue proper, since the two fights recorded in them represent the two stages in which Lancelot achieves the deliverance of the Queen.

An examination of the way the various components of the *Charrete* are related to one another shows, then, that the narrative can be divided into two parts: a preliminary account of the pursuit of Meleagant and the

Queen, and an account of the actual deliverance of Guenevere from her captor. Structurally, however, the work proves to be tripartite, since the account of the rescue proper is made up of two major components which cover the two stages in which it takes place.

As can be seen from the following diagram, the three main structural components of the *Charrete* are roughly comparable in size, which suggests that like *Erec* and *Yvain*, it too was designed to be narrated in three instalments. Of the three sections, the first is the longest by nearly 1000 lines. The other two exactly balance one another in size and composition, thus giving an unexpected symmetry to the account of the rescuing of the Queen.

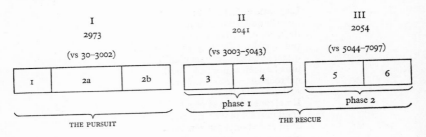

Now that the three main components of the *Charrete* have been established, the next task is to see how they are related to one another. This proves a rewarding study. It shows how Chrétien contrived to weld them into a coherent whole by ensuring that the first two sections provide adequate preparation for the events which take place later in the story.

Section I clearly functions as a preface to the rest of the romance and in particular to Section II. It explains how Lancelot comes to be crossing the swordbridge and challenging Meleagant to do battle for the Queen. At the same time, the picture it gives of Lancelot prepares the reader for much else that happens in the story of the rescue proper: for Lancelot's crossing of the bridge, for his defeat of Meleagant, and for Guenevere's acceptance of him as a lover.

As the reactions of Lancelot's two companions show (vs 3032–77), it calls for a rare degree of courage to venture along a narrow bar over a raging torrent towards two waiting lions. But Lancelot has already given evidence of such courage in tackling the assailants of the seductive damsel in Episode 2a and in dealing with the perils of the enchanted bed in Episode 1. In the one case he went to the rescue of his hostess in spite of the fact that his way was barred by two armed knights and four henchmen equipped with axes (vs 1080–180). In the other, he calmly extinguishes the fire started by the flaming lance which is hurled into his bed, flings the lance itself into the middle of the room and settles down again to sleep:

III. (a) Lancelot on the Swordbridge.
(b) Lancelot Rides in the Cart. Miniatures from the former Yates Thompson MS. of *Lancelot*; c. 1300–1320. New York, Morgan Library.

IV. Cligés and Fénice. Fénice and the Doctors. Miniature from the *Roman de la poire*; c. 1260. Paris, Bibliothèque Nationale: MS. fr. 2186.

A mie nuit, de vers les lates
vint une lance come foudre,
le fer desoz, et cuida coudre
le chevalier par mi les flans
au covertor et as dras blans
et au lit, la ou il gisoit.
En la lance un pannon avoit
qui estoit toz de feu espris;
el covertor est li feus pris
et es dras et el lit a masse.
Et li fers de la lance passe
au chevalier lez le costé
si qu'il li a del cuir osté
un po, mes n'est mie bleciez.
Et li chevaliers s'est dreciez,
s'estaint le feu et prant la lance,
en mi la sale la balance,
ne por ce son lit ne guerpi,
einz se recoucha et dormi
tot autresi seüremant
com il ot fet premieremant.                    (vs 514–34)

To crawl across a swordblade on bare hands and knees, as Lancelot does
to make sure that he reaches the other side of the river, also calls for a
rare degree of devotion:

Et cil de trespasser le gort
au mialz que il set s'aparoille,
et fet molt estrange mervoille,
que ses piez desarme, et ses mains:
n'iert mie toz antiers ne sains,
quant de l'autre part iert venus;
bien s'iert sor l'espee tenuz,
qui plus estoit tranchanz que fauz,
as mains nues et si deschauz
que il ne s'est lessiez an pié
souler, ne chauce, n'avanpié.
De ce gueres ne s'esmaioit,
s'es mains et es piez se plaioit;
mialz se voloit il mahaignier
que cheoir el pont et baignier
an l'eve don ja mes n'issist.                  (vs 3094–109)

Once again, the story of the pursuit has prepared us for just such devotion
in Lancelot. It has shown him ready to expose himself to the contempt of
the world for the sake of the Queen. For this, as Chrétien is at pains to
point out, is what is entailed by appearing in a cart:

De ce servoit charrete lores
don li pilori servent ores,
        .    .    .    .
qui a forfet estoit repris
s'estoit sor la charrete mis

E

> et menez par totes les rues;
> s'avoit totes enors perdues,
> ne puis n'estoit a cort oïz,
> ne enorez ne conjoïz.                    (vs 321–38)

This willingness to suffer humiliation and to sacrifice his standing in the world is the very sacrifice that neither Tristan nor Iseut is prepared to make when the force of the potion abates and free choice is restored to them. It suggests that Lancelot has attained the degree of self-abnegation which makes the martyr glory in the pain and degradation he suffers for his chosen cause. Indeed we find Lancelot rejoicing in the suffering he endures in crossing the bridge:

> A la grant dolor c'on li fist
> s'an passe outre et a grant destrece;
> mains et genolz et piez se blece,
> mes tot le rasoage et sainne
> Amors qui le conduist et mainne,
> si li estoit a sofrir dolz.              (vs 3110–15)

Where Lancelot's victories over Meleagant are concerned, Section I of the *Charrete* prepares us for these by revealing that he has the qualities which will make him the greatest warrior in the world.

In the first place, the tale of the pursuit establishes Lancelot as a knight who can meet the foremost warriors of the day on equal terms. As we have just seen, the quality of his courage is amply demonstrated by his reactions to the perils of the enchanted bed and to the test imposed on him at the castle of the seductive damsel. In their turn the encounter at the ford and the visit to the chapel he passes with the seductive damsel show that Lancelot is endowed with superhuman strength (which also explains why he is able to remove the iron bars from the Queen's window in Episode 5: vs 4594–638). At the ford, he almost wrenches the leg off the man who challenges him (vs 803–10). In the chapel cemetery he raises the lid of a tomb with an ease that only ten strong men could equal (vs 1910–14): a feat which reveals him to be the predestined liberator of the Queen and her fellow captives and which causes the monk who witnesses it to acclaim Lancelot as the greatest warrior ever born:

> ". . . li chevaliers fu leanz,
> si a fet mervoilles si granz
> que toz seus la lame leva
> c'onques de rien ne s'i greva,
> de sor la grant tonbe marbrine.
> Il vet secorre la reïne,
> et il la secorra sanz dote,
> et avoec li l'autre gent tote.
>
> .  .  .  .  .  .  .
>
> Onques voir d'ome ne de fame
> ne nasquié, n'en sele ne sist
> chevaliers qui cestui vausist."         (vs 1967–80)

Finally, Lancelot's skill in fighting is displayed in the two single combats he fights on the way to Bade (vs 812–99; vs 2677–750), and in the rebellion against the men of Gorre where his example and the news that he is their predestined liberator put new heart into the men of Logres:

> . . . li chevaliers s'adreça
> vers la meslee maintenant;
> s'ancontre un chevalier venant
> et joste a lui, sel fiert si fort
> par mi l'uel que il l'abat mort.
>
> .   .   .   .   .
>
> . . . molt bien s'i est maintenuz
> an la meslee une grant piece,
> qu'il ront et fant et si depiece
> escuz et lances et haubers.
> Nes garantist ne fuz ne fers,
> cui il ataint, qu'il ne l'afolt
> ou morz jus del cheval ne volt.
> Il seus si tres bien le feisoit
> que trestoz les desconfisoit,
> et cil molt bien le refeisoient,
> qui avoec lui venu estoient.
> Mes cil de Logres s'en mervoillent,
> qu'il nel conuissent, et consoillent
> de lui au fil au vavasor.
> Tant an demandent li plusor
> qu'an lor dist: "Seignor, ce est cil
> qui nos gitera toz d'essil
>
> .   .   .   .   ."
>
> N'i a celui joie n'en ait,
> quant la novele est tant alee
> que ele fu a toz contee;
> tuit l'oïrent et tuit la sorent.
> De la joie que il en orent
> lors croist force, et s'an esvertüent
> tant, que mainz des autres an tüent,
> et plus les mainnent leidemant
> por le bien feire seulemant
> d'un seul chevalier, ce me sanble,
> que por toz les autres ansanble.
> Et s'il ne fust si pres de nuit,
> desconfit s'an alassent tuit.      (vs 2382–434)

The tale of the pursuit also prepares us for Lancelot's victory by showing how powerful the incentive is which drives him to overcome Meleagant. That Lancelot's whole being is bent on rescuing the Queen is clear from the way he presses ahead of Gauvain when he has been remounted by him at the outset of the quest (vs 299–303); from his refusal to brook any delay in reaching Guenevere through following a safer but longer route to the swordbridge (vs 2144–58); from his willingness to pay any price to get news of the Queen, which leads him to agree to ride in a cart (vs 354–77) or to offer to do anything that the damsel at the crossroads may require of him (vs 606–34). But it is the way the thought of the Queen drives him to attack the assailants of the seductive damsel which best illustrates how powerful an inspiration to valour love is for Lancelot:

> Li chevaliers a l'uis s'areste
> et dit: "Dex, que porrai ge feire?
> Meüz sui por si grant afeire
> con por la reïne Guenievre.
> Ne doi mie avoir cuer de lievre
> quant por li sui an ceste queste:
> se Malvestiez son cuer me preste
> et je son comandemant faz,
> n'ateindrai pas ce que je chaz;
> honiz sui se je ci remaing.
> Molt me vient or a grant desdaing,
> quant j'ai parlé del remenoir;
> molt en ai le cuer triste et noir;
> or en ai honte, or en ai duel
> tel que je morroie mon vuel,
> quant je ai tant demoré ci."          (vs 1096–111)

After this, it is not quite so surprising to find that when Lancelot has reached the point of exhaustion in his first battle with Meleagant (vs 3622–33), the sight of the Queen gives him renewed strength to continue the fighting and, eventually, to prevail over his enemy:

> ... force et hardemanz li croist,
> qu'Amors li fet molt grant aïe
> et ce que il n'avoit haïe
> rien nule tant come celui
> qui se conbat ancontre lui.
> Amors et haïne mortex,
> si granz qu'ainz ne fu encor tex,
> le font si fier et corageus
> que de neant nel tient a geus
> Melïaganz, ainz le crient molt,
> c'onques chevalier si estolt
> n'acointa mes ne ne conut,
> ne tant ne li greva ne nut
> nus chevaliers mes, con cil fet.
> Volantiers loing de lui se tret,
> se li ganchist, et se reüse,
> que ses cos het et ses refuse.
> Et Lanceloz pas nel mennace,
> mes ferant, vers la tor le chace,
> ou la reïne ert apoiee.
>
> .    .    .    .    .
>
> Ensi Lanceloz molt sovant
> le menoit arriers et avant
> par tot la ou boen li estoit,
> et totevoies s'arestoit,
> devant la reïne sa dame
> qui li a mis el cors la flame,

por qu'il la va si regardant;
et cele flame si ardant
vers Meleagant le feisoit,
que par tot la ou li pleisoit
le pooit mener et chacier!  (vs 3720–55)

As for Guenevere's acceptance of Lancelot as a lover, the tale of the pursuit prepares the reader for this by showing Lancelot to be entirely worthy of the love of Arthur's Queen. As we have already seen, it demonstrates the intensity of his devotion and his distinction as a warrior. Furthermore, since character was all important in courtly eyes in the choice of a lover, it reveals him to be a man of principle. We find here that he possesses many of the qualities specified in the *De Amore* as essential in any man who would be found worthy to plead in the court of Love.[11]

The fact that Lancelot stops at a wayside chapel to pray, and then speaks with becoming courtesy ('molt dolcemant') to the monk he meets there, is particularly stressed to show that he treats God and his ministers with the respect that is their due:

... truevent en un leu molt bel
un mostier et, lez le chancel,
un cemetire de murs clos.
Ne fist que vilains ne que fos
li chevaliers qui el mostier
entra a pié por Deu proier.

. . . . .

Quant il ot feite sa proiere
et il s'an revenoit arriere,
si li vient uns moinnes molt vialz
a l'encontre, devant ses ialz.
Quant il l'encontre, se li prie
molt dolcemant que il li die
que par dedanz ces murs avoit.  (vs 1837–51)

His sharing the bed of the seductive damsel in spite of his overwhelming repugnance shows that Lancelot is duly scrupulous in the matter of keeping his word (which, incidentally, explains why he returns to prison after the tournament in Episode 5):

Un lit ot fet en mi la sale,

. . . . .

et la dameisele s'i couche,
mes n'oste mie sa chemise.
Et cil a molt grant poinne mise
au deschaucier et desnüer:
d'angoisse le covint süer;
totevoies par mi l'angoisse
covanz le vaint et si le froisse.
Donc est ce force? Autant le vaut;
par force covient que il s'aut
couchier avoec la dameisele;
covanz l'en semont et apele.  (vs 1195–212)

That Lancelot is a composer of disputes and is well skilled in the hand-ling of men is seen from the way he deals with the men who clamour for the honour of entertaining him after the fighting in Gorre:

> . . . herbergier le vialt chascuns
> ausi li juenes con li vialz,
> et dit chascuns: "Vos seroiz mialz
> el mien ostel que an l'autrui."
> Ce dit chascuns androit de lui;
> et li uns a l'autre le tost,
> si con chascuns avoir le vost,
> et par po qu'il ne s'an conbatent.
> Et il lor dit qu'il se debatent
> de grant oiseuse et de folie:
>
> .    .    .    .    .
> Ancor dit chascuns tote voie:
> "C'est a mon ostel. – Mes au mien.
> – Ne dites mie ancore bien,
> fet li chevaliers; a mon los,
> li plus sages de vos est fos
> de ce don ge vos oi tancier.
>
> .    .    .    .    .
> Se vos m'avïez tuit en ordre
> li uns après l'autre a devise
> fet tant d'enor et de servise
> com an porroit feire a un home,
> par toz les sainz qu'an prie a Rome,
> ja plus boen gré ne l'en savroie,
> quant la bonté prise en avroie,
> que je faz de la volanté.
> Se Dex me doint joie et santé,
> la volantez autant me haite
> con se chascuns m'avoit ja faite
> molt grant enor et grant bonté;
> si soit an leu de fet conté."
> Ensi les vaint toz et apeise.                    (vs 2448–89)

Finally, we find from the two single combats that Lancelot engages in on his way to Bade that he is a generous man, magnanimous to the defeated and generous to the suppliant. On both occasions he proves willing to spare his opponents when they sue for mercy (vs 898–910; 2852–60). On both occasions he grants the request of the young woman who approaches him after the fight, the one to beg for the liberty of her lover (vs 912–24), the other to sue for the head of her enemy (vs 2796–930). In the second case Lancelot finds himself caught between the conflicting claims of com-passion ('pitiez') and generosity ('largece'): a moral dilemma that Chrétien describes at some length (vs 2831–65), and which Lancelot resolves with the wisdom of a Solomon. He allows the man a second chance to defend himself and then presents the girl with his head when he defeats him again (vs 2866–927). Since liberality was considered so important a virtue by the courtly, Chrétien goes out of his way to call attention to a further instance of it in Lancelot. This occurs when he insists on exchanging the horse that has been presented to him by his host with the mount ridden by his young companion:

> Au departir rien ne mesprant:
> a la dame et au seignor prant,
> et a toz les autres, congié.
> Mes une chose vos cont gié
> por ce que rien ne vos trespas,
> que li chevaliers ne volt pas
> monter sor le cheval presté
> qu'an li ot a l'uis presanté;
> einz i fist, ce vos voel conter,
> un des deus chevaliers monter
> qui venu erent avoec lui.
> Et il sor le cheval celui
> monte, qu'ainsi li plot et sist.       (vs 2985–97)

Provided, then, that we are prepared to judge the story from the courtly standpoint rather than from our own, Section I of the *Charrete* makes it quite clear that as a man, a lover and a warrior, Lancelot is eminently fit to aspire to the love of Guenevere. Her returning his affection would, in fact, be a very proper case of the world's greatest lady and the world's greatest knight being in love with one another.

There are two further features in the account of Lancelot's first battle with Meleagant which come as less of a surprise because of what we have seen of him in the first section of the romance. They are his extraordinary loss of composure when he learns that he is fighting in the presence of the Queen, and his immediate compliance with her wish that he should stop fighting Meleagant.

Lancelot's reaction on finding that the Queen is watching his duel with Meleagant could well appear exaggerated to the point of being ridiculous:

> Qant Lanceloz s'oï nomer,
> ne mist gaires a lui torner:
> trestorne soi et voit a mont
> la chose de trestot le mont
> que plus desirroit a veoir,
> as loges de la tor seoir.
> Ne, puis l'ore qu'il s'aparçut
> ne se torna ne ne se mut
> de vers li ses ialz ne sa chiere,
> einz se desfandoit par derriere;
> et Meleaganz l'enchauçoit
> totes voies plus qu'il pooit,
> si est molt liez con cil qui panse
> c'or n'ait ja mes vers lui desfanse.       (vs 3669–82)

However, it is given a certain degree of credibility by the fact that we have already seen Lancelot trying to throw himself from a window when the

Queen passes out of his sight (vs 560–74), and half fainting over a comb which he is told has belonged to her:

> "Cist peignes, se j'onques soi rien,
> fu la reïne, jel sai bien;
>
> .   .   .   .   .
>
> Et li chevaliers dit: "Par foi,
> assez sont reïnes et roi;
> mes de la quel volez vos dire?"
> Et cele dit: "Par ma foi, sire,
> de la fame le roi Artu."
> Quant cil l'ot, n'a tant de vertu
> que tot nel coveigne ploier:
> par force l'estut apoier
> devant a l'arçon de la sele.          (vs 1411–27)

It hardly needs Chrétien's comment that the true lover is ever and immediately obedient to explain why Lancelot stops fighting the moment he knows this is the Queen's wish, even though Meleagant continues to attack him:

> Molt est qui aimme obeïssanz,
> et molt fet tost et volentiers,
> la ou il est amis antiers,
> ce qu'a s'amie doie plaire,
>
> .   .   .   .   .
>
> La parole oï Lanceloz:
> ne puis que li darrïens moz
> de la boche li fu colez,
> puis qu'ele ot dit: "Quant vos volez
> que il se taigne, jel voel bien",
> puis Lanceloz, por nule rien,
> nel tochast, ne ne se meüst,
> se il ocirre le deüst,
> Il nel toche ne ne se muet;
> et cil fiert lui tant com il puet.     (vs 3798–814)

Lancelot's obedience here, like his later obedience to her commands at the tournament at Pomelegoi (vs 5652–62; 5852–7), or his meekness in bearing her displeasure and her rebukes (vs 3937–64; 4484–97), is what one might expect from the man that Chrétien has already described as utterly dominated by love on three different occasions: on his getting into the cart (vs 372–7); on his rejecting the seductive damsel (vs 1223–42); and on his being lost in reverie, when, indeed, he is presented as 'cil qui force ne deffanse / n'a vers Amors qui le justise" (vs 712–3).

To pass now to Section II of the *Charrete*, we find that, in its turn, this serves as a preface to the section which follows. It not only explains how the final contest between Meleagant and Lancelot comes to be fought, but also provides an insight into the character of Meleagant which fully prepares us for his behaviour in the last part of the romance.

The character of Meleagant is established once and for all at the

beginning of Episode 3 by the conversation which takes place between
his father and himself when Lancelot succeeds in crossing the swordbridge. A preliminary comment by Chrétien presents him as thoroughly
unprincipled:

> ... deslëautez li pleisoit,
> n'onques de feire vilenie
> et traïson et felenie
> ne fu lassez ne enuiez,
>
> .    .    .    .    .
>
> Nus ne fust miaudres chevaliers,
> se fel et deslëaus ne fust;
> mes il avoit un cuer de fust
> tot sanz dolçor et sanz pitié.          (vs 3150–67)

This description of him is fully borne out by his refusal to follow his
father's suggestion that he hand the Queen over with a good grace to the
man who so richly deserves her (vs 3187–219; 3234–71) and by his
determination to hold on to his captive at all costs and by all possible
means:

> "Assez me loist ore escoter,
> et vos diroiz vostre pleisir,
> fet Meleaganz, et teisir,
> mes po m'est de quan que vos dites;
> je ne sui mie si hermites
> si prodon ne si charitables,
> ne tant ne voel estre enorables
> que la rien que plus aim li doingne.
> N'iert mie feite sa besoigne
> si tost ne si delivremant,
> einçois ira tot autremant
> qu'antre vos et lui ne cuidiez.
> Ja se contre moi li aidiez,
> por ce nel vos consantiromes;
> se de vos et de toz voz homes
> a pes et trives, moi que chaut?
> onques por ce cuers ne me faut;
> einz me plest molt, se Dex me gart,
> que il n'ait fors de moi regart,
> ne je ne vos quier por moi feire
> rien nule, ou l'an puise retreire
> deslëauté ne traïson,
> Tant con vos plest, soiez prodon,
> et moi lessiez estre cruel."          (vs 3272–95)

This initial impression of Meleagant as the arrogant and perversely
unprincipled son of a good father is borne out by what is said and seen of
him in the rest of Section II of the *Charrete*: by the report Kay has to
give of his treacherous dealings (vs 4017–57); by his insistence on fighting
Lancelot before the man's hands have had time to heal (vs 3446–59); by
his refusal to own himself defeated or to desist from attacking an un-
resisting opponent (vs 3814–46; 5019–28); or by his vindictive rage on

finding what he takes to be proof of the Queen's adultery with Kay and his insistence that the sick man defend himself against the charge (vs 4737–888).

After the picture of Meleagant's ruthlessness that we are given in Episodes 3 and 4, the abduction of Lancelot comes as no surprise in the last part of the romance. The treacherous act is utterly in character; so much so, indeed, that Meleagant is immediately suspected of being behind Lancelot's disappearance:

> N'i a un seul qui mialz ne lot
> qu'a la reïne aillent ençois:
> si le fera querre li rois;
> car il cuident qu'an traïson
> l'ait fet ses filz metre an prison,
> Meleaganz, qui molt le het.    (vs 5170–5)

Indeed, the only surprising thing is that Meleagant does not resort to murder as the most effective expedient for disposing of his opponent – until, of course, one realises that this would deprive him of the chance of gloating over his victim.

The picture that is given of Meleagant in Episodes 3 and 4 also prepares us to find him boasting, on returning to Bade from Logres, that Lancelot has taken fright and that it will be left to the great Gauvain to defend the Queen:

> "Sire, ne sai s'il vos sovient,
> .    .    .    .    .
> que devant plusors nos dist l'an
> que nos fussiens au chief de l'an
> an la cort Artus prest andui.
> G'i alai quant aler i dui,
> apareilliez et aprestez
> de ce por coi g'i ere alez;
> tot ce que je dui faire fis:
> Lancelot demandai et quis,
> contre cui je devoie ovrer;
> mes nel poi veoir ne trover:
> foïz s'an est et destornez.
> Or si m'an sui par tel tornez
> que Gauvains m'a sa foi plevie
> que se Lanceloz n'est an vie
> et se dedanz le terme mis
> ne vient, bien m'a dit et promis
> que ja respiz pris n'an sera,
> mes il meïsmes la fera
> ancontre moi por Lancelot.
> Artus n'a chevalier qu'an lot
> tant con cestui, c'est bien seü;
> mes ainz que florissent seü
> verrai ge, s'au ferir venons,
> s'au fet s'acorde li renons,
> et mon vuel seroit or androit."    (vs 6272–30£)

These insolent gibes are, again, so much in character that, as we have already seen, they immediately arouse the suspicions of his father and sister, and so lead to the frustrating of Meleagant's schemes.

A study of the means employed in the *Charrete* to ensure the cohesion of its parts, reveals that these are also bound together by the presence of three narrative themes which run right through the account of the deliverance of Guenevere, and are closely interwoven both with it and with one another.

The first of these themes is a subsidiary one: the story of Gauvain's attempt to rescue the Queen. This starts immediately after her departure from the court with Kay, for it is Gauvain who first sees the necessity of going in pursuit of them:

> La reïne au palefroi vient,
>
> . . . . . .
>
> Li seneschax, par son outrage,
> l'an mainne la ou cil l'atant;
> mes a nelui n'an pesa tant
> que del sivre s'antremeïst,
> tant que mes sire Gauvains dist
> au roi son oncle, en audïence:
> "Sire, fet il, molt grant anfance
> avez feite, et molt m'an mervoil;
> mes, se vos creez mon consoil,
> tant com il sont ancor si pres
> je et vos irïens aprés
> et cil qui i voldront venir.
> Je ne m'an porroie tenir
> qu'aprés n'alasse isnelemant:
> cel ne seroit pas avenant
> que nos aprés ax n'alessiens,
> au moins tant que nos seüssiens
> que la reïne devandra
> et comant Kex s'an contandra.                  (vs 204–38)

The initiative remains with Gauvain until he is joined by Lancelot in vs 270–3. From that moment until the end of Episode 1, when Gauvain disappears temporarily from the scene, our attention is fixed on Lancelot and Gauvain merely serves as a foil to him. In the incident with the cart, his sensible rejection of the dwarf's suggestion that he join Lancelot if he wishes to have news of the Queen (vs 378–94) shows up the self-abnegation of his companion in whom love triumphs over all thought of self.[12] In the following incident, the warmth of his reception contrasts with the cool and mocking welcome Lancelot receives (vs 435–41; 467–97). Finally, his prudent offer to do anything he can for the damsel at the crossroads shows up Lancelot's impetuosity in offering to do anything she wants if only she will give them news of the Queen:

> Et mes sire Gauvains li dist:
> "Dameisele, se Dex m'aïst,
> je vos an promet a devise
> que je mete an vostre servise,
> quant vos pleira, tot mon pooir,
> mes que vos m'an dites le voir."
> Et cil qui fu sor la charrete
> ne dit pas que il l'an promete
> tot son pooir, einçois afiche,
> come cil cui Amors fet riche
> et puissant, et hardi par tot,
> que, sanz arest et sanz redot,
> quan qu'ele voldra li promet
> et toz an son voloir se met.                    (vs 621–34)

In Section II, the story of Gauvain's quest is taken up very briefly in Episode 4 when Lancelot decides to look for Gauvain after his disastrous interview with the Queen:

> "Or soit a son comandemant",
> fet Lanceloz qui mialz ne puet,
> et dit: "Congié prandre m'estuet,
> s'irai mon seignor Gauvain querre,
> qui est antrez an ceste terre,
> et covant m'ot que il vandroit
> au Pont desoz Eve tot droit."
> A tant est de la chanbre issuz;
> devant le roi an est venuz
> et prant congié de cele voie.                   (vs 4076–85)

This decision of Lancelot's is of capital importance in the development of the main story. It leads to his being captured by Bademaguz' men who mistakenly think to please the King by so doing (vs 4119–39), and this gives rise to the rumours of Lancelot's death which so profoundly affect Guenevere's attitude to him (vs 4157–229).

Chrétien returns to the subject of Gauvain and his mission in Section III, where Episode 5 opens with Lancelot setting off once more in search of his friend when the second fight with Meleagant is over:

> Et Lanceloz, cui molt fu tart
> de mon seignor Gauvain trover,
> an vient congié querre et rover
> au roi, et puis a la reïne.
> Par le congié d'ax s'achemine
> vers le Pont soz Eve corrant.                   (vs 5044–9)

Like the first one, this second attempt to find Gauvain proves to be a turning point in the main story: it offers Meleagant the chance to have Lancelot abducted:

Ençois que pres del pont venissent
et que il veoir le poïssent,
uns nains a l'encontre lor vint

. . . . . .

Et maintenant a demandé
si com il li fu comandé:
"Li quex de voz est Lanceloz?
Nel me celez, je sui des voz;
mes dites le seüremant
que por voz granz biens le demant."
Lanceloz li respont por lui
et dit: "Il meismes je sui
cil que tu demandes et quiers.
– Ha! Lancelot, frans chevaliers,
leisse ces genz, et si me croi:
vien t'an toz seus ansanble o moi,
qu'an molt boen leu mener te voel.
Ja nus ne t'an siue por l'uel,
einz vos atandent ci androit
que nos revandrons or androit."
Cil qui de nul mal ne se dote
a fet remenoir sa gent tote
et siust le nain qui traï l'a;
et sa gent qui l'atendent la
le pueent longuemant atandre,
que cil n'ont nul talant del randre
qui l'ont pris et seisi an sont.                    (vs 5057–85)

At this point Lancelot disappears temporarily from the story, which continues to follow the fortunes of Gauvain. It tells how Lancelot's companions decide to proceed with the search for Gauvain; how they fish him out of the river 'a rains a perches et a cros'; how he is then taken to Bademaguz' Court and made welcome there; and how, when all attempts to trace Lancelot have failed, and the letters announcing his safe return to Logres arrive, it falls to Gauvain to escort the Queen back to Arthur's court, where, finally, he has to disclaim the honour of rescuing her and admit the total failure of his mission:

"Bien vaingne mes sire Gauvains,
qui la reïne a ramenee,
et mainte dame escheitivee,
et maint prison nos a randu."
Et Gauvains lor a respondu
"Seignor, de neant m'alosez;
del dire hui mes vos reposez
qu'a moi chose n'an monte.
Ceste enors me fet une honte,
que je n'i ving n'a tans n'a ore;
failli i ai par ma demore.
Mes Lanceloz a tans i vint,
cui si granz enors i avint
qu'ainz n'ot si grant nus chevaliers."      (vs 5316–29)

This admission of failure is not quite the end of Gauvain's part in the *Charrete*. When Meleagant appears in Logres to challenge Lancelot, it is Gauvain who takes up the challenge in the absence of his friend (vs 6148–213) – a fact Meleagant was to boast of, to his ultimate undoing (vs 6256–387). Finally, when the day for the battle arrives, it appears up to the very last minute that the task of defending the Queen will fall to Gauvain after all (vs 6726–84). But just as he is reaching for his shield, Lancelot appears to take the field, and he is in no mood to allow Gauvain to deprive him of the satisfaction of killing his enemy:

> "Certes, fet Lanceloz, biax sire
> . . . . . .
> . . . celui cui je n'aim de rien,
> qui cele honte et cest mesfet
> m'a porchacié, porquis, et fet,
> voldrai randre son paiemant
> or androit sanz delaiemant.
> Il l'est venuz querre et il l'ait:
> n'estuet pas que il se delait
> por l'atandre, car trop est prez;
> et je meismes resui prez;
> mes ja Dex ne doint qu'il s'an lot."
> Lors dit Gauvains a Lancelot:
> "Amis, fet il, iceste paie
> se je vostre deteur la paie,
> c'iert assez petite bontez.
> Et ausi sui je ja montez
> et toz prez, si con vos veez.
> Biax dolz amis, ne me veez
> cest don, que je requier et vuel."
> Cil dit qu'il se leiroit ainz l'uel,
> voire andeus, de la teste traire
> einz qu'a ce le poïst atraire.
> Bien jure que ja n'avandra;
> il li doit et il li randra,
> car de sa main li afïa.
> Gauvains voit bien, mestier n'i a
> riens nule que dire li sache;
> si desvest son hauberc et sache
> de son dos, et toz se desarme.
> Lanceloz de ces armes s'arme
> tot sanz delai et sanz demore;
> il ne cuide ja veoir l'ore
> qu'aquitez se soit et paiez.          (vs 6865–913)

The second narrative theme to act as a cohesive element in the *Charrete* is that of Lancelot's ride in the cart. It is introduced at the outset of the quest, and establishes from the start the quality of his devotion to the Queen. In describing the incident which wins him the title of the Knight of the Cart, Chrétien is at pains to stress the nature and the magnitude of the sacrifice Lancelot is called upon to make. The preliminary explanation of the use carts were put to in Arthur's time (vs 321–44) shows that the dwarf's suggestion that Lancelot get up behind him is nothing less than an invitation to sacrifice his standing in the world. A brief comment that his momentary hesitation will cost Lancelot dear (vs 360–4) is then followed by an analysis of the conflict that takes place in him between common sense (Reison),[13] which counsels self-interest, and love (Amor), which urges the sacrifice of self:

> Tantost a sa voie tenue
> li chevaliers que il n'i monte;
> mar le fist et mar en ot honte
> que maintenant sus ne sailli,
> qu'il s'an tendra por mal bailli;
> mes Reisons, qui d'Amors se part,
> li dit que del monter se gart,
> si le chastie et si l'anseigne
> que rien ne face ne anpreigne
> dom il ait honte ne reproche.
> N'est pas el cuer, mes an la boche,
> Reisons qui ce dire li ose;
> mes Amors est el cuer anclose
> qui li comande et semont
> que tost an la charrete mont.
> Amors le vialt et il i saut,
> que de la honte ne li chaut
> puis qu'Amors le comande et vialt.          (vs 360–77)

Finally, Chrétien drives his point home by contrasting Lancelot with Gauvain who, as we have seen, is prepared to risk death but not dishonour[14] in the service of the Queen:

> Et mes sire Gauvains s'aquialt
> aprés la charrete poignant,
> et quant il i trueve seant
> le chevalier, si s'an mervoille,
> puis li dit: "Nains, car me consoille
> de la reïne, se tu sez."
> Li nains dit: "Se tu tant te hez
> con cist chevaliers qui ci siet,
> monte avoec lui, se il te siet
> et je te manrai avoec li."
> Quant mes sire Gauvains l'oï,
> si le tint a molt grant folie
> et dit qu'il n'i montera mie,
> car trop vilain change feroit
> se charrete a cheval chanjoit.
> "Mes va quel part que tu voldras
> et g'irai la ou tu voldras."          (vs 378–94)

After this initial scene, Chrétien exploits any opportunity that presents itself in the account of the Pursuit to make his readers aware of the extent of Lancelot's sacrifice. In the following scene in Episode 1, he describes the reactions of the townsfolk who watch Lancelot driven into the castle (vs 401–17) and the mockery he has to endure from the lady of the castle (vs 484–95; 575–82). In Episode 2a, we are shown how a band of merry-makers stop their singing and dancing when the Knight of the Cart is led into their midst by the suitor of the seductive damsel (vs 1634–72). In Episode 2b, the man who challenges Lancelot to single combat on the last night of his journey to the swordbridge taunts him with his ride in the cart (vs 2589–600) – to the consternation of his hosts (vs 2603–22) – and then proves abject in defeat when he learns that he must choose between death or being paraded in a cart himself:

> ... cil dit: "Il te covandroit
> sor une charrete monter;
> a neant porroies conter
> quan que tu dire me savroies,
> s'an la charrete ne montoies
> por ce que tant fole boche as
> que vilmant la me reprochas."
> Et li chevaliers li respont:
> "Ja Deu ne place que g'i mont.
> – Non? fet cil, et vos i morroiz.
> – Sire, bien feire le porroiz,
> mes, por Deu, vos quier et demant
> merci, fors que tant seulemant
> qu'an charrete monter ne doive.
> Nus plez n'est que je n'an reçoive
> fors cestui, tant soit grief ne forz.
> Mialz voldroie estre, je cuit, morz
> que fet eüsse cest meschief.
> Ja nule autre chose si grief
> ne me diroiz, que je ne face,
> por merci et por vostre grace."                    (vs 2758–78)

The reaction of his opponent here shows, more dramatically than any other incident, that the sacrifice Lancelot made in getting into the cart was the greatest that could be asked of him. It makes it quite clear that, for a knight, death is easier to face that the scorn and contempt of his fellows.

In Section II, Chrétien reveals his particular interest in developing the theme of Lancelot's ride in the cart. At first it seems that his purpose was to make the point that nothing done for love can bring dishonour on a man. This is the conclusion that Lancelot comes to when he wonders if the Queen's displeasure at their first interview had been caused by the fact that he had been paraded in a cart:

> "Bien cuit que espoir ele sot
> que je montai sor la charrete.
> Ne sai quel blasme ele me mete
> se cestui non. Cist m'a traï.

S'ele por cestui m'a haï,
Dex, cist forfez, por coi me nut?
Onques Amors bien ne conut
qui ce me torna a reproche;
qu'an ne porroit dire de boche
riens qui de par Amors venist,
qui a reproche apartenist;
einz est amors et corteisie
quan qu'an puet feire por s'amie.

     .     .     .     .

... ne me deüst mie avoir
por ce plus vil, s'ele m'amast,
mes ami verai me clamast,
quant por li me sanbloit enors
a feire quan que vialt Amors,
nes sor la charrete monter."                    (vs 4348–71)

The second interview between Lancelot and the Queen shows, however, that this is not the conclusion Chrétien would have us draw from Lancelot's ride in the cart. The Queen explains that her anger arose from the fact that Lancelot hesitated before accepting the dwarf's invitation to ride beside him:

"Comant? Don n'eüstes vos honte
de la charrete, et si dotastes?
Molt a grant enviz i montastes
quant vos demorastes deus pas.
Por ce, voir, ne vos vos je pas
ne aresnier ne esgarder."                        (vs 4484–9)

In other words, his sacrifice, great as it was, falls short of what is expected of the perfect lover. And this rebuke Lancelot meekly accepts (vs 4490–7) – although Guenevere is in fact merely justifying a heartless caprice – so that we are left to conclude that of a 'verai ami' immediate, as well as total self-abnegation is demanded.

In Section III, Lancelot finally achieves the degree of perfection demanded of him by the Queen by his immediate obedience to her command to do his worst in the tournament at Pomelegoi:

"Sire, ma dame la reïne
par moi vos mande, et jel vos di,
que "au noauz". Quant cil l'oï,
si li dist que molt volantiers,
come cil qui est suens antiers.
Et lors contre un chevalier muet
tant con chevax porter le puet,
et faut, quant il le dut ferir;
n'onques puis jusqu'a l'anserir
ne fist s'au pis non que il pot
por ce qu'a la reïne plot.                       (vs 5652–62)

Lancelot's obedience exposes him once more to the contempt and ridicule of his fellows (vs 5674–99; 5733–61), yet, on the following day, he is equally willing to sacrifice himself again for the sake of the Queen:

> . . . ele vit le chevalier;
> si li vet tantost conseillier
> que ancor "au noauz" le face,
> s'avoir vialt l'amor et la grace
> la reïne, qu'ele li mande.
> Et cil: "Des qu'ele le comande,
> li respont, la soe merci."                    (vs 5851–7)

This ready compliance with Guenevere's wishes, which wins the admiration of her waiting-maid (vs 5908–14), forms the triumphant conclusion to the story of Lancelot's ride in the cart of ill-fame. It proves him to be the perfect 'fin amant'.

The third theme to give cohesion to Chrétien's story of the rescuing of Guenevere is the account of the love-affair which develops between Lancelot and herself at Bade. This is the underlying theme of the romance, and for most people the really important and interesting element in it: its 'substantifique moelle'. The preface to the story of Lancelot and Guenevere is contained in Section I of the *Charrete*. This provides a preliminary picture of Lancelot as a man in love with the Queen. As we have already seen, the account of the pursuit is used to stress both the intensity of Lancelot's devotion, which enables him to succeed in his mission where Gauvain fails in his, and the martial and moral qualities which make him worthy of the love of the greatest lady in the land. This portrait of Lancelot as a man in love is completed by the occasional glimpses that we get of him acting in the way all lovers, do, namely: indulging in amorous reverie; losing his composure when suddenly confronted with the beloved or with some object that reminds him of her; rejoicing over some trifle that has belonged to her; and turning from attractions that might have delighted other men.

In the incident at the ford, we find Lancelot so absorbed in thoughts of Guenevere, that he is completely oblivious of the outside world, until the shock of finding himself in the water brings him back to an awareness of it:

> . . . cil de la charrete panse
> con cil qui force ne deffanse
> n'a vers Amors qui le justise;
> et ses pansers est de tel guise
> que lui meïsmes en oblie,
> ne set s'il est, ou s'il n'est mie,
> ne ne li manbre de son non,
> ne set s'il est armez ou non,
> ne set ou va, ne set don vient;
> de rien nule ne li sovient
> fors d'une seule, et por celi
> a mis les autres en obli;

a cele seule panse tant
qu'il n'ot, ne voit, ne rien n'antant

. . . .

An cele lande avoit un gué
et d'autre part armez estoit
uns chevaliers qui le gardoit;

. . . .

Li chevax voit et bel et cler
le gué, qui molt grant soif avoit;
vers l'eve cort quant il la voit.
Et cil qui fu de l'autre part
s'escrie: "Chevaliers, ge gart
le gué, si le vos contredi."
Cil ne l'antant ne ne l'oï,
car ses pansers ne li leissa,
et totes voies s'esleissa
li chevax vers l'eve molt tost.

. . . .

et li chevax eneslepas
saut en l'eve et del chanp se soivre,
par grant talant comance a boivre.
Et cil dit qu'il le conparra,
ja li escuz ne l'an garra,
ne li haubers qu'il a el dos.
Lors met le cheval es galos,
et des galoz el cors l'anbat
et fiert celui si qu'il l'abat
en mi le gué tot estandu,
que il li avoit deffandu;
si li cheï tot a un vol
la lance et li escuz del col.
Quant cil sant l'eve, si tressaut;
toz estormiz an estant saut,
ausi come cil qui s'esvoille,
s'ot, et si voit, et se mervoille
qui puet estre qui l'a feru.               (vs 711–71)

The finding of Guenevere's comb is, as we know, an occasion for showing how profoundly a lover can be affected by being suddenly confronted with the beloved or with something that reminds him of her (vs 1411–27). It also provides Chrétien with an opportunity for showing Lancelot rejoicing, like Alexander, over a hair; although in this case the comment 'bien fet Amors d'un sage fol / quant cil fet joie d'un chevol' is implicit rather than explicit:

Et cil, qui vialt que le peigne ait,
li done, et les chevox an trait,
si soëf que nul n'an deront.
Ja mes oel d'ome ne verront
nule chose tant enorer,
qu'il les comance a aorer,
et bien .c^m. foiz les toche
et a ses ialz, et a sa boche,

> et a son front, et a sa face;
> n'est joie nule qu'il n'an face:
> molt s'an fet liez, molt s'an fet riche;
> an son soing, pres del cuer, les fiche
> entre sa chemise et sa char.
> N'en preïst pas chargié un char
> d'esmeraudes ne d'escharboncles;
> ne cuidoit mie que reoncles
> ne autres max ja més le praigne;
> dïamargareton desdaigne
> et pleüriche et tirïasque
> neïs saint Martin et saint Jasque;
> car an ces chevox tant se fie
> qu'il n'a mestier de lor aïe.          (vs 1457–78)

Lancelot's dealings with the seductive damsel show how his pre-occupation with the Queen leaves him entirely unresponsive to the attractions of another woman, however great they may be:

> ... il se couche tot a tret,
> mes sa chemise pas ne tret,
> ne plus qu'ele ot la soe feite.
> De tochier a li molt se gueite,
> einz s'an esloingne et gist anvers,
> ne ne dit mot ne c'uns convert
> cui li parlers est desfanduz,
> quant an son lit gist estanduz;
> n'onques ne torne son esgart
> ne devers li ne d'autre part.
> Bel sanblant feire ne li puet.
> Por coi? Car del cuer ne li muet,
> qu'aillors a mis del tot s'antante,
> mes ne pleist mie n'atalante
> quan qu'est bel, et gent a chascun.
> Li chevaliers n'a cuer que un
> et cil n'est mie ancor a lui,
> einz est comandez a autrui
> si qu'il nel puet aillors prester.
> Tot le fet en un leu ester
> Amors, qui toz les cuers justise.
> Toz? Nel fet, fors cez qu'ele prise.
> Et cil s'an redoit plus prisier
> cui ele daigne justisier.          (vs 1213–36)

In Section II of the *Charrete*, the subject of the love affair between Lancelot and Guenevere is brought to the fore in the fourth episode. This rounds off the account of Lancelot's first victory over Meleagant by showing how he and the Queen became lovers.

First we are told how Guenevere comes to return Lancelot's love. In this she is prompted not so much by vanity, admiration or gratitude, but, as E. Southward was the first to point out (pp. 284–5), by remorse.

Although Lancelot has set her free from bondage and covered himself in glory by defeating Meleagant, and although his crossing the sword-bridge on bare hands and knees was a most flattering demonstration of his love for her, these achievements merely leave the Queen with a complacent and half-amused satisfaction at his devotion. So much, at least, is made very clear by her treatment of Lancelot at their first meeting after his victory. For what we later learn was a sheer desire to tease him and enjoy his mortification ('et sel cuidai ge feire a gas', vs 4205) leads her to refuse to have anything to do with him:

> Quant la reïne voit le roi,
> qui tient Lancelot par le doi,
> si c'est contre le roi dreciee
> et fet sanblant de correciee,
> si s'anbruncha et ne dist mot.
> "Dame, veez ci Lancelot,
> fet li rois, qui vos vient veoir;
> ce vos doit molt pleire et seoir.
> – Moi? Sire, moi ne puet il plaire;
> de son veoir n'ai ge que faire.
> – Avoi! dame, ce dit li rois
> qui molt estoit frans et cortois,
> ou avez vos or cest cuer pris?
> Certes vos avez trop mespris
> d'ome qui tant vos a servie
> qu'an ceste oirre a sovant sa vie
> por vos mise an mortel peril,
> et de Melïagant mon fil
> vos a resqueusse et desfandue,
> qui molt iriez vos a randue.
> – Sire, voir, mal l'a enploié;
> ja par moi ne sera noié
> que je ne l'an sai point de gré."
> Ez vos Lancelot trespansé,
> se li respont molt belemant
> a meniere de fin amant:
> "Dame, certes, ce poise moi,
> ne je n'os demander por coi."
> Lanceloz molt se demantast
> se la reïne l'escoutast;
> mes por lui grever et confondre,
> ne li vialt un seul mot respondre,
> einz est an une chanbre antree.          (vs 3937–69)

The change in attitude from amused satisfaction to a reciprocal desire, freely and fully acknowledged, is brought about by the reports that Lancelot has been killed whilst looking for Gauvain. Guenevere's reactions to the news, which are reported in full by Chrétien, show how the shock makes her face up to the irresponsible heartlessness of her behaviour at the interview:

> "Ha! lasse! De coi me sovint,
> quant mes amis devant moi vint,
> que je nel deignai conjoïr
> ne ne le vos onques oïr!
> *Quant mon esgart et ma parole*
> *li veai, ne fis je que fole?*
> *Que fole? Ainz fis, si m'aïst Dex,*
> *que felenesse et que cruex;*
> *et sel cuidai ge feire a gas,*
> mes ensi nel cuida il pas,
> se nel m'a mie pardoné.
> Nus fors moi ne li a doné
> le mortel cop, mien escïant.
> *Quant il vint devant moi riant*
> *et cuida que je li feïsse*
> *grant joie, et que je le veïsse,*
> *et onques veoir ne le vos,*
> *ne li fu ce donc mortex cos?*
> Quant ma parole li veai,
> tantost, ce cuit, le dessevrai
> del cuer et de la vie ansanble."        (vs 4197–217)

The very natural remorse Guenevere feels here leads her, equally naturally, to regret that she had not granted Lancelot his heart's desire at least once before his death:

> "Et Dex! Avrai ge reançon
> de cest murtre, de cest pechié?
> Nenil voir, ainz seront sechié
> tuit li flueve, et la mers tarie!
> Ha! lasse! Con fusse garie
> et com me fust granz reconforz
> se une foiz, ainz qu'il fust morz,
> l'eüsse antre mes braz tenu."        (vs 4220–7)

Then, struck by the full implications of this admission, Guenevere finds herself accepting the idea of their being lovers:

> "Comant? Certes, tot nu a nu,
> por ce que plus an fusse a eise."        (vs 4228–9)

– an acceptance made easier perhaps by the feeling that, now Lancelot is dead, such desires can be safely indulged and given full play.

Once Guenevere has admitted to such desires in herself, it is inevitable, given the courtly attitude to love, that she and Lancelot should become lovers when and as circumstances permit. How this is achieved, and what consequences stem from it, is told in the rest of Episode 4. First comes the account of the meeting which takes place between the lovers when Lancelot is brought back to Bade by Bademaguz' men (vs 4458–532). Here we see how Guenevere's gracious welcome, which contrasts so sharply with her previous reception of him, encourages Lancelot to ask for the cause of her earlier displeasure (vs 4460–82). As we already know, Guenevere justifies her caprice by giving him to understand that he had fallen short of the perfection to be expected of a truly courtly lover by his momentary hesitation before getting into the cart: a rebuke that Lancelot accepts at its face value so that the lovers are reconciled (vs 4484–500). The reconciliation further emboldens Lancelot to ask for a more private meeting with the Queen, which is granted and arranged with exemplary discretion:

> "Dame, fet il, vostre merci;
> mes je ne vos puis mie ci
> tot dire quan que ge voldroie;
> volantiers a vos parleroie
> plus a leisir, s'il pooit estre."
> Et la reïne une fenestre
> li mostre, a l'uel, non mie au doi,
> et dit: "Venez parler a moi
> a cele fenestre anquenuit,
> quant par ceanz dormiront tuit,
> et si vanroiz par cel vergier.
> Ceanz antrer, ne herbergier
> ne porroiz mie vostre cors;
> je serai anz, et vos defors
> que ceanz ne porroiz venir."          (vs 4501–15)

The account of this second meeting between Lancelot and his lady is followed in vs 4536–67 by a description of Lancelot's impatient desire for nightfall and his attempts to avoid arousing the suspicions of the curious (which Chrétien suggests are tactics familiar enough to some at least of his audience: 'Bien poez antendre et gloser, / vos qui avez fet autretel'). Then comes the account of the nocturnal rendezvous where the lovers, fired by an equal desire, proceed from such embraces as are possible through a barred window (vs 4583–93), to the full consummation of their love when it is found that the iron bars need prove no barrier between them:

> Or a Lanceloz quan qu'il vialt
> quant la reïne an gré requialt
> sa conpaignie et son solaz,
> quant il la tient antre ses braz
> et ele lui antre les suens.
> Tant li est ses jeus dolz et buens,
> et del beisier, et del santir,
> que il lor avint sanz mantir
> une joie et une mervoille
> tel c'onques ancor sa paroille
> ne fu oïe ne seüe;
> mes toz jorz iert par moi teüe,
> qu'an conte ne doit estre dite.
> Des joies fu la plus eslite
> et la plus delitable cele
> que li contes nos test et cele.          (vs 4669–84)

Finally, we see the price the lovers have to pay for the joy they have together. For the Queen's bed is stained with blood from the wounds that Lancelot received in removing the iron bars from her window (vs 4699–701) and the next day the stains are noticed by Meleagant who takes them as proof of her adultery with Kay who sleeps in her chamber and whose sheets are similarly stained (vs 4737–900). So that Episode 4 ends with Lancelot having to vindicate the Queen's innocence and honour in a second battle against Meleagant (vs 4901–5043).

The story of Lancelot and Guenevere does not close with Lancelot's successful defence of the Queen and Kay, still less with the night at Bade as some critics maintain.[15] It is continued in the third section of the *Charrete*, which provides it with a conclusion by presenting Lancelot and the Queen as the ideal lovers of the canon subscribed to in this particular romance.

In the case of Lancelot, Chrétien clearly uses the tournament of Pomelegoi to exalt him as the perfect courtly lover, as the truly 'fin amant'. As we know, it is here that Lancelot achieves the ultimate degree of perfection demanded of him by the Queen. For his ready compliance with her command "au noauz" proves him capable of immediate as well as total self-abnegation on her behalf, and rightly merits the following eulogy from her waiting-maid:

> ... "Dame, onques ne vi
> nul chevalier tant deboneire,
> qu'il vialt si oltreemant feire
> trestot quan que vos li mandez;
> que, se le voir m'an demandez,
> autel chiere tot par igal
> fet il del bien come del mal." (vs 5908–14)

The tournament is also used to present Lancelot as the man all women would choose as a husband or a lover. By the time he has fulfilled the predictions of the herald and proved himself the best knight in the land, the damsels who have attended the tournament with a view to choosing themselves husbands have eyes only for Lancelot. They are ready to forswear marriage for the time being if they cannot become his wife, though they realise there is little enough chance of his deigning to consider any one of them:

> Et les dameiseles disoient,
> qui a mervoilles l'esgardoient,
> que cil les tolt a marïer;
> car tant ne s'osoient fïer
> en lor biautez n'an lor richeces,
> n'an lor pooirs, n'an lor hauteces,
> que por biauté ne por avoir
> deignast nule d'eles avoir
> cil chevaliers, que trop est prouz.
> Et neporquant se font tex vouz
> les plusors d'eles, qu'eles dïent

> que s'an cestui ne se marïent
> ne seront ouan marïees,
> n'a mari n'a seignor donees.
> Et la reïne qui antant
> ce dom eles se vont vantant,
> a soi meïsme an rit et gabe;
> bien set que por tot l'or d'Arrabe,
> qui trestot devant li metroit,
> la meillor d'eles ne prandroit;
> la plus bele ne la plus gente,
> cil qui a totes atalante.
> Et lor volentez est comune
> si qu'avoir le voldroit chascune;
> et l'une est de l'autre jalouse
> si con s'ele fust ja s'espouse,
> por ce que si adroit le voient,
> qu'eles ne pansent ne ne croient
> que nus d'armes, tant lor pleisoit,
> poïst ce feire qu'il feisoit.          (vs 5993–6022)

As for Guenevere, the last part of the *Charrete* presents her as the accomplished courtly lady whose discretion complements and matches the prowess and the devotion of her lover. There are two occasions in it which augur well for the relationship between Lancelot and herself by showing that their secret is safe in her hands. The first occurs at the tournament where the order sent to Lancelot is one which he alone will be willing to obey for her sake. As such it is the surest and most discreet method of ascertaining his identity that she could devise. It is not intended, as some critics maintain, to demonstrate her power over him – although she may yield somewhat to that temptation in sending the maiden a second time with the command "au noauz", and must naturally be gratified by his response:

> . . . la pucele s'an repaire,
> s'est a la reïne venue,
> qui molt l'a corte et pres tenue
> tant que la responsse ot oïe,
> dom ele s'est molt esjoïe
> *por ce c'or set ele sanz dote*
> *que ce est cil cui ele est tote*
> *et il toz suens sanz nule faille.*          (vs 5868–75)

The second occasion for demonstrating the exemplary discretion of the Queen comes with Lancelot's last minute arrival at court in Episode 6. Chrétien's successor dwells at some length on the way the Queen gives no outward sign of her inward joy, but is content to await a more suitable opportunity for welcoming him as her heart would wish:

> Et la reïne n'i est ele
> a cele joie qu'an demainne?
> Oïl voir, tote premerainne.

Comant? Dex, ou fust ele donques?
Ele n'ot mes si grant joie onques
com or a de sa bien venue
et ele a lui ne fust venue?
Si est voir, ele an est si pres
qu'a po se tient, molt s'an va pres,
que li cors le cuer ne sivoit.
Ou est donc li cuers? Il beisoit
et conjoïssoit Lancelot.
Et li cors, por coi se celot?
N'estoit bien la joie anterine?
A y donc corroz ne haïne?
Nenil certes, ne tant ne quant,
mes puet cel estre, li auquant:
li rois, li autre, qui la sont,
qui lor ialz espanduz i ont,
aparceüssent tost l'afeire,
s'ainsi, veant toz, volsist feire
tot si con li cuers le volsist;
et se reisons ne li tolsist
ce fol panser et cele rage,
se veïssent tot son corage;
lors si fust trop granz la folie.
Por ce reisons anferme et lie
son fol cuer, et son fol pansé;
si l'a un petit racenssé
et a mis la chose an respit
jusque tant que voie et espit
un boen leu et un plus privé,
ou il soient mialz arivé
que il or ne sont a ceste ore.        (vs 6820–53)

On reading this passage one is reminded, inevitably, of Tristan and Iseut whose imprudence betrayed their secret to the rest of the world:

Ha! Dex, qui puet amor tenir
un an ou deus sanz descovrir?
Car amors ne se puet celer:
Sovent cline l'un vers son per,
sovent vienent a parlement,
et a celé et voiant gent.
Par tot ne püent aise atendre,
maint parlement lor estuet prendre.

(Beroul, *Tristran* vs 573–80)

Inevitably one feels that it was the author's intention to demonstrate the superiority of his hero and heroine over the Cornish lovers by this implicit contrast. Indeed, one is very aware here, as elsewhere, of the didactic purpose behind the story of Lancelot and Guenevere. But this is a subject outside the scope of the present essay. For the time being it is enough to see how the story of the lovers runs through the *Charrete* to give it added cohesion as well as interest.

After analysing the *Charrete* one finds that it has been as carefully and as skilfully contructed as either *Erec* or *Yvain*.

1. The organising of its two principal themes has been carefully synchronised. On the one hand, the three main structural divisions of the *Charrete* correspond to the three stages in the deliverance of the Queen; on the other, they provide the preface, main narrative and conclusion of the story of her relationship with Lancelot.

2. The various themes that run through the romance have been skilfully interwoven to produce a close-textured narrative. The interweaving is particularly successful in the case of the two main themes: first one and then the other comes to the fore, and each in turn affects the development of the other. It is Lancelot's love for the Queen which gives him the determination and the strength to succeed in his mission. In its turn, his success in the initial battle against Meleagant leads to the interview with Guenevere that results, eventually, in their becoming lovers – a development which in courtly eyes was the proper sequel to his victory. In the account of the second phase of the rescue, it is the natural desire of a lover to appear to advantage in his lady's eyes which makes Lancelot contrive to attend the tournament in Logres. This, of course, is the immediate cause for the decision to have him removed to a more secure prison which ultimately leads to the frustrating of Meleagant's schemes.

The subsidiary theme of Gauvain's quest is fused initially with the story of Lancelot's mission. It is Gauvain who provides Lancelot with a fresh mount when he first comes rushing to Guenevere's rescue, and, until their ways separate, it is Gauvain who serves as a foil to his companion and so enables us to form some estimate of his quality. On the three other occasions when Gauvain comes indirectly or directly into the story, it is to have a shaping influence on the course events take (a point overlooked by those who feel Gauvain has no 'structural significance' in the *Charrete*[16]). Lancelot's first attempt to find him produces the situation which causes the Queen to accept the idea of being in love with Lancelot. The second attempt provides Meleagant with an opportunity to abduct his adversary. Finally, Gauvain's offer in Episode 6 to meet Meleagant in Lancelot's stead is the occasion of the boasting that leads to Meleagant's downfall.

As for the theme of the ride in the cart which threads its way through the romance, this is an essential element in the story of the love affair between Lancelot and the Queen. It enables Chrétien to trace the development of Lancelot from the near-perfect to the perfect lover (which doubtless is why it has given the romance its name[17]); it also provides the Queen with an excuse for her heartless treatment of Lancelot, and later, with the means of ascertaining his identity at the tournament.

3. For all Gaston Paris' complaints or Mario Roques' bewilderment, the *Charrete* lacks neither clarity nor coherence.

In most cases, the features which have been criticised in the first part of it serve a very definite purpose; that of achieving a gradual clarification of the situation resolved in the second part. They also serve to bring about that marriage of Celtic magic and twelfth-century rationalism which is a feature of Chrétien's romances. For they create an atmosphere of mystery which makes it possible to introduce so fantastic an element as a sword-bridge into a tale that has otherwise to do with the very human realities of love, selfless generosity, arrogance and spite.

The second part of the *Charrete*, the tale of the rescue proper, is particularly remarkable for its clarity and coherence. This is due to a large extent to the care that Chrétien takes to see that we understand the behaviour and the reactions of his protagonists. The picture of Lancelot which is gradually built up as the tale of the pursuit unfolds prepares us for what we find him doing in the story of the rescue proper. The Queen's reflections on hearing of Lancelot's 'death' provide the clue to her previous attitude towards him, and prepare us for the developments that take place later at Bade. The discussion Meleagant has with his father at the beginning of Episode 3 supplies an insight into his character which explains his subsequent actions. The same discussion establishes Bademaguz as a man of principle and honour. Thereafter we are ready for his constant generosity towards Lancelot: the cordial welcome he extends to him on his arrival (vs 3303–422; 3478–88); his attempts to make peace between him and Meleagant (vs 3423–49); his rage when his subjects take Lancelot prisoner (vs 4143–56; 4442–54); his attempts to trace him when he is abducted by Meleagant (vs 5205–28); and his angry defence of Lancelot when Meleagant brags that he has been scared into hiding from him (vs 6354–73). The introductory impression of Bademaguz as a man 'qui molt ert soutix et aguz / a tote enor et a tot bien' also prepares us for the courtesy and protection he extends at all times to the Queen, and which explains why she is willing on two occasions to respect his feelings as a father and call a halt to the fighting between Lancelot and Meleagant.

The care taken in the *Charrete* to achieve coherence by making sure that the motivation of every major event is fully explained is seen, finally, in the way Chrétien's successor is at pains to account for the interest Meleagant's sister takes in Lancelot. She was, we discover, the maiden whom he had earlier presented with the head of her enemy:

> "Je sui cele qui vos rové
> quant au Pont de l'Espee alastes
> un don, et vos le me donastes
> molt volantiers quant jel vos quis:
> ce fu del chevalier conquis
> le chief, que je vos fis tranchier,
> que je nes point n'avoie chier.
> Por ce don, et por ce servise
> me sui an ceste poinne mise:
> por ce vos metrai fors de ci."    (vs 6572–81)

Indeed, the only loose end left in the story of the rescue proper is the inexplicable failure of Gauvain to look for Lancelot once it is known that the letters announcing his return to Logres were forgeries. Arthur's failure to send out a search party is explained away as the natural ingratitude of a man who forgets his obligations in the enjoyment of more immediate pleasures (vs 5344–58); but in Gauvain's case, the ties of friendship between Lancelot and himself render his inactivity as inexplicable to us as it seems to Lancelot in his tower (vs 6483–522).

At this point, it may seem a little surprising that the majority of critics should have subscribed for so long to the view that the *Charrete* is ill-constructed and incomplete. But the generally adverse opinions of the work can be explained on two counts.

In some cases the critics have attempted to interpret the romance in terms of its underlying theme, whereas an understanding of its organisation must start from an analysis of it as an adventure story. This is clearly what has happened with Southward:

> What I would like to do, however, is to show that the *Lancelot* as we have it tells a story which does not depend on either of these two elements [the abduction story and "amour courtois"] but which alone explains the form, sequence and incomplete state of the romance. I think it is quite clear that Chrétien was setting out primarily to tell the story of how Guinevere became unfaithful to Arthur. *The whole unity of the romance and every inconsistent detail of its construction depend upon this interpretation,* and although the other factors also enter the picture, they are not the dominating consideration (p. 282, my italics).

It is hardly surprising that for this critic the romance should end once Guenevere has admitted her love for Lancelot, or that her study of it should conclude as follows:

> From this point in the story Chrétien's ideas seem slowly to fade. There is the episode of Lancelot's visit to the queen at night. . . . Then we slide away into the commonplaces of Arthurian romance: tournaments, combats, adventuring, seeking. Chrétien has, in short, attained his object: Guinevere is now in love with Lancelot, and admits her love. Once attained, this object does not permit of any further step, and Chrétien can think of no conclusion to his story. At the beginning of the poem Guinevere was a banal queen – the beautiful wife of a famous king; . . . Now, she is a woman in love with one of the King's own knights, and from this situation there is no way out. In a few thousand lines of verse, Chrétien has succeeded in creating one of the great tragedies of European literature (p. 289).

It is true that the romance might have ended a little later for Southward had she seen it as the study of a mutual enthralment. She might then have felt with Cross and Nitze that the story ends where Chrétien leaves it: at the tournament.[18] But even so, her conclusion would probably have been the same:

> So we can begin to see why Chrétien never finished the *Lancelot*: there was no final scene possible. Any conventionally happy ending would be an anti-

climax, and so in fact Godefroy de Leigni's conclusion remains. Chrétien is said to have agreed to his successor's work; this is not impossible, perhaps, but it is easy to understand that Chrétien himself would not relish such artistic hypocrisy (p. 289).

Elsewhere, the adverse opinions of the structure of the *Charrete* seem to stem from the critics' dislike of the work which blinds them to its merits and leads them into an almost wilful misinterpretation of its author's intentions. This appears to have been the case with Gaston Paris, who admits that the romance is logical enough in its broad outlines, but rejects it on points of detail as incoherent and utterly absurd:

> On ne peut contester qu'elle [l'oeuvre de Chrétien et de Godefroi] ne présente une certaine unité. . . . *Mais si le plan général du récit est simple et clair, il n'en est pas de même d'un grand nombre des traits dont ce récit se compose.* D'abord plusieurs épisodes sont absolument inutiles: la première partie du roman, prise en bloc, n'a aucun lien avec la seconde. La demoiselle au lit périlleux, celle qui soumet Lancelot à une si rude épreuve, le chevalier qui veut la ravir . . . apparaissent et disparaissent sans qu'on comprenne leur raison d'être et d'agir. La charrette elle-même est inexpliquée: qui était ce nain qui la conduisait? quel interêt avait-il à contraindre Lancelot à un acte déshonorant? comment la reine a-t-elle connu cette aventure? nous ne l'apprenons nulle part. Ce qui est plus singulier encore, c'est l'obscurité qui règne sur la conduite du héros principal: d'où arrivait-il, sur son cheval essoufflé, quand il rencontre Gauvain et lui emprunte un de ses destriers? Il volait évidemment à la poursuite de Méléaguant; mais qui donc l'avait prévenu de l'enlèvement de la reine? Plus tard il faut supposer qu'attiré dans le bois où Ké venait déjà d'être blessé et fait prisonnier, il a soutenu un combat acharné contre Méléaguant et toute sa troupe, combat dans lequel il a eu son cheval tué . . . et a dû, contraint par le nombre, laisser s'éloigner ses ennemis, emmenant leur proie; cependant nulle part dans la suite il n'est fait allusion à ce combat, et on ne s'explique pas comment Méléaguant et ses gens, qui portent Ké blessé dans une litière, ont pu s'éloigner assez vite pour que Lancelot perde complètement leurs traces et soit obligé de monter sur la charrette pour reprendre la piste; cette piste une fois ressaisie, il la laisse d'ailleurs s'effacer, et il s'inquiète non plus du chemin qu'a pris la reine, mais du moyen de pénétrer dans le royaume de Gorre. Le personnage de Bademagu n'est pas clair non plus. . . . (pp. 482–4, my italics).

The reasons behind the dislike so generally felt for the *Charrete* are easy enough to understand. For some people, the unvarying perfections of the hero prove a strain on credulity and patience alike. Lancelot's sole interest is that he represents the ideal lover as conceived by a certain section of society in a bygone age. In himself he is an unmitigated bore who makes one long for the touch of reality that is found in the imperfections of an Erec or an Yvain. For others, a work that exalts adultery, as this one undoubtedly does, is obviously distasteful. At times the distaste expresses itself explicitly, as in the following passage:

> . . . an interpretation which showed the "courtly love" in the *Roman* to be merely a feature of the *cortex* would constitute an act of kindness to Chrétien

and to his Lady. . . . As the matter now stands among most critics, the poet is made out to be a heretic of a very peculiar kind, guilty of writing an empty fable which is indeed "porcorum cibus", and his Lady is accused of foisting upon him, his rather silly heresy.[19]

Elsewhere it betrays itself in the attempts made to excuse Guenevere's behaviour or to tone down the adulterous nature of her relationship with Lancelot, regardless of the fact that in the eyes of the public for whom the work was intended no such palliation or justification was necessary. The following passage can be taken as typical:

> Il y a, à la vérité, la nuit de passion chez Bademagu, à la fois soudaine, violente et révélatrice d'amour réciproque, mais c'est la récompense inespérée d'un amour qui est une religion secrète, telle une "grâce" subite d'en haut qui couronne une "foi" mystique.
>
> Des commentateurs se demandent si cette scène ardente, lorsque Lancelot et Guenièvre auront tous deux retrouvé leur place à la cour d'Artur, ne va pas être suivie de la régulière banalité d'un adultère; mais Chrétien n'en laisse rien supposer, et ce n'est pas une nécessité. Tristan et Iseut, même après les sublimes moments du Morois, n'ont-ils pas fini par vivre encore, plus ou moins séparés avant leur réunion dans la mort? La nuit chez Bademagu peut n'avoir pas été précédée ni devoir être suivie d'autres pareilles, malgré la passion des deux héros.[20]

In themselves, these adverse reactions to the *Charrete* are legitimate enough. It is in fact a tribute to Chrétien that his work can so affect twentieth-century readers. It shows that the problems he deals with are with us today and are not merely of antiquarian interest. However, our exasperation with the "rather silly heresy" put forward in this romance, or with its even sillier hero, should not blind us to the fact that technically the work cannot be faulted. As a composition, it takes its place beside *Erec* and *Yvain* as a 'molt bele conjointure'.

All that is needed now to complete this investigation into the organisation of the *Charrete* is for my findings to be compared with those of the three other critics who have considered this aspect of the romance.

Where the division of the work into its basic components is concerned, it will be found that my analysis tallies for the most part with the views outlined by Voretzsch in his summary of its plot:

> The plot of the *Lancelot*, in spite of its numerous adventures and the profusion of its fictitious elements, comprises five rather distinct parts. The exposition narrates the abduction of Queen Guinevere by Meleagant. Then, as second part, follows the adventurous journey of Lancelot and Gauvain to free the queen. Gauvain's journey to the subaqueous bridge, *ponz evages*, is briefly described; that of Lancelot to the sword bridge, *ponz de l'espee*, is, on the other hand, related in detail. The main action or third part, falls into two sections: the liberation of the queen by Lancelot who crosses the *ponz de l'espee* and vanquishes Meleagant; and – after being rejected, at first, and again separated from her – the final granting by the queen of the highest reward to her liberator. The fourth part, intended to retard the progress of the main action, tells how

Lancelot is decoyed into prison and incarcerated by Meleagant, describes Gauvain's reappearance, the queen's return home, and the wedding-tourney. In the fifth and last part Lancelot's final victory over Meleagant at the court of King Arthur is portrayed (p. 292).

If Voretzsch seems to differ from me in dividing the *Charrete* into five parts where I divide it into six, the difference is more apparent than real. It arises from the fact that he recognises the close connection between what he calls the liberation of the Queen (my Episode 3) and the rewarding of Lancelot (my Episode 4), and treats them as the two halves of his third component. It is interesting to note that he does not see that the imprisonment of Lancelot and his final victory over Meleagant (my Episodes 5 and 6) are equally closely connected and could also be treated as the halves of a larger unit.

Where Voretzsch and I may differ is over the nature of the first component. For him, this seems to consist solely of the abduction of the Queen (vs 30–219). For me, it also comprises the initial search by Gauvain and Lancelot for news of the Queen, which Voretzsch appears to include in his second component. But in the absence of any line references, it is not possible to be specific about this.

My analysis also confirms the views on the bipartition of the *Charrete* contained in the following statement by Frappier:

> Un contraste s'accuse dans la composition du roman entre la première partie et la seconde, avant et après le passage du pont de l'épée.[21]

The relationships between the six basic components of the *Charrete* have proved to be such that it falls into two main parts, which do indeed cover the events before and after the crossing of the swordbridge (as opposed to Bezzola's contention that 'la première partie s'achève par la délivrance de la reine').[22]

Where Frappier differs from Gaston Paris in his estimate of the first part of the *Charrete*, my findings show that he was justified in countering the charge that it is illogical and irrelevant. They support him when he claims with Foerster that we are dealing here with 'un art des explications suspendues' and endorse the suggestion that there is 'une conformité entre les aventures prodigieuses, mais presque saugrenues parfois, et l'âme du héros étrange et magnifique' by showing that they do indeed reveal 'sa trempe exceptionnelle'.[23]

Although I accept the *Charrete* as bipartite from one standpoint, the fact that its second part contains two components of major proportions means that I agree with Kelly in seeing it as structurally tripartite. But here all resemblance between our views on its organisation ends. Over the details of its tripartition as over the question of its symmetry, we differ entirely.

The essential differences between our views on the main divisions of the

*Charrete* can be seen from the following diagram where our respective findings are presented in the form adopted by Kelly on pp. 168–9 of his book.

| KELLY | ZADDY |
|---|---|
| I. OPENING SCENE: THE ABDUCTION (vs 30–223) 194 lines | |
| DIVISION A: LANCELOT'S QUEST (vs 224–3135) 2912 lines | SECTION 1: THE PURSUIT (vs 30–3002) 2973 lines |
| DIVISION B: LANCELOT AT BATH (vs 3136–5358) 2223 lines | SECTION 2: THE RESCUE: STAGE 1 (vs 3003–5043) 2041 lines |
| DIVISION C: LANCELOT'S IMPRISONMENT (vs 5359–6725) 1367 lines | SECTION 3: THE RESCUE: STAGE 2 (vs 5044–7097) 2054 lines |
| II. CLOSING SCENE: DEFEAT OF MELEAGANT (vs 6726–7097) 372 lines | |

From this it is clear that Kelly and myself differ over (i) the treatment of the abduction of Guenevere as an independent structural element in the romance; (ii) the point of demarcation between the first and the second of its main components; (iii) the point of demarcation between the second and third main component; and (iv) the treatment of Meleagant's final defeat as an independent structural element.

As I see it, there are no satisfactory grounds for isolating the abduction scene from the main body of the text. As the starting point of the tale of the pursuit, it is an essential part of it, and cannot be detached from it as a separate and independent element in the same way as the prologue (vs 1–29) can. Kelly's grounds for doing so are, seemingly, that it is an Arthurian scene and that according to Kellermann, such scenes have a structural significance in Chrétien's romances. For, having presented his plan of the *Charrete* on pp. 168–9, he continues:

The symmetry of this plan will be confirmed by what follows.

*Kellermann*
  Kellerman has called attention to the significance of the scenes which take place at Arthur's court as structural turning points in Chrétien's poems. It is therefore indicative of one of the fundamental differences between the *Charrete* and his other works that there are in fact only two structurally significant Arthurian scenes in the former – the one at the beginning and the one at the end – whereas all the others contain four. This difference is explained by the fact that the *Charrete* has but one plot, which begins in the first scene with Meleagant's challenge and ends in the last one with his death. In Chrétien's other works, a first adventure or plot begins at Arthur's court, and returns there about one-third of the way through the poem to culminate in the main Arthurian scene; the second adventure or plot grows out of this scene, moves the action away from the court, and then returns there briefly in a third

F

Arthurian scene; afterwards the action again takes place away from the court to return there at the end of the poem, where the second adventure ends (cf. Kellermann, *Aufbaustil*, pp. 11–13). But the *Charrete* is different. It has one adventure, divided structurally into three divisions. To have had division A (Lancelot's quest) conclude at Arthur's court was impossible as far as the narrative is concerned, first because it would have necessitated an awkward displacement of the leading characters, and second because it would have obliged Chrétien to bring about a dénouement to the problem of the prisoners if the central Arthurian scene were to be like that in his other poems (p. 169).

Kelly's case here is not very convincing. It reads as if he has attempted to interpret the *Charrete* in terms of a preconceived pattern which, from his account of it, does not sound as if it applies to *Cligés* or, entirely, to *Yvain*. It does not seem to have occurred to him that the fact that an incident is a turning point in a work does not necessarily mean that it forms an independent component there.

As for the point of demarcation between the first and the second main component of the *Charrete*, we find that Kelly's first component ends at vs 3135 (after the crossing of the swordbridge) and mine at vs 3002 (with Lancelot's arrival at the bridge.) It is true that one cannot be dogmatic over this point. There is no clear indication (such as a break in the time sequence or an explicit statement) to show where one component ends and the other begins. Indeed, they have been carefully dovetailed, as might be expected from the fact that the account of the pursuit is not a self-contained narrative, like Part I of *Yvain* or Episode 1 of *Erec*, but a prelude to the account of the rescue proper which only fully makes sense when read in the context of the rest of the romance. Nevertheless, I feel that the evidence of the text suggests that the crossing of the swordbridge should be included in the second, rather than the first section of the *Charrete*. In the first place, it is one of Lancelot's most spectacular exploits. According to Bademaguz, it is 'le plus grant hardemant / qui onques fust mes nes pansez' (vs 3192-3), and makes Lancelot 'li miaudres chevaliers del monde' (vs 3219). It seems more logical, then, to include it in the same part of the romance as his initial victory over Meleagant, than to place it in the first component with all the preliminary adventures which serve precisely to prepare us for these two outstanding achievements. In the second place, the crossing of the bridge provides the Queen herself with ocular proof of Lancelot's worth and devotion, whereas his previous exploits merely served to establish him in the reader's eyes as a warrior and a lover. Its place, therefore, would seem to be in that section of the romance which tells how the couple came to be lovers.

Turning now to the point of demarcation between the second and the third main component, we find that the second component ends for Kelly at vs 5358 (after the return of the Queen and the other prisoners to Logres), and for me at vs 5043 (after the Queen and Kay have been cleared of the charges brought against them by Meleagant). This time the case against Kelly's position is a clear one. As I have already pointed out,[24] vs 5044-538 tell how Lancelot came to be kidnapped when he set out a second time to look for Gauvain, and was then left behind in Gorre when the others were tricked into returning to Arthur's court without him. They constitute, therefore, the beginning of the account of Lancelot's imprisonment and belong, logically, to the third section of the romance.

Kelly's reason for including vs 5044–358 in his second major component is, one gathers, that as the account of Lancelot's departure from Bath, they balance the account of his arrival in that city. This gives his second component (his Division B) a symmetry that is discussed at length in pp. 178–82 of his study, and is presented in diagrammatic form on p. 178:

DIVISION B: LANCELOT AT BATH (vs 3136–5358)

a. Arrival of Lancelot (vs 3136–3488)
b. First interrupted combat between Lancelot and Meleagant (vs 3489–3898)
c. Guenevere's rejection of Lancelot's service (vs 3899–4082)
d. First search for Gauvain (vs 4083–4458)
c. Guenevere rewards Lancelot's service (vs 4458–4736)
b. Second interrupted combat between Lancelot and Meleagant (vs 4737–5043)
a. Departure and disappearance of Lancelot (vs 5044–5358)

To my mind, however, the symmetry that Kelly is able to claim for his Division B, by including vs 5044–358 in it, is no justification for ignoring the obvious logic of Chrétien's narrative.

The case against isolating Meleagant's final defeat as a separate component in the *Charrete* is an equally clear one. It cannot, any more than the abduction of Guenevere, be detached from the main body of the text simply on the score that it is an Arthurian scene. The account of Lancelot's final victory over Meleagant is the climax of the story of the rescue proper, and as such it is an integral part of it, in fact, it is the essential part. Indeed, it is this duel which makes sense of all the events that follow Lancelot's defence of Kay and the Queen; it sets them in train in the first place, and they serve, in their turn, as a prelude to it.[25] Furthermore, it is the connection between this contest and the first one fought in Episode 3 which provides the link between the two halves of the story of the rescue proper.[26]

The weakness of Kelly's case for treating the combat at Arthur's court as an independent component in the *Charrete* can be gauged from the justification he is left to give for taking the – decapitated – account of Lancelot's imprisonment as his third major component of that romance:

> But structural division of the main plot into Lancelot's quest and Lancelot's imprisonment, with the section at Bath between them, can be justified on the grounds of Lancelot's immediate motivation. In the first part Lancelot is bent on reaching the Queen by the shortest and quickest way possible so as to free her and the other prisoners from the "custom" of Gorre. Most of the time Meleagant plays no direct role in motivating him. . . . This is just the reverse of the situation in the third or imprisonment part. *Lancelot is here struggling not so much*

*to save Guenevere and the prisoners as to escape from Meleagant's prison.* Even in the tournament, his temporary freedom, though brought about by his desire to appear before Guenevere, is obtained by getting around Meleagant's orders. The same is true at the end of the poem, where Lancelot hastens to Arthur's court not so much to see Guenevere as to fight Meleagant (p. 168, my italics).

Kelly's attempt to justify the way he divides the *Charrete* on the grounds of Lancelot's immediate motivation in each section seems particularly inappropriate in the case of the 'imprisonment part' where Lancelot's feelings count for so little in determining the course of events. Except for his participation in the tournament, Lancelot's role here is necessarily a passive one; the initiative lies with Meleagant and with his sister – as Kelly is ready enough to admit elsewhere.[27] In this passage, as throughout his discussion of the main structural divisions of the *Charrete*, one is left feeling that although Kelly gives an accurate enough account of its individual incidents (pp. 102–47), the basic facts of the general organisation of the romance have eluded him.

Where the symmetry of the *Charrete* is concerned, my findings do not support Kelly's views. The fact that I see vs 5044–358 as belonging to the third rather than the second main component of the romance means that I cannot accept Kelly's claim that the second component is symmetrically constructed around the first search for Gauvain – or in his own words, 'has a striking symmetrical arrangement of [its] different episodes around a common center' (p. 178). Nor again can I agree with his further claim that the whole romance is symmetrically constructed around this same centre:

> . . . the poem is built upon a symmetrical pattern with the scene in which Lancelot and Guenevere confess and analyze their love as the core. This episode is found in the center of the central structural division. . . . (p. 184).

The similarity Kelly finds in the composition of his first and third components is only achieved by excluding vs 5044–358 from the third component against the logic of Chrétien's narrative.

Where Kelly sees the search for Gauvain as the structural centre of the *Charrete*, I have found that the two main divisions of the romance both have their own symmetry. In the account of the pursuit, a relatively longer central episode is flanked by two relatively shorter ones. And in the account of the rescue proper, the two main components neatly balance one another in size and in make-up.

Over the question of its symmetry, as over the question of its partitioning, one is left with the feeling that Kelly has been a little too anxious to find certain preconceived patterns in the *Charrete*, and too little concerned with the actual facts of its organisation. If this judgement seems unduly harsh, an illustration of this tendency can be seen in Kelly's analysis of the first major component of the romance (his Division A, Lancelot's quest).

Like myself, he recognises that there are three stages in the journey to Gorre, but these he characterises by the companions who travel with Lancelot:

> Structurally, the quest falls into three parts, each corresponding to the particular companion Lancelot has. In the first part Gawain accompanies Lancelot (vs 224–709), in the second part an attractive maiden (vs 931–2011), and in the third part the two sons of the first vavassor (vs 2012–3133) (p. 172).

As Kelly admits, the weakness of this scheme is that it 'leaves [out] the adventure at the ford (vss 710–931), at which time Lancelot is alone' (p. 172). But although he also admits that the incident 'marks in fact the true beginning of Lancelot's quest in so far that it is the first encounter he has while actually on his way towards Gorre' (p. 172), we find it rather vaguely associated with the first, or 'Gawain' part of the quest rather than the second or 'maiden' part in the diagrams given on pp. 175 and 184. The reason for this, as one realises from Kelly's discussion of his last two components, is that, by excluding the ford incident from the second, 'maiden', part, he can claim that it, like the 'companion' part, is constructed strictly in accordance with Saran's ABABA formula:

> Structurally the two parts which follow [the 'Gawain' part] are very much alike. Each begins with a main episode, followed by an interlocking or alternating pattern for the rest of the episodes; in this pattern one episode is interrupted before its conclusion by another, after which the first episode is resumed. This structural pattern was first identified by Franz Saran, and is expressed by the formula, ABABA; he found it especially common in courtly epic, and Kellermann has shown that it is frequent in Chrétien's writings . . . though he makes reservations as to its uniqueness and to the rigidity of its application. The truth is that Chrétien uses this basic scheme in various modifications of which we find several in the *Charrette* itself (p. 173).

One could wish that Kelly had shared Kellermann's reservations about applying Saran's formula too rigidly, and that here, as elsewhere in his analysis of the *Charrete*, he had looked to the plot itself to see where its main divisions come.

A further illustration of this tendency to interpret the *Charrete* in terms of preconceived patterns occurs when Kelly comes to justify his scheme for dividing the romance into its main structural components. As we have seen, he first claims that his recognition of an opening and closing Arthurian scene is 'confirmed by' Kellermann. He then proceeds to justify his three major divisions on the grounds that they correspond to the three components which figure in the common structural pattern Frappier attributes to *Erec*, *Yvain* and the *Graal* – provided that pattern is read in reverse:

> Frappier's version of the typical structural pattern for Chrétien's courtly epic resembles the *Charrette* more closely [than Kellermann's], since it places less emphasis on the turning points in the plot than on the nature of the narrative between the turning points.

Dans l'*Erec*, l'*Yvain*, le *Conte du graal* lui-même, des parallélismes indiquent une préférence réfléchie pour un certain type de structure. Ce schéma . . . se caractérise par une composition en triptyque: une première aventure s'achève par le bonheur amoureux d'un héros ou d'une héroïne; une crise, qui unit un drame psychologique à un conflit d'ordre moral ou social, fait rebondir l'action; une troisième partie, la plus ample, marquée par une suite progressive d'aventures, dont une mystérieuse et magique entre toutes . . . aboutit à un dénouement heureux, la parfaite réconciliation des amants. Ce plan méthodique s'assouplit et souffre des variantes. Mais d'un roman à l'autre les lignes générales se reconnaissent (*Chrétien*, p. 227).

Except for the necessary changes resulting in large part from the presence of only one adventure from beginning to end in the *Charrette*, we have in Frappier's summation the essential features of our poem's structure. It has a tripartite structure, with a crisis in the central part. The first part does lead to the happiness of Lancelot and Guenevere, but happiness which follows a re-conciliation; this makes the first part of the *Charrette* similar to the third part of Chrétien's other poems. Its similarity to the third part is enhanced by the suite of adventures which take place in the first part rather than in the third. But the crisis at Bath, rather than resolve one adventure and create a new one, does exactly the opposite, delaying the climax till the end of the plot. The third part of the *Charrette* is in turn similar to the first part in Chrétien's other poems. Lancelot is victorious in the tournament, as was Erec in the sparrow-hawk episode. . . . He gains thereby the complete devotion of his lady, which lasts beyond the conclusion of the poem; this is also typical of Chrétien's other writings. *The poet has merely reversed the order of the main divisions of his usual structural pattern and limited the narrative to one adventure*, ample proof of Frappier's assertion that "Chrétien n'était pas tenu à ne jamais modifier son art" (*Chrétien*, p. 173) (pp. 171–2; my italics).

Since Frappier himself sees the *Charrete* as bipartite, it is a little piquant that he should have been taken up in this manner.

But if Kelly's interpretation of the *Charrete* is often more ingenious than convincing, there can be no quarrelling with his general conclusion. My findings have confirmed that the romance has 'a well thought-out plot with a carefully constructed structural foundation' (p. 238). Technically, it has proved a masterpiece and no failure.

## NOTES

1. See Paris' 'Études sur les romans de la Table Ronde. Lancelot du Lac: II: Le conte de la Charrette', Romania 12 (1883), pp. 464–84.
2. See Foerster's edition of Christian von Troyes, *Der Karrenritter* (*Lancelot*) *und das Wilhelmsleben* (*Guillaume d'Angleterre*) (Halle, 1899), pp. lxxxv–lxxxvi.
3. *Der Karrenritter*, p. lxxxvii.
4. See for example: J. D. Bruce: '*Lancelot* is the poorest in construction of all the works of this author' (*The Evolution of Arthurian Romance from the Beginnings down to the Year 1300* (Göttingen, 1923), vol. I, p. 195); T. P. Cross and W. A. Nitze: 'The *Charrete* is by no means his best composition, as all who have the fortitude to read through our first chapter will realize' (*Lancelot and Guenevere*.

*A Study on the Origins of Courtly Love* (Chicago, 1930), p. 2); E. Southward's views on the defects of the *Charrete* are quoted on pp. 147–8 of this study. They were taken from her article 'The Unity of Chrétien's Lancelot' in *Mélanges de linguistique et de littérature romanes offerts à Mario Roques* (Paris, 1950–1953), vol. II, p. 289.

5. See for example: K. Voretzsch, *Introduction to the Study of Old French Literature*, translated by F. M. du Mont (New York, 1931), pp. 292–3; J. Frappier, *Chrétien de Troyes*, pp. 132–4.

6. See Roques' edition of Chrétien de Troyes, *Le Chevalier de la charrete* (Paris, 1958), p. x. The same views are expressed in his article 'Pour l'interprétation du "Chevalier de la charrete" de Chrétien de Troyes', *Cahiers de Civilisation Médiévale* I (1958), p. 143.

7. F. D. Kelly, '*Sens*' and '*Conjointure*' in the '*Chevalier de la Charrette*' (The Hague, 1966).

8. These line references are those given by Kelly in the analysis of his Division B of the *Charrete* on p. 178 of '*Sens*' and '*Conjointure*'.

9. A point recognised by Frappier. See *Chrétien de Troyes*, p. 133.

10. For convenience, quotations from this treatise will be taken from J. J. Parry's translation, Andreas Capellanus, *The Art of Courtly Love* (New York, 1959). The original text can be consulted in E. Trojel's edition, Andreae Capellani regii Francorum De amore libri tres (Copenhagen, 1892).

11. See the *Art of Courtly Love*, pp. 59–61, 151–3.

12. See below, pp. 132–3, for a full discussion of this point.

13. For the interpretation of 'reison' as 'common sense' in this passage, see Appendix 2, pp. 190–2.

14. A point missed by Roques who claims that if Gauvain refuses to get into the cart 'ce n'est pas à cause de la honte qui s'y attache, mais seulement parce qu'il préfère raisonnablement un bon cheval à un mauvais tombereau' ('Pour l'interprétation du "Chevalier de la charrete" ', p. 151).

15. See for example Southward quoted on p. 147 of the present essay.

16. See for example Kelly, '*Sens*' and '*Conjointure*', p. 187: '. . . a reconsideration of Gawain's part in the *Charrete* shows that we can in fact attribute little *structural* significance to him . . .' Kelly continues: 'This is not to say that Chrétien introduces Gawain into the poem for no reason at all. He . . . provides contrast for Lancelot – but he is a contrast of more significance for the *sens* of the *Charrette* than for its structure'.

17. A rather different justification for the title of the romance is put forward by Roques in his discussion of the Queen's treatment of Lancelot. His argument suggests, however, that he has not fully appreciated the role of the cart incident in the *Charrete*. In his eyes, its main importance lies in being taken by Guenevere as a token of Lancelot's devotion which moves her to look more favourably on him:

> On peut noter surtout . . . que Guenièvre n'a fait aucune allusion du type de celle de la demoiselle hôtesse de Lancelot et de Gauvain. . . . N'est-ce pas qu'elle a compris que Lancelot n'a accepté cette honte que pour elle . . . Et on s'expliquerait bien aussi comment Guenièvre, accueillant un peu plus tard ouvertement Lancelot, ne lui parlera de la "charrete" que pour lui faire remarquer, par une taquinerie amusée, qu'il a eu une légère hésitation avant d'y sauter. Cela prouve au moins qu'elle a réfléchi à l'incident, et ne peut douter de l'amour qu'il atteste chez Lancelot, amour qui mérite d'être payé de quelque retour: nous sommes loin de l'indifférence au moins apparente du début.
>
> Ainsi le chevalier "honni" de presque tous pourra devenir le chevalier "aimé" de Guenièvre, et la suite fidèle de son service d'amour et de ses exploits amènera celle-ci à lui consentir la faveur de l'entretien secret à la

fenêtre: alors pourra jaillir l'étincelle de passion qui éclairera et enflammera l'âme de la reine elle-même. . . .

Cette interprétation pourrait rendre compte du titre, *Le Chevalier de la charrete*, et de la place qu'y tient ce véhicule infâmant . . . qui ne joue aucun rôle utile après les premières scènes . . . ('Pour l'interprétation du "Chevalier de la charrete" ', pp. 150–1).

18. Speaking of the tournament where Lancelot has proved to the Queen that 'he is indeed her *amis antiers*', these authors claim: 'Here the romance ends for Chrétien. . . . The close of the story is banal and adds nothing to its meaning. The real *Roman de la Charrete* had closed, not with the rescue of the Queen from her Otherworld abductor, but with her complete enthralment of Lancelot' (*Lancelot and Guenevere*, pp. 77–8).

19. D. W. Robertson, 'Some Medieval Literary Terminology with Special Reference to Chrétien de Troyes', *Studies in Philology* 48 (1951), p. 691.

20. Roques, 'Pour l'interprétation du "Chevalier de la charrete" ', pp. 149–50. He plainly overlooks vs 6846–53 which describe how the Queen restrains herself from welcoming Lancelot as she would choose until a more favourable occasion presents itself. Adler likewise finds it necessary to prove that 'though an adulteress, [Guenevere] can be shown to be *almost* justified'. See 'A Note on the Composition of Chrétien's "Charrette" ', *Modern Language Review* 45 (1950), pp. 35–7.

21. Frappier, *Chrétien de Troyes*, p. 132.

22. R. R. Bezzola, *Le sens de l'aventure et de l'amour*, p. 81.

23. *Chrétien de Troyes*, pp. 132–3.

24. See above, p. 111.

25. See above, pp. 116–7.

26. See above, p. 117.

27. See the accounts of 'Meleagant's Treachery' and of 'The Rescue of Lancelot' in his discussion of the plot of the *Charrete*, '*Sens*' and '*Conjointure*', pp. 144–6.

# The Structure of *Cligés*

THE structure of *Cligés* is a subject that has not received much attention so far. Chrétien himself announces at the beginning of the romance (vs 8–13) that it contains two stories: the hero's and his father's. For their part, the critics have mostly been content to follow Chrétien's lead and describe the work as bipartite – with the announcement of Cligés' birth marking the division between his father's story and his own:

> Chrétien . . . ne manque pas non plus, à la manière d'un Virgile au début de l'*Enéide*, de résumer son sujet et de préciser son plan, en signalant tout de suite sa division en deux parties: "je vais raconter", nous dit-il (vers 9–17) "l'histoire d'un jeune prince grec qui appartenait au lignage d'Arthur . . . mais avant que je vous dise rien de lui, vous m'entendrez parler de son père, des circonstances de sa vie et de son lignage. Vous saurez qu'il fut preux et de cœur fier, et que, pour acquérir prestige et renommée, il alla de Grèce en Angleterre qui s'appelait alors Bretagne." De fait, Chrétien a consacré un peu plus du tiers de son roman, exactement [2344] vers sur [6664], aux amours et au mariage des parents de Cligés avant d'aborder l'histoire dont ce dernier est le héros et Fénice l'héroïne.[1]

Apart from this, they have usually gone no further than summarising its contents.[2] The only person to embark on a more ambitious analysis seems to be Karl Voretzsch. In the brief outline of the romance found in his *Introduction to the Study of Old French Literature*, the story of Cligés proper is divided into five parts: a beginning, middle and end, and, in addition, two episodes which serve 'to retard the main story' – or, as Gaston Paris put it,[3] 'to pad it out':

> We have here – excepting the history of the hero's parents – a plot in five parts: the exposition [vs 2345–4192], the main or central action [vs 5059–6336], the conclusion [vs 6586–6664], and the two secondary episodes (the hero's sojourn in England [vs 4193–5058] – the discovery and flight of the lovers [vs 6337–6585]) inserted to retard the main story.[4]

In the circumstances, I feel it would be of interest to make a detailed investigation into the organisation of *Cligés*, and to see how it compares with that of Chrétien's other romances.

An examination of the plot of *Cligés* suggests that it is made up of eight episodes. Of these, four are structurally of very minor importance, whilst the others prove to be compound episodes containing elements which may themselves be of major structural importance.

*Episode 1 (vs 43–265)* is a minor component of 223 lines. It is an account of the departure from Greece of Prince Alexander, the hero's father, and it tells how he prevailed upon the emperor to let him go to Arthur's court to prove his mettle.

*Episode 2 (vs 266–2350)* is a very long one of 2085 lines which tells the story of Alexander's exploits at Arthur's court. It comprises four components:

*Episode 2a (vs 266–415)*. This is a very short one of a mere 150 lines. It describes Alexander's arrival at Arthur's court and the favourable reception he received there.

*Episode 2b (vs 416–1041)* is a medium sized component of 626 lines which tells how Alexander and Gauvain's sister, Soredamors, fell in love with one another during the visit the court paid to Brittany. A descriptive sequence of rhetorical as well as psychological interest, it portrays the lovers' reactions at their first meeting, and then the frustrations, inner conflicts and fantasies that beset them when Soredamors finds herself obliged to abandon her adolescent stand of being above love, and Alexander, inhibited by an over scrupulous diffidence from making his desires known, is driven to look for solace in reverie.

*Episode 2c (vs 1042–2199)*, a major component of 1158 lines, is an account of the campaign against Arthur's regent, Count Angres, and of the part Alexander played in it. It tells how Arthur returned to Britain on learning that the Count was attempting to usurp the throne; how Alexander and his companions persuaded the King to dub them so that they could take part in the campaign; how they proved their mettle in a preliminary skirmish outside Windsor castle, the rebel stronghold; how the fate of the prisoners they took in the skirmish drove the rebels to break out of the castle in a vain attempt to surprise the besieging host; and how Alexander pursued the Count into the castle to take him and his men prisoner, thus winning a gold cup and the right to ask for any boon – save the crown and the Queen – that Arthur had offered as a reward for seizing the rebel stronghold.

*Episode 2d (vs 2200–2350)* is a short component of only 151 lines which describes how Alexander was rewarded for his achievements by being given Soredamors' hand in marriage. It tells how he was too scrupulous to seek her hand until the Queen emboldened him to do so; how his request was readily granted, and how, in the fullness of time, Soredamors bore him a son whom they christened Cligés.

From the description of it that has been given here, it might well seem that Episode 2 is lacking in cohesion. It has, however, a unity that has been achieved by the skilful interweaving of the two themes which appear in it: the theme of Alexander's fortunes as a lover and that of his fortunes as a soldier. For the story of his love for Soredamors continues beyond Episode 2b and threads its way through the long account of his military exploits (Episode 2c) before it reaches its fulfilment in Episode 2d.

On the dubbing of Alexander, for example, the Queen sends him a shirt made by Soredamors, who has worked one of her golden hairs into the embroidery around the collar and cuffs. This is an occasion for Chrétien to comment on the pleasure it would have given both lovers to know that Alexander possessed something of Soredamors' (vs 1139–75).

Again, Alexander sends his prisoners to the Queen after his success in the preliminary skirmish with the rebels and pays a courtesy visit to her tent. This proves to be a chance for Chrétien to depict the timidity and the bashfulness of the lovers who eventually find themselves alone together. For his part, Alexander is too diffident to speak. As for Soredamors, who sees he is wearing her shirt and so has a topic she could discuss with him, she misses her chance to do so by hesitating too long over the correct way to address him (vs 1354–401).

At the end of the second day's fighting, Alexander pays a further visit to the Queen's tent. This time Chrétien seizes the opportunity to show how lovers can betray themselves to an observant eye. For now it is the Queen who notices that he is wearing Soredamors' shirt and the thought makes her smile. When asked the reason for her smile, she calls Soredamors to her to let her do the explaining, and the confusion of the lovers on finding themselves together is enough to make their secret known to Guenevere (vs 1535–80). Chrétien also uses this second visit as an occasion for portraying the reactions of a lover who finds himself in possession of a token of the beloved. He gives a full description of Alexander's behaviour on learning that his shirt contains one of Soredamors' golden hairs and concludes with the dry, but not unkindly comment: 'bien fet Amors d'un sage fol, / quant cil fet joie d'un chevol' (vs 1581–624).

Finally, the two themes of Alexander's fortunes in love and war come together and fuse when his successes in the campaign against Count Angres give him the right to ask for Soredamors' hand in marriage (vs 2180–99).

*Episode 3* (*vs 2351–2556*), a short component of 206 lines, is an account of Alexander's return to Constantinople to claim his inheritance. It tells how the embassy sent to recall him to Greece on his father's death was shipwrecked; how the sole survivor contrived to get his younger brother, Alis, crowned in his stead; how Alexander set off to claim his throne on hearing this news, and how it was decided between the brothers that Alexander should wield the power, but Alis retain the title of Emperor and the crown – on condition that he forswore marriage and adopted Cligés as his heir.

*Episode 4* (*vs 2557–4169*) is a very long one of 1613 lines, and is the story of the marriage of Alis to Fénice, the daughter of the Emperor of Germany. It contains four components:

*Episode 4a* (*2557–2661*), a very minor component of 105 lines, is an account of Alis' decision to marry the German princess. It tells how he was persuaded, after his brother's death, to break his oath and take a wife; how it was agreed that he should marry Fénice although she had already been promised to the Duke of Saxony; and how he set off for

Germany with sufficient men to thwart any attempt of the Duke's to capture his bride.

*Episode 4b (vs 2662–2924)* is a short episode of 263 lines describing how Cligés and Fénice fell in love. A passage of chiefly rhetorical and psychological interest, it tells how they were immediately attracted to one another when the Greek and German courts met at Cologne; and how Fénice's attraction to Cligés was confirmed by the prowess he displayed in jousting against the envoy sent by the Duke of Saxony to press his claim to Fénice.

*Episode 4c (vs 2925–3330)*, a somewhat longer component of 406 lines, is an account of the measures taken to protect Fénice against the unwelcome attentions of her husband. It tells how Fénice came to inform her nurse, Thessala, of her distress at having to marry the uncle of the man she loved; how Thessala prepared a potion that would save her from the attentions of Alis; how it was handed to Alis by Cligés on the night of the wedding, and how, on that and on every subsequent night, it caused Alis to dream that he had successfully made love to his wife.

*Episode 4d (vs 3331–4169)* is a major component of 839 lines. It is an account of Cligés' success in foiling the attempts made by the Duke of Saxony to carry off Fénice. It tells how Cligés acquitted himself when the Greek party was ambushed by the Saxons on the journey back to Constantinople; how he rescued Fénice when the Duke's men succeeded in abducting her, and how he finally vindicated his uncle's claim to Fénice by defeating the Duke himself in single combat.

Like Episode 2, Episode 4 has a cohesion that is not apparent from an analysis of its various components.

In the case of Episodes 4b and 4c, cohesion is ensured by the causal links that connect them. Given Thessala's magical powers, the deception of Alis follows naturally enough on Fénice's enthralment by his nephew; whilst the conversation that leads to the brewing of the potion arises out of the changes Thessala sees in Fénice and which have been brought about by the prospect of having to marry Alis instead of Cligés (vs 2947–76).

For the most part, however, cohesion is achieved in Episode 4, as in Episode 2, by the interweaving of its two narrative themes: the dispute between Alis and the Duke of Saxony over the possession of Fénice, and the love of Fénice and Cligés. In Episode 4b, for example, the arrival of a Saxon at Cologne with an ultimatum from his master brings the theme of the political rivalry into the account of the mutual enthralment of the lovers (vs 2819–37). The two themes then coalesce, temporarily, when the envoy challenges Cligés to joust (vs 2838–40). For Cligés eagerly accepts the challenge in his desire to show to advantage in his lady's eyes (vs 2874–9), whilst she goes to watch the jousting equally eagerly in her desire to see her partiality for the handsome stranger justified (vs 2851–73). In its turn, the love theme is worked into Episode 4d which is mainly concerned with the struggle between the Greeks and the Saxons for the possession of Fénice. Thus, in describing the attempt to abduct Fénice, Chrétien shows how love spurs Cligés on to her rescue (vs 3654–67; 3707–18), and explains how Fénice is torn between her wish that it should be Cligés who is acquitting himself so gloriously on her behalf and the hope that he is not the man who is putting his life in such jeopardy (vs 3745–51). Later, the silence that falls over the lovers as they ride back to join the Greeks proves to be an occasion for Chrétien to discourse at length on the importance of fear in love and to justify the timidity of Cligés (vs 3773–860) – though he hastens to add that his hero would have made his feelings known had he not had scruples about making advances to his uncle's wife (vs 3861–8). The love theme appears once again in Episode 4d when Cligés' feelings for Fénice prove to be the deciding factor in his duel with the Duke. It is Fénice's distress on seeing her lover felled to the ground (vs 4054–73) which rallies him and gives him the strength that will enable him to prevail against his opponent:

> Clygés, quant Fenice cria,
> l'oï molt bien et antendi;
> sa voiz force et cuer li randi;
> si resaut sus isnelemant,
> et vint au duc irieemant,
> si le requiert et envaïst,
> que li dus toz s'an esbaïst;
> car plus le trueve bateillant,
> fort, et legier, et conbatant,
> que il n'avoit fet, ce li sanble,
> quant il vindrent premiers ansanble.    (vs 4074–84)

*Episode 5 (vs 4170–5007)* is a major component of 838 lines. It describes the visit Cligés paid to Arthur's court, and comprises three components which cover the various stages of the visit:

*Episode 5a (vs 4170–4243)* is a very minor component of 74 lines which tells how Cligés decided not to return to Constantinople with the rest of the Greeks, but to go to Britain, as his father had once suggested, to prove himself against Arthur's knights.

*Episode 5b (vs 4244–4529)*, a minor component of 286 lines, is a passage of rhetorical and psychological interest. It describes the leave-taking of the lovers and the reflections this later evokes in Fénice as she sits in lonely splendour in Constantinople.

*Episode 5c (vs 4530–5007)*, a rather longer component of 478 lines, is an account of Cligés' exploits in Britain. It tells how he proved his mettle against all Arthur's knights in the three-day tournament at Wallingford, and how he was welcomed by Arthur and Gauvain when he eventually made himself known to them.

*Episode 6 (vs 5008–5096)* is a very minor component of 89 lines. It is the account of Cligés' return to Greece. It tells how he was driven back to Constantinople when the strain of separation from Fénice proved unendurable; and how he was welcomed there by Alis and Fénice.

*Episode 7 (vs 5097–6551)*. This is a very long episode of 1455 lines and is the story of the elopement of the lovers. It comprises two components which cover the two phases of the elopement:

*Episode 7a (vs 5097–6258)* is a major component of 1162 lines. It describes the removal of Fénice from the court to a secret hideout outside Constantinople. It tells how the lovers eventually came to confess their love to one another; how Fénice refused to incur the odium of an elopement; and how it was agreed, with the co-operation of Thessala and of Cligés' artificer, Jean, that she should sham dead and be removed from her tomb to a secret apartment in a tower constructed by Jean. The rest of the episode then relates how this plan was put into action; how it nearly miscarried when three physicians arrived at the court and almost killed Fénice in their attempts to force her to confess that she was shamming dead; how she was rescued in time by the ladies of the court; how she was duly buried in the tomb specially prepared by Jean, and then removed to the tower where the lovers were united at last in a life of bliss.

*Episode 7b (vs 6259–6551)* is a short one of 293 lines, and is an account of the discovery and flight of the lovers. It tells how Fénice eventually tired of being confined; how her desire for an orchard was met by Jean, and how the lovers were discovered there one day and denounced to Alis; how Alis succeeded in capturing Jean – from whom he learnt how he had been duped – but failed to catch Fénice and Cligés who made good their escape with Thessala's aid.

*Episode 8 (vs 6552–6664)*, a very minor component of 113 lines describes the lovers' triumphant return to Greece. It tells how Cligés prepared to invade Greece and reclaim his throne with Arthur's help; how an embassy arrived in time to inform him of Alis' death – from sheer mortification – and how he and Fénice returned to Constantinople to be married and crowned Emperor and Empress of Greece.

When one comes to examine relationships between its eight episodes, *Cligés* proves to be structurally quadripartite with four main components.

i. The first three episodes form a connected series where Episode 1 (Alexander's departure from Greece) and Episode 3 (his return to Greece) balance one another as the introduction and conclusion to the account of his exploits in Britain. As the history of Alexander, the three episodes together constitute Section I of *Cligés*, its first main structural division.

ii. Episodes 4 and 5 (the marriage of Alis and Fénice, and Cligés' visit to Britain), which are both components of major structural importance, from Sections II and III of the romance respectively.

iii. The last three episodes form a connected series. Episode 6, which explains how love finally drove Cligés back to Greece, provides a natural introduction to the story of the lovers' elopement, whilst Episode 8 supplies it with its 'happy ending'. As the story of the lovers' union, the three episodes constitute Section IV of *Cligés*, its last main structural division.

If *Cligés* is structurally quadripartite, thematically it is, of course, bipartite – just as we were warned to expect by the prologue.

i. Section I obviously forms a self-contained whole. Like the account of the winning of Enide or of Laudine, the history of Alexander could exist perfectly well as an independent tale in its own right.

ii. Equally obviously, Sections II, III and IV belong together as parts of a greater whole. Though self-contained in varying degrees, they only fully make sense when seen as the three phases in the story of Fénice and Cligés.

Section II clearly represents the preliminary stage in that story. By the time Alis leaves Germany with his bride, she and Cligés have fallen in love (vs 2667–924), the steps have been taken to render his marriage null and void (vs 2925–3332) and the stage is set for Cligés to make a move to remedy the position in which he finds himself. In addition, we have been given a clear idea of the fiercely uncompromising idealism of Fénice which prepares us for the stand she takes later in the story. Her conversation with Thessala in Episode 4c reveals that she will not countenance adultery as a solution for an unhappy marriage. Rather than become a second Iseut, indulging in sexual relations with two men, she would, one gathers, sacrifice her love for Cligés:

> "... l'empereres me marie,
> don je sui iriee et dolante,
> por ce que cil qui m'atalante
> est niés celui que prendre doi.
> *Et se cil a joie de moi,*
> *donc ai ge la moie perdue,*
> *ne je n'i ai nule atandue.*
> Mialz voldroie estre desmanbree
> que de nos deus fust remanbree
> l'amors d'Ysolt et de Tristan,
>
> .     .     .     .     .
>
> Ja ne m'i porroie acorder
> a la vie qu'Isolz mena.
> Amors en li trop vilena,
> que ses cuers fu a un entiers,
> et ses cors fu a deus rentiers.
> Ensi tote sa vie usa
> n'onques les deus ne refusa.
>
> .     .     .     .     .
>
> *Ja mes cors n'iert voir garçoniers,*
> *n'il n'i avra deus parçoniers.*
> Qui a le cuer, cil a le cors,
> toz les autres an met defors.
> Mes ce ne puis je pas savoir
> comant puisse le cors avoir
> cil a cui mes cuers s'abandone
> quant mes peres autrui me done,
> ne je ne li os contredire.

> *Et quant il est de mon cors sire,*
> *s'il an fet chose que ne vuelle,*
> *n'est pas droiz c'un autre i acuelle."*    (vs 3098–132)

After this, the sacrifice that Fénice is prepared to make and the risks she is ready to run in order to safeguard her reputation in vs 5199–211 and vs 5249–301 come as no surprise.

Turning now to Section III, it might seem from some critics that its chief purpose is to 'retard' the lovers' story.[5] In point of fact, Cligés' visit to Britain represents an intermediary phase in it: a first, unsuccessful attempt on Cligés' part to extricate himself from an intolerable situation. This one realises as soon as the visit is viewed in the light of what comes before and after it. One then sees that it is motivated, not so much by Cligés' desire to obey his father's injunctions to prove himself against Arthur's knights (which is what he alleges in vs 4170–221 and vs 4269–75), as by the need to remove himself from the temptation to betray Alis. For Cligés' embarrassment at finding himself so attracted to his uncle's wife was revealed in the previous episode – when Chrétien stated that this is what kept him from declaring his love to Fénice after rescuing her from the Saxons:

> Donc ne fausse ne mesprant mie
> Cligés, s'il redote s'amie.
> Mes por ce ne leissast il pas
> qu'il ne l'eüst eneslepas
> d'amors aresniee et requise,
> comant que la chose an fust prise,
> s'ele ne fust fame son oncle.
> Por ce sa plaie li reoncle,
> et plus li grieve et plus li dialt,
> qu'il n'ose dire ce qu'il vialt.    (vs 3859–68)

Again, the explanation given in the following episode (6) for Cligés return to Greece strongly suggests that his main reason for going to Britain had been to put Fénice out of his mind:

> . . . l'amor don il est plaiez
> ne li aliege n'asoage;
> la volanté de son corage
> toz jorz en un panser le tient:
> de Fenice li resovient
> qui loing de lui se retravaille.
> Talanz li prant que il s'an aille,
> car trop a fet grant consirree
> de veoir la plus desirree
> c'onques nus puisse desirrer.
> ne s'an voldra plus consirrer.
> De raler an Grece s'atorne,
> congié a pris, si s'an retorne.    (vs 5014–26)

When Section III is seen in its context, it seems more appropriate, in fact, to define it as the flight from Fénice or as the separation of the lovers.

Once it is viewed in this light, the long description of their leave-taking and of Fénice's reactions to it acquires a new relevance.

Section IV represents the final stage in the lovers' story: the resolution of their problems, first by Fénice's fake death – a stratagem which safeguards their reputation for the time being – and then by the open elopement Fénice had sought to avoid, but which precipitates the 'happy ending' of their affairs.

At first, one might well be tempted to think that this section of the romance could stand, like the first, as an independent tale. On second thoughts, one realises that it has to be seen in context if it is to be understood as Chrétien intended his readers to understand it. Taken by itself, the account of the union of Fénice and Cligés might well appear to be the story of a husband hoodwinked by an unscrupulous wife and an ungrateful nephew. This indeed is how it is presented in the following passage and its accompanying footnote:

> La transformation même que Chrétien a fait subir au thème [de la "fausse morte"], en appelant la sympathie sur les amants, n'a pas été effectuée avec beaucoup d'art. *Les relations de Cligés avec Alis*[2] *sont louches:* Cligés accepte l'amitié de son oncle, ses faveurs et ses riches présents; il ne proteste pas contre son mariage et ne vient que longtemps après, quand il a enlevé Fénice, dénoncer ce mariage à Arthur comme un manquement de foi. Les sentiments de Fénice . . . ne sont pas non plus sans incohérence: l'amour soudain dont elle se prend pour un inconnu, uniquement à cause de sa beauté, n'est pas fort touchant, *et ses relations avec son mari, qui n'a aucun tort envers elle, manquent de loyauté.*
>
> [2] Le caractère d'Alis est tracé d'une façon tres incertaine, et je ne puis trouver avec M. Förster (grande éd., p. xvii) que "du commencement à la fin il possède notre complet mépris": sauf son manque de foi (dû à de mauvais conseils), il est peint de couleurs très favorables, bon, généreux, aimant tendrement et sa femme et son neveu; à la fin seulement, quand il apprend les tromperies dont il a été victime, il se montre violent et vindicatif.[6]

Certainly, the warmth with which Alis receives his nephew on his return to Greece gives colour to the criticism of Cligés voiced here:

> . . . ses oncles li abandone
> tot quanqu'il a, fors la corone;
> bien vialt qu'il praingne a son pleisir
> quanqu'il voldra por lui servir,
> ou soit d'argent, ou de tresor.  (vs 5083–7)

In the same way, Alis' distress at Fénice's illness and death (vs 5627–30, 5686–94) lends support to the description of him as an affectionate husband "qui n'a aucun tort envers elle". But when Section IV of *Cligés* is set against the sections which precede it, it emerges clearly enough as the story of a wrong redressed. From the time of their first meeting (vs 2667–946) the lovers are presented as an ideal couple, a second Erec and Enide, perfectly matched in every respect – in beauty, breeding, rank and worth.

The portrait of Cligés (vs 2721–52) shows him to be endowed with every physical, moral and social virtue ('. . . an lui ot / san et biauté, largesce et force' vs 2746–7). And particular pains are taken to emphasise Fénice's satisfaction on finding her affections so worthily bestowed:

> . . . . . . par tote la cité
> an sevent tuit la verité,
> et le suen non, et le son pere,
> et le covant que l'emperere
> li avoit fet et otroié;
> s'est ja tant dit et puepleié
> que neïs cele dire l'ot
> qui an son cuer grant joie en ot,
> por ce c'or ne puet ele mie
> dire qu'Amors l'ait eschernie,
> ne de rien ne se puet clamer;
> car le plus bel li fet amer,
> le plus cortois et le plus preu
> que l'en poïst trover nul leu.           (vs 2933–46)

In the circumstances, Alis' marriage is presented as a further, though unwitting, usurpation of his nephew's place. Above all, it is shown as an outrage understandably resented by his wife – provided one is prepared to recognise that forcing a woman into intimacy with a man she does not want is a form of rape, even though the Church may give its sanction and its blessing.[7] Accordingly, the union of Fénice and Cligés does not appear as the triumph of low cunning over indulgent benevolence. It is made to seem a very satisfactory righting of a wrong – except of course to the more zealous defenders of the rights of husbands. Where they are concerned, it is entirely useless for Chrétien to claim that Love acted in a way entirely worthy of himself in bringing such a couple together:

> Certes, de rien ne s'avilla
> Amors, quant il les mist ansanble.           (vs 6252–3)

In their eyes, Cligés can only be the nephew who betrays his uncle, and Fénice the woman who violates the most sacred laws of marriage:

> Il y a quelque chose de choquant à voir Fénice, au sortir de l'église où elle a juré devant Dieu fidélité à son mari, entrer avec ce mari, dont elle a trouvé moyen de ne pas être la femme, dans le lit conjugal que viennent de "signer et bénir" des évêques et des abbés.[8]
>
> Si Cligés et Tristan sont différents dans leur comportement, il n'en reste pas moins que tous deux finissent par commettre un péché (du point de vue de la loi et de l'Église) ils enlèvent la femme au mari. . . .
>
> .   .   .   .   .   .   .
>
> Fondamentalement . . . la situation de Fénice et d'Iseut est identique. . . . Du point de vue chrétien, social et juridique, Fénice est la femme d'Alis, et peu importe qu'elle ait vécu conjugalement avec lui ou non. En se faisant passer

pour "morte", pour vivre avec Cligès, elle n'a pas cessé (juridiquement et religieusement) d'être la femme d'Alis. Elle commet un adultère.[9]

To complete this survey of the organisation of *Cligés*, it only remains now to see how its two main thematic components are linked together.

It has been claimed that *Cligés* 'exhibits a manifest want of unity' on the grounds that, where Tristan's whole life 'is determined by the tragical fate of Rivalin and Blanchefleur . . . there is no such relation between the stories of Cligés and his parents'.[10] This criticism of Chrétien's romance, however, totally overlooks the fact that the histories of Alexander and Cligés happen to be linked by a common narrative theme which arises in the one and continues through the other. The theme in question is the one that critics of *Cligés* mostly tend to play down, namely, his dispossession by Alis.[11] This issue first arises in the concluding episode of Alexander's story (Episode 3) which opens with Alis being crowned Emperor in his stead, and closes with the pact that leaves Alis with the title of Emperor, but guarantees the succession for Cligés:

> Alys par un suen conestable
> mande Alixandre qu'a lui veigne
> et tote la terre mainteigne,
> mes que tant li face d'enor
> qu'il lest le non d'empereor
> et la corone avoec li lest;
> einsi puet estre, se lui plest,
> entr'aus deus la chose bien feite.
>
> .   .   .   .   .   .
>
> Mes Alixandre ne plest mie,
> quant il ot la parole oïe
> que ses freres ait la corone,
> se sa fïance ne li done
> que ja fame n'esposera,
> mes aprés lui Cligés sera
> de Costantinoble emperere.
> Ensi sont acordé li frere.
> Alixandres li eschevist,
> et cil li otroie et plevist
> que ja en trestot son aage
> n'avra fame par mariage.                    (vs 2518–42)

Alis' dispossession of his nephew is carried a stage further at the beginning of the second part of the romance. For the starting point of Cligés' own story is his uncle's decision to take a wife, although this is a flagrant violation of his oath – a crime that is minimised by the defenders of Alis who speak only of his unremitting benevolence towards Cligés:[12]

> . . . l'empereres s'est tenuz
> lonc tans aprés de fame prandre,
> car a leauté voloit tandre;
> mes il n'a cort an tot le monde

> qui de mauvés consoil soit monde.
> Par le mauvés consoil qu'il croient
> li baron sovant se desvoient,
> si que leauté ne maintienent.
> Sovant a l'empereor vienent
> si home qui consoil li donent;
> de prandre fame le semonent,
> si li enortent et anpressent,
> et chascun jor tant l'en apressent
> que par lor grant engresseté
> l'ont de sa fïance gité,
> et lor voloir lor acreante.                    (vs 2592–607)

Once Cligés meets Fénice, the theme of his dispossession coalesces with the theme of their love – as is obvious from the fact that in defrauding Alis of his conjugal rights, Fénice's intention is as much to safeguard her lover's inheritance as to avoid any commerce with a man she does not love:

> ". . . ce ne puis je pas savoir
> comant puisse le cors avoir
> cil a cui mes cuers s'abandone,
> quant mes peres autrui me done,
> ne je ne li os contredire.
>         .   .   .   .
> Mes se vos tant savïez d'art
> que ja cil an moi n'eüst part
> cui je sui donee et plevie,
> molt m'avrïez an gré servie.
> Mestre, car i metez antante
> que cil sa fïance ne mante
> qui au pere Clygés plevi,
> si com il meïsme eschevi,
> que ja n'avroit fame esposee.
> Sa fïance en iert reüsee,
> car adés m'espousera il.
> Mes je n'ai pas Cligés si vil
> que mialz ne vuelle estre anterree
> que ja par moi perde danree
> de l'enor qui soe doit estre.
> Ja de moi ne puisse anfes nestre
> par cui il soit desheritez.
> Mestre, or vos an entremetez,
> por ce que toz jorz vostre soie."          (vs 3125–55)

In the end, the two themes of Cligés' dispossession and of his love for Fénice are brought to a simultaneous conclusion when he makes ready with Arthur to assert his right to the throne and to Fénice (vs 6552–85), only to learn that Alis has died in the meanwhile. So that the romance closes with the marriage and the joint coronation of the lovers:

> Ja devoient la mer passer,
> quant de Grece vindrent message

qui respitierent le passage,
et le roi et ses genz retindrent.

. . . . .

Li message haut home estoient
de Grece, qui Cligés queroient.

. . . . .

Si li ont dit: "Dex vos saut, sire,
de par toz ces de vostre empire.
Grece vos est abandonee
et Costantinoble donee
por le droit que vos i avez.
Morz est (mes vos ne le savez)
vostre oncles del duel que il ot,
por ce que trouver ne vos pot.

. . . . .

Biax sire, or vos an revenez,
car tuit vostre baron vos mandent,
molt vos desirrent et demandent,
empereor vos voelent feire."

. . . . .

Et Cligés se haste et atorne,
qu'an Grece s'en vialt retorner,
n'a cure de plus sejorner.
Atornez s'est, congié a pris
au roi et a toz ses amis;
Fenice an mainne, si s'en vont,
ne finent tant qu'an Grece sont,
et a grant joie le reçurent,
si con lor seignor feire durent,
et s'amie a fame li donent,
endeus ansanble les coronent.          (vs 6586–632)

From the discussion of the theme which links its two main thematic components, it is clear that, in the last analysis, *Cligés* is the story of a man who eventually gains possession of the kingdom and the wife that his uncle has usurped and that should by rights be his. As such, the romance proves to be something of a *tour de force*. For Chrétien has succeeded here in producing a variant of the Tristan–Mark–Iseut situation that has nothing to offend courtly propriety – always excepting his denunciation of adultery (as an indulging in sexual relations with two partners rather than a breaking of marriage vows). On the one hand, it avoids the tragedy of the Tristan story since the uncle is manifestly in the wrong both as regards his nephew and his wife. On the other hand, it is saved from the gross cynicism of the *fabliaux* by the fierce purity of the heroine. Although one shares Gaston Paris' preference for the original Tristan legend, it has to be admitted that, by courtly standards, *Cligés* was a satisfactory reworking of that old, barbaric tale.

Their common narrative theme is not the only link between the two parts of *Cligés*. The work also derives a very definite unity from being a demonstration of Chrétien's virtuosity in presenting themes with which his public were thoroughly familiar in a new and unexpected guise. One is first aware of this aspect of *Cligés* in the passages which describe the reactions of the various lovers. In many cases, these are of rhetorical rather than psychological interest. Their main function is not to provide a new insight into the workings of the human heart, but to display Chrétien's skill in elaborating on Ovidian motifs – such as the migrant heart or the nature of love's wounds – which had already become the vogue with *Eneas*.[13] The most obvious example of this is Alexander's attempt to explain how Love's arrows can harm the heart but leave the eyes unscathed (vs 684–700). The conceit of the inward wound that has no outward trace had already been used by Eneas in complaining of the harm done him by the arrow that brought Lavinia's message:

> "La saiete qui trete fu
> m'a malemant el cors feru.
> – Tu manz, molt cheï loing de toi.
> – Ele aportot ma mort o soi,
> angoisosemant me navra.
> – Ne sez que diz, ne te tocha.
> – Non voir, cop ne plaie n'i pert,
> mais li brievez qui antor ert
> m'a molt navré dedanz le cors.
> – Li cuirs est toz sains de defors;
> li briés coment? – Ja me mostra
> ce que Lavine me manda.
> – Donc n'iés tu autremant navré
> se del brief non qui t'a mostré
> que Lavine te vialt amer?"
>
> (*Eneas*, edited by J. J. Salverda de Grave, vs 8965–79)

When Chrétien's hero comes to take up the conceit of the arrows that bring pain only to the heart, he justifies it first in terms of the current psycho-physiological theories,[14] interpreting the arrows as the visual images the eyes reveal to the heart as the principle of perception and desire:

> "A l'uel ne m'a il rien grevé,
> mes au cuer me grieve formant.
> Or me di donc reison comant
> li darz est par mi l'uel passez,
> qu'il n'an est bleciez ne quassez.
> Se li darz parmi l'uel i antre,
> li cuers por coi s'an dialt el vantre,
> que li ialz ausi ne s'an dialt,
> qui le premier cop an requialt?
> De ce sai ge bien reison randre:
> li ialz n'a soin de rien antandre,
> ne rien ne puet feire a nul fuer,
> mes c'est li mereors au cuer,
> et par ce mireor trespasse,
> si qu'il ne blesce ne ne quasse,

le san don li cuers est espris.

. . . . .

726 ... es ialz se fiert la luiserne
ou li cuers se remire, et voit
l'uevre de fors, quex qu'ele soit;
si voit maintes oevres diverses,
les unes verz, les autres perses,
l'une vermoille, et l'autre bloe,
l'une blasme, et l'autre loe,
l'une tient vil, et l'autre chiere.
Mes tiex li mostre bele chiere
el mireor, quant il l'esgarde,
qui le traïst, s'il ne s'i garde."                    (vs 692–736)

At this point Alexander proceeds to denounce his own eyes for deceiving his heart and leading it to play traitor to him. Then, in vs 762–852, he employs himself in interpreting the dart that has struck him in terms of his lady-love and her beauty. ('Or vos reparlerai del dart / qui m'est comandez et bailliez, / comant il est fez et tailliez'). For Alexander this is an opportunity to dwell – very chastely – on the charms of Soredamors. For Chrétien, it is an opportunity to produce a variant of the stock description of female beauty (which we meet in its standard form in the description of Enide, *Erec* vs 411–41):

"La floiche et li penon ansanble
sont si pres, qui bien les ravise,
que il n'i a c'une devise
ausi con d'une greve estroite;
mes ele est si polie et droite
qu'an la rote sanz demander
n'a rien qui face a amander.
Li penon sont si coloré
con s'il estoient tuit doré,
mes doreüre n'i fet rien,
car li penon, ce savez bien,
estoient plus luisant ancores.
Li penon sont les treces sores
que je vi l'autre jor an mer,
c'est li darz qui me fet amer.
Dex, con tres precïeus avoir!
Qui tel tresor porroit avoir,
por qu'avroit an tote sa vie
de nule autre richesce anvie?

. . . . .

Et quant ces deus choses en pris
(qui porroit esligier le pris
de ce?) que vaut li remenanz,
qui tant est biax et avenanz,
et tant boens, et tant precïeus,
que desirranz et anvïeus
sui ancor de moi remirer
el front que Dex a fet tant cler
que nule rien n'i feroit glace,

ne esmeraude, ne topace?
Mes an tot ce n'a riens a dire,
qui la clarté des ialz remire;
car a toz ces qui les esgardent
sanblent deus chandoiles qui ardent
Et qui a boche si delivre,
qui la face poïst descrivre,
le nes bien fet, et le cler vis,

. . . . . .
et de la bochete riant
que Dex fist tele a esciant,
por ce que nus ne la veïst
qui ne cuidast qu'ele reïst?

. . . . .
825    Tant a a dire et a retraire
an chascune chose a portraire,
et el manton, et es oroilles,
qu'il ne seroit pas granz mervoilles,
se aucune chose i trespas.
De la boche ne di ge pas
que vers li ne soit cristax trobles;
li cors est plus blans quatre dobles;
plus clere d'ivoire est la trece.
Tant com il a des la chevece
jusqu'au fermail d'antroverture,
vi del piz nu sanz coverture
plus blanc que n'est la nois negiee.
Bien fust ma dolors alegiee,
se tot le dart veü eüsse.
Molt volantiers, se je seüsse,
deïsse quex an est la floiche:

. . . . .
Ne m'an mostra Amors adons
fors que la coche et les penons,
car la fleche ert el coivre mise:
c'est li bliauz et la chemise,
don la pucele estoit vestue.
Par foi, c'est li max qui me tue,
ce est li darz, ce est li rais,
don trop vilainnemant m'irais."          (vs 770–852)

To a modern reader, Alexander's musings seem distinctly tedious. But one can see that they might have been rather more to the taste of a public used to gauging the skill of its 'singers of tales' by their originality in handling stock motifs.

The demonstration of Chrétien's virtuosity in ringing the changes on stock themes and situations is by no means restricted to the 'Ovidian' passages in *Cligés*. On reading the romance one realises that it is not just a general restatement of the Tristan situation, but that, in minor as in major matters, it is a systematic transposition of the whole Tristan story – and more particularly of Thomas' version of it[15] – episode by episode and theme by theme.

On comparing the first part of Chrétien's work with Thomas',[16] one finds that the visit Alexander pays to Arthur's court is a faithful echo of the one Tristan's father, Rivalen, pays to Mark's (Bédier, pp. 4–25). The motive behind the two visits is much the same; both men meet with a gracious reception from their host; both distinguish themselves in the service of their master; and both eventually return to their native-land to safeguard their interests, Rivalen to repel an invader and Alexander to claim the throne from the brother who has usurped his place. Finally, both heroes are alike in falling in love during their sojourn abroad. But here the similarities end. Where the love of Rivalen and Mark's sister, Blanchefleur, takes a tragic turn, so that their son is born in pain and sorrow, the love of Alexander and Soredamors follows a happier course, and the birth of their son is a joyous, and more decorously timed event. As regards the use Chrétien makes in Alexander's story of individual motifs from *Tristan*, one finds that: (a) the play on the words la mer, *l'amer* (love) and *l'amer* (the tang of the sea air) which Iseut uses in trying to make her feelings known to Tristan (Bédier, p. 146) is worked into the explanation that Chrétien gives for Guenevere's failure to realise what is happening to Alexander and Soredamors aboard the royal barge; (b) the golden hair which leads in the more primitive versions of the Tristan story to the quest for Iseut (Bédier, p. 110) has become the golden hair threaded through the collar of Alexander's shirt; (c) the laugh that arouses the suspicions of Tristan's brother-in-law (Bédier, pp. 323–5) reappears as the smile which leads Alexander to discover who made his shirt; (d) the advice Roald gives Rivalen on the desirability of marrying Blanchefleur (Bédier, p. 22) has become the counsel Guenevere gives her protégé in very different circumstances. Indeed her warnings seem to refer directly to the unhappiness caused by Rivalen's failure to avow his love for Mark's sister (Bédier, pp. 16–7, 19–20).

As for the second part of *Cligés*, this, as we have seen, is a complete transmogrification of Tristan's story. The lovers have no cause for guilt or shame, since Alis is squarely in the wrong, whilst they, having had no potion to numb their self-respect, are at all times mindful of what is owing to their position. As regards the fortunes of individual themes and motifs in the story of Cligés, one finds that: (a) the various descriptions Thomas gives of Tristan and his accomplishments (Bédier, pp. 28–9, 34, 43–7, 51–4) are echoed in the portrait Chrétien paints of his hero; (b) the tournament at which Rivalen completes the conquest of Blanchefleur (Bédier, pp. 9–14) reappears as the joust which confirms Fénice in her love for Cligés. In both cases the hero wins the admiration and arouses the curiosity of the spectators; in both cases, there is a brief encounter between the lovers as he rides from the field; (c) the potion Iseut's mother brews to ensure the happiness of her daughter with Mark has become the potion that is to save Fénice from Alis. As in Mark's case, it is handed to Alis by his nephew on the night of the wedding, with results very similar to those obtained by the substitution of Bringvain for Iseut (Bédier, pp. 156–7); (d) Tristan's duel with the Morholt (Bédier, pp. 71–91) is represented by the duel between Cligés and the Duke of Saxony. In both cases, the hero takes the field against a seasoned warrior; in both cases he is a mere stripling, freshly dubbed for the occasion; in both cases he undertakes the duel on behalf of his uncle, but against that uncle's will. At the same time, the duel between Cligés and the Duke is a transposition of Tristan's fight with the dragon, which was also undertaken in order to secure a bride for his uncle; (e) Rivalen's perplexity over the meaning of Blanchefleur's words to him after the tournament (Bédier, pp. 15–6) reappears as Fénice's musings over Cligés' parting words to her; (f) the life in the forest of Morrois has been transmogrified as the idyllic existence of the lovers in Jean's tower, complete with luxuries and facilities unobtainable even in the *fossure a la gent amant* of Thomas' tale – though they may well have been provided in the *salle aux images* that Tristan's tame giant constructs for him there (Bédier, pp. 304–6, 309–13); (g) Mark's discovery of the lovers in the forest has become the surprising of Fénice and Cligés in their orchard, where a bower, skilfully fashioned from the boughs of a living tree and offering complete protection against the sun, replaces Tristan's inadequate shelter. The glove that wakens Iseut has become the pear that falls on Fénice, and the sword which separates the sleeping lovers and convinces Mark of their innocence reappears as the sword that Cligés uses to good effect against the intruder who disturbs his slumbers; (h) the lovers fleeing from a Mark all too disposed to receive them back into favour are now the lovers flying, with good reason, from the wrath of Alis; and finally, (i) the death of the lovers from pain and grief has been transposed as the death of Alis from sheer mortification.

That *Cligés* is a systematic transposition of *Tristan* has long been known.[17] It has long been recognised that it was intended to be 'une oeuvre de controverse et d'émulation littéraire'.[18] What has not, perhaps, been seen is that it is as an exhibition piece, as a virtuoso performance in presenting the familiar in an unfamiliar guise, that *Cligés* acquires an additional unity – a unity that could well justify its being subtitled 'a metamorphosis of *Tristan*'.

The most interesting point to emerge from this investigation into the structure of *Cligés* is that it is something of an exception among Chrétien's romances.

Where *Erec*, *Yvain*, and the *Charrete* are found to contain three main structural components, *Cligés* proves to be structurally quadripartite. As one can see from the accompanying diagram, its second narrative element consists of two components of equal size joined by one of half their length:

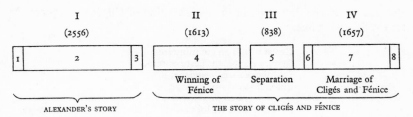

From one point of view, however, it might be claimed that *Cligés* is merely a variant of the tripartite pattern that characterises Chrétien's other works. For the purposes of public narration, a reading of Section III could well be combined with a reading of either Section II or Section IV. In both cases this would give an instalment of around 2400 lines, which seems to be what Chrétien envisaged as a session of average length for his narrators.

A second distinctive feature in *Cligés* is the way its main sections dovetail into one another. Where the breaks between such components are usually clearly marked in the other romances, it is difficult in *Cligés* to see exactly where one ends and the other begins.

(a) Section I has been shown here as ending at vs 2556, which marks the settlement between the dispute between the brothers. But one might well argue that Alexander's story is brought to a close at vs 2585 with Soredamor's death (following on his own). On the other hand, I cannot accept the prevailing view (illustrated in the following quotation) that Alexander's story ends with the birth of his son, and that the account of his return to Greece (my Episode 3) forms part of the story of Cligés:

> C'est un roman en deux parties, histoire d'abord des parents du héros. Alexandre, fils de l'empereur grec, quitte Constantinople pour se rendre auprès du roi Artus: il y prend part à une expédition guerrière, se couvre de gloire, devient amoureux de la jolie Soredamors, et finit par l'épouser. De ce mariage naît Cligés.
>
> Après cette première partie, que Chrétien a soigneusement séparée de la suite, commence le roman principal. L'empereur meurt, et Alexandre doit lui succéder. Mais avant qu'il n'arrive à Constantinople, le bruit de sa mort s'y répand, et son frère cadet Alis est couronné. Au retour d'Alexandre, les deux frères font un traité: Alis garde le titre sans le pouvoir, qu'il passe à Alexandre; il ne se mariera pas, n'aura donc pas d'héritier, et tout l'empire reviendra à Cligés. Alexandre meurt bientôt, après avoir recommandé à son fils Cligés d'aller à la cour d'Artus pour éprouver sa chevalerie.[19]

*A priori*, it may seem logical enough for Cligés' story to start from the time of his birth. In point of fact, however, this means depriving his father's story of its natural conclusion which balances the opening account of his departure from Greece. It also means losing the link that connects the stories of the father and the son. For, as we have seen, it is precisely in

Episode 3 that the first stage in the disinheriting of Cligés takes place. As for the following lines:

Ce est Cligés an cui mimoire
fu mise an romans ceste estoire.
De lui et de son vasselage,
quant il iert venuz en aage
que il devra en pris monter,
m'orroiz adés de lui conter.                    (vs 2345–50)

these should not be taken as the opening of the second part of the romance, but merely as an anticipatory comment, such as one is accustomed to find in the epics, inserted into Alexander's story.

(b) Again, Section II has been shown here as ending at vs 4169 with the parting of the two emperors. A case could be made for making it finish instead at vs 4154, which marks the end of the Duke's attempt to secure Fénice. I cannot agree, however, with Voretzsch's view that the first part of Cligés' story ends at vs 4192. This line comes in the middle of his attempt to obtain leave of Alis to go to Britain. As I see it, vs 4170–92 are an essential part of the introduction to Section III.

(c) Finally, there is some doubt in my mind over the ending of Section III. I have shown it as coming at vs 5007, which marks Cligés' triumphant reception by Arthur and the successful accomplishment of his father's injunctions. It could be argued that the explanation for his departure from Britain also forms part of the account of the visit to Arthur, and that therefore vs 5008–24 should be included in Section III. Voretzsch, indeed, makes the account of the visit end at vs 5058 with the satisfaction of Alis and Fénice at Cligés' safe arrival in Greece. But I feel that the journey from Britain to Greece, at least, forms a necessary introduction to Section IV.

The third and last feature which sets *Cligés* apart from *Erec, Yvain* and the *Charrete* is the wholly novel unity it derives from being a conscious demonstration of Chrétien's ability to take a well-known work and transform it completely, episode by episode, and theme by theme. It is perhaps this virtuosity which constitutes Chrétien's main achievement in this romance. In itself, *Cligés* is, perhaps, the least interesting of his works. But as a *Tristan* metamorphosed – and as an *Eneas* revitalised – it is, as Frappier says, "une prouesse littéraire".[20]

## NOTES

1. J. Frappier, *Le roman breton: Chrétien de Troyes. Cligès* (Paris, 1951), p. 28. The line references in the quotation refer to Micha's edition of *Cligés*, those in the original text to Foerster's. For similar views see: G. Paris, 'Cligès' in *Mélanges de littérature française du Moyen Age*, edited by M. Roques (Paris, 1912), Vol. I,

pp. 271–2; M. Borodine, *La femme et l'amour au XII^e siècle d'après les poèmes de Chrétien de Troyes*, p. 77; G. Cohen, *Un grand romancier d'amour et d'aventure au XII^e siècle. Chrétien de Troyes et son oeuvre*, p. 188; K. Voretzsch, *Introduction to the Study of Old French Literature*, pp. 287–8; R. R. Bezzola, *Le sens de l'aventure et de l'amour (Chrétien de Troyes)*, p. 81; A. Pauphilet, *Le legs du Moyen Age. Études de littérature médiévale* (Melun, 1950), pp. 154–5; A. Micha in his edition of Chrétien de Troyes, *Cligés* (Paris, 1957), pp. xi–xii.

2. See: Paris, 'Cligès', pp. 269–306; Borodine, pp. 77–148; Cohen, pp. 169–210; Pauphilet, pp. 154–5; Micha, *Cligés*, pp. iii–viii; Frappier, *Le roman breton. Cligès*, pp. 28–38 and *Chrétien de Troyes*, pp. 106–9.

3. See 'Cligès', pp. 271–2: '*Cligès* est composé comme plus d'un roman du moyen âge: le thème choisi ne suffisant pas à fournir un récit assez étendu – les romans devaient avoir au moins six à sept mille vers – le poète l'allonge soit en y introduisant des épisodes qu'il invente, soit en lui donnant pour préambule l'histoire du père de son héros. Chrétien s'est servi des deux moyens; il a inséré divers hors-d'oeuvre dans l'histoire propre de Cligès, et il a fait précéder l'histoire de Cligès de celle de ses parents'.

4. Voretzsch, p. 289. The line references given in the quotation refer to the Micha edition, those given by Voretzsch (in his synopsis of *Cligés* on p. 288) to the Foerster edition.

5. This is the opinion of Paris (see above, note 3) and Voretzsch (see above, p. 159). It is also that of J. D. Bruce, who says of the love affair of Cligés and Fénice: 'This main story Chrétien has complicated and retarded by the episode of the hero's visit to Arthur's court, the most interesting feature of which is the well-known Three Tournaments motif. . . .' (*Evolution of Arthurian Romance*, p. 118).

6. Paris, 'Cligès', pp. 307–8 (my italics). For a similar view of *Cligés* as little more than a fabliaux see M. Lazar, *Amour Courtois et "Fin' Amors" dans la littérature du XII^e siècle*, p. 229.

7. This is a point Micha is prepared to recognise – with certain reservations: 'D'autre part le mariage de convenance, ou plus exactement le mariage de raison d'état, comme celui d'Alis et de Fenice . . . est un attentat au droit élémentaire qu'a l'individu de disposer de lui-même, et le désir de refaire sa vie avec un être d'élection, sans être une excuse aux manquements à la foi conjugale, bénéficie dès lors de circonstances atténuantes. Le coeur a ses droits que le droit ne connaît pas. Il convient sans doute de ne pas forcer la note, de ne pas grossir la voix de Chrétien en y voulant entendre d'anachroniques accents revendicateurs; l'individualisme n'est pas dans la "couleur du temps" au XII^e siècle, il n'a pas la force de faire éclater les cadres sociaux ni les morales reçues' ('Tristan et Cligès', *Neophilologus* 36 (1952), p. 10).

8. Paris, 'Cligès', p. 291, note 2. The passage to which the note refers repudiates the idea that Fénice's conduct is inspired by any more lofty conception than that of the paramountcy of sexual desire, of 'l'amour tout court . . . pour lequel mariage et adultère sont des considérations tout à fait accessoires et même négligeables, la seule chose essentielle étant la pleine et exclusive possession des amants l'un par l'autre' (p. 292).

9. Lazar, pp. 227–8. A similar line is taken by Micha in the beginning of his article, 'Tristan et Cligès' (pp. 5–6). But his strictures are followed by an interesting 'recantation' on pp. 9–10, part of which has already been cited in note 7.

10. Bruce, p. 118.

11. That Alis' usurpation of his brother's throne provides the link between the two parts of *Cligés* is recognised by Micha (though it is by no means clear whether he sees the passage (vs 2351–585 on pp. iv–v of his synopsis) as part of the story of Cligés or as a link passage): 'Un lien assez solide unit les deux parties [de *Cligés*]:

la première amène l'usurpation d'Alis et par suite sa promesse de ne pas se marier, d'importance capitale pour le développement de l'histoire' (*Cligés*, p. xii).

12. See Paris' assessment of Alis quoted on p. 167; and his further statement: 'en toute rencontre il lui témoigne la plus sincère affection' ('Cligès', p. 307, note 3).

13. Chrétien's debt to *Eneas* is discussed in detail by Micha in his article 'Enéas et Cligès' in *Mélanges de philologie romane et de littérature médiévale offerts à Ernest Hoepffner* (Paris, 1949), pp. 237–43.

14. A similar attempt to justify a cliché in terms of the current psycho-physiological theories occurs in *Yvain* vs 149–70 where Calogrenant explains why he should command the hearts as well as the ears of his hearers.

15. In seeing *Cligés* as a reworking of Thomas' *Tristan*, I subscribe to the view held by Paris ('Cligès', pp. 272, 280–2); A. G. Van Hamel ('Cligès et Tristan', *Romania* 33 (1904, pp. 473, 486, note 1); and Frappier (*Le roman breton. Cligès*, p. 46 and *Chrétien de Troyes*, pp. 105–6). The contrary opinion will be found in Hoepffner's article 'Chrétien de Troyes et Thomas d'Angleterre', *Romania* 55 (1929), pp. 1–16.

16. The text used in this study is that of Bédier (*Le roman de Tristan par Thomas. Poème du XIIᵉ siècle* (Paris, 1902–5, vol. I). This provides a reconstruction of the missing passages of Thomas' romance based on extant translations of that work and on the other versions of the story.

17. The subject of the transpositions is dealt with in greater or lesser detail by Paris ('Cligés', pp. 272, 276, 279–82); Van Hamel ('Cligès et Tristan', pp. 465–86); Micha (*Cligés*, pp. x–xi); and Frappier (*Le roman breton. Cligès*, pp. 46–51 and *Chrétien de Troyes*, pp. 111–2). The list of transpositions given here is far from complete – since only the more obvious have been given and in the barest outline – nevertheless, it contains a number of points not mentioned by my predecessors.

18. Van Hamel, p. 486. This point is developed more fully by him on p. 473: 'Je crois donc qu'on est parfaitement fondé à admettre que Chrétien de Troyes, sous l'impression du *Tristan* de Thomas . . . a voulu opposer à cette histoire d'amour une autre histoire d'amour, de même nature, comme contenu, et cependant foncière-ment différente comme tendance. Peut-être même pouvons-nous songer à un débat littéraire dans lequel Chrétien se sera entendu adresser le mot d'Oronte à Alceste: "Je voudrais bien, pour voir, que de votre manière Vous en composassiez sur la même matière." Le poète aura relevé le défi, ou, si l'on veut, accepté la gageure.' A similar view will be found in Frappier: 'Ce roman a été conçu comme une réponse au *Tristan*. Celui-ci a été transformé, presque donnée par donnée, et orienté vers un *sen* nouveau compatible avec les valeurs courtoises' (*Chrétien de Troyes*, p. 105).

19. Pauphilet, *Legs du Moyen Age*, pp. 154–5. The only critics who do not see vs 2345–556 as part of Cligés' story seem to be Borodine and Bruce, who treat it as a linking passage between the two main stories. See: *La femme et l'amour au XIIᵉ siècle*, p. 97: 'Depuis ce moment [the birth of Cligés], l'histoire d'Alexandre et de Soredamors peut être considérée comme finie, car les événements qui suivent ne forment qu'une transition au récit des aventures de Cligès'; *The Evolution of Arthurian Romance*, pp. 113–4: 'This [the birth of Cligès] ends the first division of the poem, and next comes the connecting link [the return of Alexander and his activities up to the time of his death]. . . . Now follows the second and main division of the poem'.

20. Frappier, *Chrétien de Troyes*, p. 121.

# Conclusion

SINCE only some and not all of the questions concerning the form and content of Chrétien's romances have been considered here, it is not possible, as yet, to offer a complete picture of his art and achievement. However, some general points have already emerged from the present studies and some conclusions can be drawn from them.

1. Contrary to the opinion of those who feel that Chrétien's works are only meaningful at an allegorical level, the texts studied here have been found to make perfectly good sense, both thematically and structurally, at the literal level. In each case, the various adventures befalling the hero are contained within, or alternatively contain, the story of his private and personal life which gives the work meaning and shape.

It may well be, of course, that Chrétien also intended his romances to be open to an allegorical interpretation. Nevertheless, I strongly suspect that his immediate public was more concerned with the problems he deals with at the literal level, namely, the ideals of worldly chivalry and the nature of the perfect love-relationship, than with the more edifying subjects some critics feel to be rather worthier of his talents and their own interests.

2. It has been claimed that Chrétien's romances are constructed according to a common pattern, but this does not prove to be the case. Although they all seem to be organised to allow for narration in three sessions, the works studied here differ widely in the details of their organisation:

*Erec* consists thematically of three adventure stories contained within a study of a love-relationship. Structurally, the work is made up of three main components which correspond to the beginning, middle and end of its overall theme.

*Cligés* comprises two self-contained stories. These concern two different heroes – a father and his son – and are connected by the fact that the one arises out of the other. Structurally, the work is made up of four main components. The first and largest corresponds to the father's story. The next three, consisting of two major components joined by one half their size, correspond to the three phases in the story of the son's fortunes.

The *Charrete* has two major themes which run concurrently through it: a rescue story and the account of a love affair. Structurally, it is made up of three main components which correspond to the three phases of the rescue story.

*Yvain* consists of two self-contained stories. These concern the same hero and are connected by the fact that the one leads to the other. Structurally, the romance is made up of three main components. The first and largest corresponds to the first tale. The second and third components correspond to the two halves into which the second tale is divided for the convenience, one suspects, of a narrator.

3. The present studies have also illustrated the dangers of approaching Chrétien's texts – or, indeed, those of any writer – with too rigid an idea of what one expects to find there. Interpreting a work in terms of a preconceived idea can so often lead to a distortion or to a total misunderstanding of the author's intentions. On the one hand, we so readily contrive to see what we are looking for: subconsciously or even consciously any discordant facts tend to be disregarded – as can be seen from some of the attempts to present Yvain as a Christian hero or as a man who sets out to redeem himself. On the other hand, the pattern that is being read into the text may well be inappropriate. It may, for instance, seem reasonable enough to assume that a man will repeat himself from one work to another. But such consistency is not inevitable. The very different structural patterns of Chrétien's romances show that a writer may equally well change his techniques or his ideas in the course of his career. Nor do the tastes or the identity of his public necessarily remain the same. Again, it may seem reasonable to suppose that a man will conform to what are recognised as the norms of behaviour and the canons of taste for his day and age. But we must be prepared for the occasional maverick. The mediocre will tend to conform, since they can only follow established patterns. The more gifted may well prove to be innovators, exceptions to the general rule – which is what Chrétien shows himself to be in his views on ideal love in *Erec*, *Cligés* and *Yvain*. Finally, it must not be forgotten that what we take to be the recognised norms and the established canons for another culture are concepts to be discarded or adapted, like any other hypothesis, when they no longer accommodate the available data. Indeed, when we are faced with a recalcitrant fact, it is better, perhaps, for us to question the validity of our general assumptions than to doubt or deny the evidence of the texts. This certainly proves the wiser course when Erec and Yvain fail to behave as courtly heroes are commonly expected to do.

The need to beware of trying to impose alien patterns on to the texts we study is a constant one. It is particularly great in the case of medieval works. In dealing with one of these, as in dealing with the product of any alien culture, we must first try, by patient analysis, to determine what its particular features are, and then proceed, with the help of workers in the other disciplines involved, to reconstruct the context to which it belongs. This exercise demands two qualities: accuracy of observation and the suppleness of mind to revise any concept or assumption which fails to make sense of the facts of a given case.

4. Finally, the present studies have illustrated the danger of approaching a text through the critics. The case of the *Charrete* shows that one thereby

runs the risk of inheriting difficulties which may turn out to be pseudo-problems, arising not so much from the work itself as from some limitation in a critic or from his particular conditioning. The sounder, indeed, the only, approach is to begin by examining the text itself and acquiring a first-hand knowledge of the problems it contains. These may be resolved later on consulting the critics or in discussions with colleagues, who, as outsiders, are well placed to detect any unsuspected blind-spots in oneself or to find the unjustified assumptions in one's thinking.

That the texts, the primary sources, should be the starting point and the main concern of scholarship is not, of course, a new idea. But since it is a point which is frequently forgotten, it might, perhaps, be appropriate to end here by recalling the advice La Bruyère gave the scholars of his own generation:

> L'étude des textes ne peut jamais être assez recommandée: c'est le chemin le plus court, le plus sûr et le plus agréable pour tout genre d'érudition. Ayez les choses de la première main; puisez à la source; maniez, remaniez le texte . . . songez surtout à en pénétrer le sens dans toute son étendue et dans ses circonstances; conciliez un auteur original, ajustez ses principes, tirez vous-même les conclusions. Les premiers commentateurs se sont trouvés dans le cas où je désire que vous soyez; n'empruntez leurs lumières et ne suivez leurs vues qu'où les vôtres seraient trop courtes.[1]

For all they were written in the seventeenth century, these words form a most apposite conclusion to this first series of Chrétien studies.

## NOTE

1. *Les caractères*, edited by R. Barthes, '*De quelques usages*', p. 409.

# Appendix 1

## *Esprover* and its uses in Chrétien de Troyes[1]

FOR many people the question of the motive behind Erec's second quest is one that must be finally decided by the way the verb *esprover* is used in vs 5096–8:

> Or ne li set que reprochier
> Erec, qui bien l'a esprovee:
> vers li a grant amor trovee.

It follows, then, that a knowledge of the different meanings the verb had in Old French is essential for a proper understanding of *Erec*. It therefore seems appropriate here to set down the various uses of the word that are to be found in the romances of Chrétien de Troyes. Such a survey will show that the verb had a far wider range of meanings than one might be led to suspect by Tobler – Lommatzsch or Godefroy. It will certainly serve to illustrate the rashness of claiming, as certain critics have done, that the 'sens normal' of *esprover* is 'mettre à l'épreuve'.[2]

(Abbreviations: obj. object; sub. subject; v.t. verb transitive.)

ESPROVER v.t.

1. To prove something in the sense of deliberately demonstrating something about it, viz: its quality, validity, worth etc. (cf N.E.D. 'Prove' 6, 7).

*Obj.: the power Death would show it wields over men.*
"Ce que Morz a acostumé / ne puet müer qu'ele ne face: / toz jorz a son pooir esface / le mialz que ele puet trover. / Or vialt son pooir esprover, / s'a pris plus de bien en un cors / qu'ele n'en a lessié defors; / s'ele eüst tot le monde pris, / n'eüst ele mie fet pis" (*Cligés* 5772–80).

2. To prove something in the sense of making something known about it, viz: its quality, worth, validity etc., but without deliberate intent (cf N.E.D. 'Prove' 6, 7).

*Obj.: swords used against the enemy to good purpose.*
Li traïtor molt s'an esmaient, / si s'escrïent: "Traï, traï!", / mes cil ne sont pas esbahi, / car tant con desarmez les truevent, / lor espees bien i espruevent; / car les trois en ont si charmez, / de ces qu'il troverent armez, / qu'il n'an i ont que cinc lessiez (*Cligés* 1866–73).

3. To make trial of, test or try something in the sense of carrying out a deliberate test to ascertain something about it, viz: its quality, worth, validity, etc. (cf Godefroy, IX, p. 550b, 'Esprover' ('soumettre une personne, une chose à certaines expériences'); N.E.D. 'Prove' 1).

*Obj.: people being sounded to ascertain their intentions and reactions.*
L'empereres de l'autre part / apele cez ou plus se fie, / de son frere qui le desfie / lor quiert consoil, et vialt savoir / s'il puet en aus fïance avoir, / que ses frere a ceste anvaïe / n'ait par aus force ne aïe, / et si vialt esprover chascun (*Cligés* 2488–95).

"Mes or le voldrai esprover, / et se je i puis foi trover, / lui et ses oirs toz franchirai" (*Cligés* 5329–31).

*Obj.: the qualities (courage and strength) that men wish to test in themselves.*
"Et que voldroies tu trover?" / "Avantures por esprover / ma proesce et mon hardemant" (*Yvain* 361–3).

"Mes d'une chose me mervoil, / se vos n'an avez quis consoil / a la cort le buen roi Artu. / Nus hon n'est de si grant vertu / qu'a sa cort ne poïst trover / tes, qui voldroient esprover / lor vertu ancontre la soe" (*Yvain* 3905–11).

4. To make trial of something by tasting or smelling. To smell or taste (cf N.E.D. 'Prove' 2).

*Obj.: the aroma of spices in a drink.*
". . . por ce que vos esprovastes / et santistes au vant de l'air / des boenes espices le flair, / et por ce que cler le veïstes, / le vin an sa coupe meïstes" (*Cligés* 3254–8).

5. (e. de) To test something for a given quality.

*Obj.: a warrior whose prowess needs no establishing.*
"... il est chevaliers si buens / qu'an ne porroit meillor trover / ne n'est or pas a esprover / de bonté ne de vaselage" (*Erec* 6248–51).

6. (e. + noun clause) To ascertain a given point, to try to establish it by deliberate experiment or investigation (cf Godefroy, IX, p. 550b. 'Esprover' ('constater par une expérience')).

*Obj.: an indirect question.*
"Ne vos ai rien dit par orguel, / mes por savoir et esprover / se je porroie an vos trover / que vos m'amessiez de boen cuer" (*Erec* 3360–3).

S'avoit antrecosu par leus / lez l'or de son chief un chevol, / et as deus manches et au col, / por savoir et por esprover / se ja porroit home trover / qui l'un de l'autre devisast / tant cleremant i avisast (*Cligés* 1152–8).

7. To learn, to find something out, by experience (cf Petit Robert, 'Éprouver' 3°; N.E.D. 'Prove' 3).

*Obj.: a truth which has been confirmed, but not by deliberately checking its validity.*
"Ainz boens teisirs home ne nut, / mes parlers nuist mainte foiee; / ceste chose ai bien essaiee / et esprovee an mainte guise" (*Erec* 4592–5).

8. (e. + noun clause) To prove a given fact in the sense of finding it out from experience (cf Petit Robert 'Éprouver' 3°; N.E.D. 'Prove' 3).

*Obj.: an indirect statement*
De ce furent tuit escherni / qu'il n'i ont pas Erec trové. / Lors a bien li cuens esprové / que la dame l'a deceü (*Erec* 3516–9).

*Obj.: an indirect question*
Li vilains dit bien voir qu'a poinne / puet an mes un ami trover; / de legier puet an esprover / au besoing qui est boens amis (*Charrete* 6502–5).

9. To assess, to recognise or come to know the worth or character of a person (cf Godefroy, IX, p. 550b, 'Esprover' ('apprécier')).

*Obj.: a friend whose worth, according to the adage, can only be recognised in adversity.*

"... se De plest, ore i verrons / vostre consoil et vostre san; / qu'au besoing, toz jorz le dit an, / doit an son ami esprover" (*Yvain* 6598–01).

*Obj.: a person who has not – from the context – been subjected to any deliberate testing.*

"Mestre, fet ele, je sai bien / que chose que je ci vos die / n'iert ja par vos avant oïe, / car molt vos ai bien esprovee / et molt vos ai sage trovee: / tant m'avez fet que molt vos aim" (*Cligés* 5350–5).

10.  To encounter, to meet with something (?)

*Obj.: a warrior who has not been deliberately sought out or 'tested' in battle.*

"Hui matin ne cuidoie mie / c'uns seus hom par chevalerie / me poïst vaintre; or ai trové / meillor de moi et esprové: / molt estes chevaliers vaillanz" (*Erec* 1043–7).

11.  To experience or to have experience of an emotion etc. (cf N.E.D. 'Prove' 3).

*Obj.: love*

"Comant? Set donc Amors mal faire? / Don n'est il dolz et debonaire? / Je cuidoie que il eüst / en Amor rien qui boen ne fust, / mes je l'ai molt felon trové. / Nel set qui ne l'a esprové, / de quex jeus Amors s'antremet" (*Cligés* 659–65).


S'ESPROVER


1.  To prove oneself in the sense of demonstrating one's abilities and quality, but not necessarily with deliberate intent.

*Sub.: an abstraction (Valour) described as having manifested itself in the person of a dead man.*

"... an toi s'estoit biautez miree, / proesce s'iert esprovee, / savoirs t'avoit son cuer doné" (*Erec* 4601–3).

2.  To prove one's mettle in battle, but not necessarily with deliberate intent.

*Sub.: a warrior who has distinguished himself in battle, but not necessarily with the intention of giving proof of his mettle.*

Ne por che ne laissa il mie / a requerre chevalerie; / et les estranges aventures, / les felenesses et les dures, / aloit querant, et s'en trova, / tant que molt bien s'i esprova. / Soissante chevaliers de pris / a la cort le roi Artu pris / dedens cinc ans i envoia (*Perceval* 6225–35)[3].

3. To prove oneself in the sense of deliberately testing one's capacities and quality.

*Sub.: a young man wishing to find his own measure.*
"Por ce toche an l'or a l'essai / que l'an conoisse s'il est fins. / Ausi voel je, c'en est la fins, / moi essaier et esprover, / la ou je cuit l'essai trover. / An Bretaigne, se je sui preuz, / me porrai tochier a la queuz / et a l'essai fin et verai, / o ma proesce esproverai / qu'an Bretaigne sont li prodome / qu'enors et proesce renome" (*Cligés* 4202–12).

4. (s'e. à) To measure oneself against another warrior in order to test one's mettle.

*Sub.: warriors urged, or wishing to match themselves against others in battle.*
Et mes sire Gauvains a dit / que tel josteor mes ne vit, / et por ce qu'il voldroit avoir / s'acointance et son non savoir, / dit qu'il iert, l'andemain, premiers / a l'asanbler des chevaliers. / Mes il ne se vante de rien, / einçois panse et si cuide bien / que tot le mialz et les vantences / avra cil au ferir des lences, / mes a l'espee puet cel estre, / ne sera il mie ses mestre, / c'onques ne pot mestre trover. / Or se revoldra esprover / demain au chevalier estrange (*Cligés* 4835–49).

"Biax filz Cligés, ja ne savras / conuistre con bien tu vaudras / de proesce ne de vertu, / se a la cort le roi Artu / ne te vas esprover einçois / et as Bretons et as Einglois. / Se avanture la te mainne, / ensi te contien et demainne / que tu n'i soies coneüz, / jusqu'a tant qu'as plus esleüz / de la cort esprovez te soies. / . . . / et s'an leu viens, ja ne t'esmaies / que a ton oncle ne t'essaies, / mon seignor Gauvain. . . ." (*Cligés* 2565–79).

5. (s'e. à) To attempt an undertaking, but not with the express intention of testing one's capacities to accomplish it (cf N.E.D. 'Prove' 4; 'Assay' 17).

*Sub.: a man invited to see if he can discover a secret section of a building.*
"Encor i a de tex reduiz / que nus hom ne porroit trover; / et se vos i loist esprover / au mialz que vos porroiz cerchier, / ja n'i savroiz tant reverchier, / ne nus, tant soit soutix et sages, / que plus trovast ceanz estages, / s'ançois ne li mostre molt bien" (*Cligés* 5508–15).

6. (s'e. à) To fight against someone (i.e. to match oneself against an opponent, but not necessarily in order to test one's mettle against his (cf N.E.D. 'Assay' 14).

> *Sub.: a warrior promising to take on two giants*
> "Dameisele, g'irai aprés, / fet Erec, quant vos m'an proiez, / et tote seüre soiez / que tot mon pooir an ferai: / . . . / Se li jaiant le leissent vivre / tant que je les puisse trover, / bien me cuit a ax esprover" (*Erec* 4330–8).

> *Sub.: a warrior who has just fought a battle.*
> "Ne vivrai pas, se com je quit, / que je trovai un chevalier / preu et hardi et fort et fier; / onques si vaillant ne trovai / ne a si fort ne m'esprovai" (*Perceval* 6608–12).

> *Sub.: a young man who is to be allowed to fight a certain warrior if it seems the match will be a fair one.*
> "De tel estre et de tel sanblant / le porrïens nos tost trover / que je t'i leiroie esprover / et conbatre a ta volanté" (*Charrete* 1806–9).

A survey of the way the verb *esprover* is used by Chrétien does not enable us to establish all its meanings in Old French. It does, however, suggest that the word had much the same range of uses as the English verb 'to prove'. It also suggests that, like its counterpart, *esprover* had two principal meanings, namely 'to demonstrate' and 'to test', from which the rest are derived.

Furthermore, one can see from the passages quoted here that the meanings of *esprover* which developed out of its use in the sense of 'testing' did so when the verb became associated either with the activities involved in a particular test (clearly the origin of its use in the senses of 'smelling' or 'fighting'), or with the activities resulting from a particular test (clearly the origin of its use in the senses of 'learning', 'finding out', 'meeting with', 'experiencing', or 'assessing the worth etc. of a person or thing').

Finally, it is clear that where *esprover* is used in the senses of 'knowing', 'discovering' or 'assessing', it is of no importance whether the knowledge has been acquired fortuitously or by deliberate experiment. And it is precisely this point that is vital for an understanding of vs 5097 of *Erec*, and so for an understanding of the motive behind Erec's quest.

## NOTES

1. The material presented here first appeared as an article: 'Chrétien de Troyes and the verb *Esprover*', in *Medium Aevum* 37 (1968), pp. 263–71.
2. See, for example, A. R. Press, 'Le comportement d'Erec envers Enide', p. 538.
3. Edited by W. Roach, Textes Littéraires Français (Genève, 1956).

# Appendix 2

## The Significance of *Reison* in vs 365–76 of *Le Chevalier de la charrete*

WHEN Lancelot is told by the dwarf to get into the cart if he wishes to have news of the Queen, Chrétien describes him as caught between Reason and Love:

> ... Reisons, qui d'Amors se part,
> li dit que del monter se gart,
> si le chastie et si l'anseigne
> que rien ne face ne anpreigne
> dom il ait honte ne reproche.
> N'est pas el cuer, mes an la boche,
> Reisons qui ce dire li ose;
> mes Amors est el cuer anclose
> qui li comande et semont
> que tost an la charrete mont.
> Amors le vialt et il i saut,
> que de la honte ne li chaut. (vs 365–76)

The tendency among critics has been to interpret 'reison' here as (knightly) honour or duty. In Frappier's view, for example, 'une courte lutte s'engage dans le coeur de Lancelot entre l'amour et la raison, ici l'honneur chevaleresque' (*Chrétien de Troyes*, p. 126); whilst Kelly claims that 'the contrast between the commands of Love and the duties of the knight has been vividly drawn in this scene' (*'Sens' and 'Conjointure'*, p. 110).

For my part, I see the conflict as one between the dictates of love and those of prudence or common sense. My grounds for doing so are as follows:

In the treatises dealing with the mental faculties which were current in Chrétien's day, reason is presented as the faculty which enables men – at the purely human level – to act as much in a prudent as in a moral fashion. The twelfth-century writer Alcher, for example, describes reason as the power men have to distinguish between the expedient and the inexpedient as well as between right and wrong, falsehood and truth:

> Quaedam ergo sunt infra rationem, quaedam juxta rationem, quaedam supra rationem. Infra rationem sunt quae sensu percipimus, ... *Juxta rationem sunt et pervia rationi, quae ratione percipimus, sicut commoda et incommoda, vera et falsa, justa et injusta.* ... Supra rationem sunt quae ... divina revelatione comprehenduntur.
>
> ('De spiritu et anima' in *Patrologiae Latinae*, edited by J. P. Migne, XL, col. 788. My italics)

Elsewhere (col. 787), Alcher speaks of reason as the faculty which endows men with prudence ('facitque ratio scientiam sive prudentiam'), which is itself defined in col. 794 both as the recognition of the feasible ('prudentia est scire quod possit') and as the choice of what is fitting or just ('prudentiae est nihil poenitendum appetere, et nihil praeter justum velle facere'). From this it would appear that in certain contexts in twelfth-century texts, 'ratio' and its French equivalent 'reison' may perfectly well be translated by 'common sense'. This rendering is entirely in accord with what the twelfth century saw as one aspect of rational activity.

To turn now to vs 365–76 of the *Charrete*, the evidence indicates that Chrétien is here concerned with reason in its prudential rather than its moral role. The presence of the verb 'oser' in the statement 'n'est pas el cuer, mes an la boche, / Reisons qui ce dire li ose'[1] shows clearly enough that Chrétien condemns Reason for warning Lancelot against doing anything that will bring disgrace upon himself.[2] Now in a courtly text one would not expect a man to be criticized for following the counsels of duty or honour. He is far more likely to be censured for listening to those of self-interest. Nor would one expect the *Charrete* to prove an exception in this respect. For love and duty are not shown in conflict elsewhere in that story. On the contrary, we find love acting there as a spur to duty – as it does in driving Lancelot to undertake the defence of the seductive damsel (vs 1096–111). Indeed, what is demanded of the perfect lover in the *Charrete* is not in fact the dereliction of duty, but total self-abnegation: a willingness to sacrifice not merely life and limb in the service of the beloved, but even one's standing in the world. And this surely is what is being asked of Lancelot in this scene, with Reason telling him to think of himself and Love urging him on to the greatest sacrifice of all.

## NOTES

1. In opposing heart and mouth here, Chrétien's intention is surely to show that the considerations urged on Lancelot by 'reison' are of peripheral rather than of central importance to him. A more appropriate use of the same conceit occurs in *Erec* vs 3376 ('ce panse cuers que ne dit boche') to indicate the discrepancy between Enide's protestations to the amorous count and her real intentions towards him.

2. This is a point that A. H. Diverres overlooks in claiming that 'no word of either praise or blame of the action is included' in Chrétien's account of Lancelot's reaction to the dwarf's offer ('Some Thoughts on the *Sens* of *Le Chevalier de la charrette*', *Forum for Modern Language Studies* 6 (1970), p. 25). He then proceeds to argue from Gauvain's reaction to a similar suggestion from the dwarf that Chrétien's intention was to 'imply, therefore, that Lancelot has foregone *raison* and committed *folie* at the dictates of *amor*'. But here he overlooks the evidence that comes later in the story and which shows that Gauvain's role in the *Charrete* is to emphasise the perfections not the folly of Lancelot. I refer to the fact that

Lancelot's impetuosity in his dealings with the maiden at the crossroads is favourably compared with his companion's more circumspect behaviour: 'Et cil qui fu sor la charrete / ne dit pas que il l'an promete / tot son pooir, einçois afiche, / *come cil cui Amors fet riche* / *et puissant, et hardi par tot,* / que, sanz arest et sanz redot, / quan qu'ele voldra li promet / et toz an son voloir se met' (vs 627–34).

# Select Bibliography

ADLER, ALFRED. 'Sovereignty as the Principle of Unity in *Erec.*' *Publications of the Modern Language Association of America* 60 (1945), pp. 917–36.

'Sovereignty in Chrétien's *Yvain.*' *Publications of the Modern Language Association of America* 62 (1947), pp. 281–305.

'A note on the composition of Chrétien's "Charrette." ' *Modern Language Review* 45 (1950), pp. 33–39.

ANDREAS CAPELLANUS. *The Art of Courtly Love.* Translated by John Jay Parry. New York: Frederick Ungar Publishing Co., 1959.

BEZZOLA, RETO R. *Le sens de l'aventure et de l'amour (Chrétien de Troyes).* Paris: La Jeune Parque, 1947.

BORODINE, MYRRHA. *La femme et l'amour au XII*e *siècle, d'après les poèmes de Chrétien de Troyes.* Paris: A. Picard et Fils, 1909.

BRUCE, JAMES DOUGLAS. *The Evolution of Arthurian Romance from the Beginnings down to the Year 1300.* Vol. I. Göttingen: Vandenhoeck & Ruprecht; Baltimore: The Johns Hopkins Press, 1923.

COHEN, GUSTAVE. *Un grand romancier d'amour et d'aventure au XII*e *siècle, Chrétien de Troyes et son oeuvre.* Paris: Boivin et Cie, 1931.

COLLAS, J. P. 'The Romantic Hero of the Twelfth Century' in *Medieval Miscellany Presented to Eugène Vinaver by Pupils, Colleagues and Friends.* Edited by F. Whitehead, A. H. Diverres and F. E. Sutcliffe. Manchester: Manchester University Press, 1965, pp. 80–96.

CROSS, TOM PEETE and NITZE, WILLIAM ALBERT. *Lancelot and Guenevere: a Study on the Origins of Courtly Love.* Chicago: University of Chicago Press, 1930.

DUGGAN, JOSEPH J. 'Yvain's Good Name: The Unity of Chrétien de Troyes' "Chevalier au lion".' *Orbis Litterarum* 24 (1969), pp. 112–29.

FOERSTER, WENDELIN, editor. *Erec und Enide.* Christian von Troyes Sämtliche Werke nach allen bekannten Handschriften. III Erec. Halle: Niemeyer, 1890.

editor. *Der Karrenritter (Lancelot) und das Wilhelmsleben (Guillaume d'Angleterre).* Christian von Troyes Sämtliche Erhaltene Werke nach allen bekannten Handschriften. IV: Karrenritter und Wilhelmsleben. Halle: Niemeyer, 1899.

FRAPPIER, JEAN. *Le roman breton: Chrétien de Troyes, Cligès.* Paris: Centre de Documentation Universitaire, 1951.

*Le roman breton: Yvain ou le Chevalier au lion.* Paris: Centre de Documentation Universitaire, 1952.

'Chrétien de Troyes' in *Arthurian Literature in the Middle Ages. A Collaborative History.* Edited by Roger Sherman Loomis. Oxford: Clarendon Press, 1959, pp. 157–91.

*Chrétien de Troyes: nouvelle édition revue et augmentée, illustrée.* Connaissance des Lettres 50. 1st ed. rev. Paris: Hatier, 1968.

*Étude sur Yvain ou le Chevalier au lion de Chrétien de Troyes.* Paris: Société d'Édition d'Enseignement Supérieur, 1969.

HARRIS, JULIAN. 'The Rôle of the Lion in Chrétien de Troyes' *Yvain.' Publications of the Modern Language Association of America* 64 (1949), pp. 1143–63.

HATTO, A. T. 'Der Aventure Meine' in Hartman's *Iwein'* in *Medieval German Studies Presented to Frederick Norman Professor of German in the University of London by his Students, Colleagues and Friends on the Occasion of his Retirement.* London: University of London Institute of Germanic Studies, 1965, 94–103.

HOEPFFNER, ERNEST. ' "Matière et sens" dans le roman d'Erec et Enide.' *Archivum Romanicum* 18 (1934), pp. 433–50.

'Chrétien de Troyes et Thomas d'Angleterre' *Romania* 55 (1929), pp. 1–16.

HOFER, STEPHAN. 'Les Romans du Graal dans la littérature des XIIᵉ et XIIIᵉ siècles' in *Colloques internationaux du Centre National de la Recherche Scientifique.* Vol. III. Paris: Éditions du Centre National de la Recherche Scientifique, 1956, pp. 15–26.

KELLY, F. DOUGLAS. *'Sens'* and *'Conjointure'* in the *'Chevalier de la Charrette'.* The Hague – Paris: Mouton & Co., 1966.

LAZAR, MOSHÉ. *Amour courtois et 'fin'amors' dans la littérature du XIIᵉ siècle.* Paris: C. Klincksieck, 1964.

LOT, FERDINAND. 'Nouvelles études sur la provenance du cycle arthurien: l'épisode des larmes d'Enide dans *Erec.' Romania* 28 (1899), pp. 333–35.

LYONS, FAITH. 'Sentiment et rhétorique dans l'*Yvain.' Romania* 83 (1962), pp. 370–77.

MICHA, ALEXANDRE, editor. *Les Romans de Chrétien de Troyes édités d'après la copie de Guiot (Bibl. nat. fr. 794), vol. II: Cligés.* Classiques Français du Moyen Age 84. Paris: Librairie Ancienne Honoré Champion, 1957.

'Tristan et Cligès.' *Neophilologus* 36 (1952), pp. 1–10.

'Enéas et Cligès' in *Mélanges de philologie romane et de littérature médiévale offerts à Ernest Hoepffner, membre de l'Académie des Inscriptions et Belles-lettres, Doyen honoraire de la Faculté des Lettres de Strasbourg, par ses élèves et ses amis.* Publications de la Faculté des Lettres de l'Université de Strasbourg Fascicule 113. Paris: Société d'Édition: Les Belles Lettres, 1949, pp. 237–43.

NITZE, WILLIAM ALBERT. 'The Romance of Erec, Son of Lac.' *Modern Philology* 11 (1914), pp. 445–89.
'Erec's Treatment of Enide.' *Romanic Review* 10 (1919), pp. 26–37.
'Erec and the Joy of the Court.' *Speculum* 29 (1954), pp. 691–701.

PARIS, GASTON. 'Compte rendu *Erec und Enide*, von Christian von Troyes, herausgegeben von Wendelin Foerster. Halle, Niemeyer, 1890, 8°, LV–361 pages (*Christian von Troyes Sämtliche Werke*, III).' *Romania* 20 (1891), pp. 148–66.
'Études sur les romans de la Table Ronde, Lancelot du Lac: II: Le Conte de la Charrette.' *Romania* 12 (1883), pp. 459–534.
'Cligès' in *Mélanges de littérature française du Moyen Age*. Edited by Mario Roques. Paris: Honoré Champion, Libraire-Editeur, 1912, pp. 229–327.

PAUPHILET, ALBERT. *Le legs du Moyen Age: études de littérature médiévale*. Bibliothèque Elzévirienne, nouvelle série: Etudes et Documents. Melun: Librairie d'Argences, 1950.

PHILIPOT, EMMANUEL. 'Un épisode d'Erec et Enide, La Joie de la Cour: – Mabon l'Enchanteur.' *Romania* 25 (1896), pp. 258–94.

PRESS, A. R. 'Le comportement d'Erec envers Enide dans le roman de Chrétien de Troyes.' *Romania* 90 (1969), pp. 529–38.

REASON, JOSEPH H. *An Inquiry into the Structural Style and Originality of Chrestien's Yvain*. The Catholic University of America, Studies in Romance Languages and Literatures Vol. no. LVII. Washington, D.C.: The Catholic University of America Press, 1958.

REID, T. B. W. editor. Chrestien de Troyes, *Yvain (Le Chevalier au lion)*. *The critical text of Wendelin Foerster with introduction, notes and glossary*. 2nd ed. Manchester: Manchester University Press, 1948.

ROBERTSON, D. W., Jr. 'Some Medieval Literary Terminology with Special Reference to Chrétien de Troyes.' *Studies in Philology* 48 (1951), pp. 669–92.

ROBSON, C. A. 'The Technique of Symmetrical Composition in Medieval Narrative Poetry' in *Studies in Medieval French Presented to Alfred Ewert in Honour of his Seventieth Birthday*. Edited by E. A. Francis. Oxford: Clarendon Press, 1961, pp. 26–70.

ROQUES, MARIO. 'Compte rendu *La femme et l'amour au XII^e siècle d'après les poèmes de Chrétien de Troyes*, par Myrrha Borodine, Paris, Picard, 1909. In-8, vi–285 pages.' *Romania* 39 (1910), pp. 377–83.
Editor. *Les romans de Chrétien de Troyes, édités d'après la copie de Guiot (Bibl. nat. fr. 794); vol. I: Erec et Enide*. Classiques Français du Moyen Age 80. Paris: Librairie Ancienne Honoré Champion, Éditeur, 1952.
'Pour l'interprétation du "Chevalier de la Charrete" de Chrétien de Troyes.' *Cahiers de Civilisation Médiévale* I (1958), pp. 141–52.
Editor. *Les romans de Chrétien de Troyes, édités d'après la copie de Guiot (Bibl. nat. fr. 794); IV: Le Chevalier au lion (Yvain)*. Classiques

Français du Moyen Age 89. Paris: Librairie Ancienne Honoré Champion, Éditeur, 1960.

SHELDON, E. S. 'Why does Chrétien's Erec treat Enide so harshly?' *Romanic Review* 5 (1914), pp. 115–26.

SOUTHWARD, ELAINE. 'The Unity of Chrétien's Lancelot' in *Mélanges de linguistique et de littérature romanes offerts à Mario Roques, professeur honoraire au Collège de France, membre de l'Institut, par ses collègues et ses anciens élèves de France et de l'étranger.* Vol. II. Bade: Éditions Art et Science; Paris: Librairie Marcel Didier, 1952, pp. 281–90.

VAN HAMEL, A. G. 'Cligès et Tristan.' *Romania* 33 (1904), pp. 465–89.

VORETZSCH, KARL. *Introduction to the Study of Old French Literature,* translated by F. M. du Mont. New York: G. E. Stechert & Co. 1931.

WHITEHEAD, F. 'The *Joie de la Cour* Episode in *Erec* and its bearing on Chrétien's ideas on love.' *Bibliographical Bulletin of the International Arthurian Society* 21 (1969), pp. 142–43.

WOODBRIDGE, BENJAMIN M. 'Chrétien's Erec as a Cornelian Hero.' *Romanic Review* 6 (1915), pp. 434–42.

WOODS, WILLIAM S. 'The Plot Structure in Four Romances of Chrestien de Troyes.' *Studies in Philology* 50 (1953), pp. 1–15.

ZADDY, Z. P. 'Pourquoi Erec se décide-t-il à partir en voyage avec Enide?' *Cahiers de Civilisation Médiévale* 7 (1964), pp. 179–85.

'The Structure of Chrétien's *Erec*.' *Modern Language Review* 62 (1967), pp. 608–19.

'Chrétien de Troyes and the verb *Esprover*.' *Medium Aevum* 37 (1968), pp. 263–71.

'The Structure of Chrétien's *Yvain*.' *Modern Language Review* 65 (1970), pp. 523–40.